HISTORY OF THE WESTERN WORLD
General Editor: John Roberts

The Age of Absolutism
1648 -1775

Overleaf Louis XIV departing for the war in
the Netherlands in 1672. Before he leaves, he
authorizes the establishment of a military
hospital – L'Hôtel des Invalides – in Paris.

Plan
Pour l'Hostel
Royal des
Invalides.

The Age
of Absolutism
1648-1775

Maurice Ashley

G. & C. Merriam Company, Publishers
Springfield, Massachusetts

Library of Congress Cataloging in Publication Data
  Ashley, Maurice Percy.
   The age of absolutism, 1648–1775.
   (History of the Western World, v. 3)
   Bibliography: p.309
   1. Europe—History—1648–1789. I. Title. II. Series.
D273.A79   940.2′5   73–17239
ISBN 0–87779–061–2

Contents

List of Maps

Introduction

We are all familiar with the idea of a 'Western world', though we may find it hard to agree upon its outline. Yet it is a very recent idea. At the moment in the seventeenth century when Dr Ashley's study begins, it would not yet have been intelligible. People would have spoken readily enough of Europe (or, to use an older term, of Christendom); these would have been familiar ideas to the educated. There was already in existence a Western world wider than Europe, but it was only just there. By 1775, something quite different in scale and quality had come into existence, an Atlantic community which is still the kernel of the Western world. The age discussed here by Dr Ashley is therefore crucial in the evolution of our own. It belongs to both yesterday and today. In the seventeenth and eighteenth centuries there crystallized, though in elementary forms, the fundamental structures of a world we can recognize because it provides the ground-plan of our own.

Dates are often less helpful as dividers of historical themes than is thought, but in this case they are good markers. On 24 October 1648, after five years of negotiations, documents were signed which we call the treaty of Westphalia. They closed thirty years of European war. They defined the future; on what was then decided the public law of Europe was to rest until the French Revolution. Because of this, some have seen this year as the end of the Middle Ages; it was a triumph of new centralized states – notably France – and a new international system at the expense of the old Holy Roman Empire. In the next century it would become clear that Spain had lost for ever the military dominance which the English Commonwealth still contested and Prussia would appear as a great power of the future. Habsburg-Bourbon rivalry would give way to one of Habsburg with Hohenzollern. By this time another great issue of the past would be dead, too; Westphalia was the last general peace at which one of the main things to be settled was religious difference.

At Westphalia only continental European states mattered. One nation, England, had not been involved at all, but by 1775 she was a world power and the Western world had become an oceanic community. Much was to follow from the events of that year. As Dr Ashley points out, from what happened on 19 April at Concord, no one could then have inferred that the insurrection of a few North American colonials would lead to the emergence of the most powerful state on earth. Yet there were by then already two million people on the other side of the Atlantic – nearly a third of the population of England at that moment – and in the century and a quarter since Westphalia a Western world still not very different in extent from medieval Christendom had grown to span the Atlantic. Insofar as the ministers of George III were resisting the implications of this, they were bound to fail. As the lines on the memorial to the British soldiers killed at Concord bridge put it,

> They came three thousand miles to die,
> To keep the past upon its throne.

Like the English, the Russians had not been involved in Westphalia. Yet in 1775 they, too, were a great power. Since 1648 they had moved east and west out of old Muscovy. They had settlements on the Pacific coast and had just exacted from Turkey a treaty which announced the beginning of the Eastern Question which was to tax statesmen for a century and a half. A few years before, Russian troops had made their first appearance as conquerors in Berlin.

Military power was the most obvious sign of a new historical role for Russia but she had changed in other ways, too. If one ruler stands out in these pages as a creative genius it is Peter the Great, who, as a later Russian put it, wrote indelibly the words 'Europe' and 'Occident' on the page of Russian history. Today, he seems more interesting than ever, one of the first of those modernizers who have grappled with the problems of political power and progressive change in backward societies. He achieved much, not only by setting Russia on the road to territorial security, but by opening a door to the West never to be quite closed after him. Indeed, eighteenth-century Russia was in some ways more a part of the Western world than ever afterwards because she was more akin to much of the rest of it than she was later to become.

American revolution and a new Russia were two signs of a new world in 1775. Another was the consolidation in the eighteenth century of a Western technical superiority with deep roots in the past. The platform was being made ready for the great take-off of the next century. This was one aspect of a great cultural leap forward, too. Intellectual capital was being laid down on which interest would be drawn right through the nineteenth century. It was to be fundamental to the always-growing confidence with which the West approached and exploited the rest of the world. Although at the end of this period China was still aloof and un-harmed, India after Aurungzebe was only a bone for French and English to dispute at leisure. The greatest age of imperial suprem-acy lay ahead – somewhat ironically, in view of the approaching collapse of colonial rule within so large a part of the Western world, the Thirteen Colonies.

Such changes are epoch-marking. We are tempted therefore always to exaggerate their impact on the men who lived through them. But the eighteenth century was still subject to immense historical inertia by comparison with our own day. In 1775 as in 1648, by far the majority of inhabitants of the Western world lived by agriculture. The news of the American rebellion could travel no faster from Paris to Madrid than had done that of Westphalia. Monarchs were still deeply respected; the revolutionary act of the English in cutting off a king's head in 1649 was thought so shock-ing that it was a century and a half before their example was followed. Like medieval monarchs, eighteenth-century rulers still had some magic about them; Queen Anne still touched her subjects who hoped thus to be cured of the 'King's Evil'. As late as 1745 the new United Kingdom had its last feudal rebellion.

Such things are not trivial even if they seem to run against the general tide of events. They speak of the weight of the past in men's minds, of the huge deposit of customary thinking and feeling which would have to be eroded by rationalism and enlightenment, by efficient government and brute force. Even in the fertile and creative age described by Dr Ashley, most men lived narrow, routine-dogged lives. This unchanging reality must never be lost to sight if we are to grasp how much of the future was already in existence by 1775.

JOHN ROBERTS

1 The Western World after the Thirty Years' War 1648-61

Of what did the Western world consist in the mid-seventeenth century? Essentially it was still a Christian world; and it was composed out of the old Europe and of the new Europe which was then being colonized across the Atlantic in the Americas, both of which were destined to complete the Western world of modern times.

In the early days of Western civilization, long after the flood described in the Old Testament, geographers had divided the globe into three parts, identified by the Jews with the sons of Noah; Shem stood for Asia, Ham for Africa and Japhet for Europe. Then medieval Christians became accustomed to equating Europe or the West with Christendom. The Greek Church converted Russia and the Balkans, while the Latin Church converted the rest of Europe. Thus by the thirteenth century AD the Cross was the universal symbol of a Christendom stretching from the Atlantic to the Black Sea and from the Baltic to the Mediterranean. The Christians of Africa and Asia were deemed to be of little significance. The attempt made by the crusaders to subject and convert Asia having failed, the Ottoman Turks by conquering Constantinople in 1453 defined the eastern boundary of the Western world. But the Turks tolerated the Christians of the Balkans. So Europe west of the Balkans evolved a pattern of unity.

The discovery of the American continent by the beginning of the sixteenth century enlarged the map of mankind: but the West was not yet considered to embrace the New World. In 1625 Samuel Purchas, a compiler of early seventeenth-century works on travel and discovery, wrote:

Europe is taught the way to scale Heaven, not by mathematical principles, but by divine verity. Jesus Christ is their way, their truth, their life; who hath long been given a bill of divorce to ungrateful Asia, where He was born, and Africa the place of His flight and refuge, and is become almost wholly and only European. For little do we find of this name in Asia, less in Africa and nothing at all in America, but later European gleanings.

Since the Protestant Reformation Christendom had been divided. To the Greek and Latin Churches were now added the Lutheran Church, the Calvinist Church and that curious compromise, the Church of England. Protestantism had opened the way to dissent. The nuances of the Christian faith were infinite, were far more varied than they had been even among the heretics of the Middle Ages. Christian beliefs in fact comprised at their most radical end the millenarians and chiliasts of every hue who based their lives on trust in the imminent return of Christ to earth, as well as the Socinians who did not believe in the doctrine of the Holy Trinity; then arose the Quakers and Quietists who were convinced that the spirit of God manifested itself in their gatherings and required mankind to live together in a pure state of love far different from that normally followed upon the political battlefields of Europe. But after 1648 the religious frontiers remained practically unchanged for many years. It was only in the Americas that new and permanent Christian communities were to be established. By the seventeenth century a New England, a New France, a New Spain and a New Netherlands were created. The Portuguese, pioneers of exploration in this new world, had christened Brazil, where they founded a magnificent colony in the sixteenth century, 'the Land of the True Cross'.

Before the vast area of this expanding Western world is surveyed it is necessary to consider the old 'Europe', a word not frequently employed before the Renaissance. From ancient times Europe and Asia were reckoned as being divided by the river Don, which flows from south of Moscow to the Sea of Azov. Muscovy itself was long regarded as a wild, barbaric and oriental land by the rulers of western Europe, typified by the cruel and superstitious Ivan IV (or the Terrible), the first Tsar or Caesar, who died in 1584. The sovereigns of Russia had previously been known simply as the Lords or Grand Dukes of Muscovy. After a Time of Troubles, which succeeded Ivan's death, the family of the Romanovs emerged in the early seventeenth century as hereditary Tsars. Gradually during this century the first Romanov Tsars extended their interests into western Europe, while Muscovy companies were set up there to trade with Russia, known to be rich in minerals, furs and wheat. By the time of Peter the Great, who became Tsar in 1694, Russia may be said to have 'entered' Europe. But until then it was generally thought to be doubtful whether Russia

14

belonged to the Western world at all; indeed it never did so completely either in reality or in spirit. Most of it was in Asia; Okhotsk, which was to become a busy port in the Pacific, was founded in 1648 and thus Asiatic Russia became a valuable source of furs. But it was significant that, also in 1648, the Russians and the English were the most notable absentees from the congresses which drew up the peace of Westphalia at the end of the Thirty Years' War.

Some modern historians have actually argued that in those days neither Russia nor England could be described as forming a true part of Europe or at any rate of European civilization. The English (and Scots) were cut off by the Channel from the 'continental' mainland and could enjoy, if they wished, a culture of their own, nurtured in glorious isolation from Europe as a whole. As to Russia there was the saying 'Scratch a Russian and you will find a Tartar', that is to say a savage. But England had in fact been European in every sense of the word since the days of the Danish and Norman invasions. English and French cultures had long intermingled. By the seventeenth century Shakespeare and Rabelais, to take two obvious examples, contributed equally to Western culture.

During the time of Ivan IV in the late sixteenth century, Muscovy increasingly began to consider itself as the spiritual heir of Byzantium. By the Time of Troubles in the early seventeenth century, the Russian Patriarch, who helped to found and sustain the Romanov dynasty, was head of an influential offshoot from the Greek Orthodox Church. It is true that Arnold Toynbee, in distinguishing civilizations as intelligible units of historical study, separated what he called Western civilization from the Orthodox Christendom centred upon the Muscovite Empire. Still, if it is agreed that Christendom was indeed the principal unifying factor in the Western world during the later part of the seventeenth century, then surely it must be conceded that Russia, both historically and potentially, came within the Western world.

But Russia was still sparsely populated and politically inchoate. Although early modern statistics are largely a matter of guesswork, the population of Europe in the mid-seventeenth century could be estimated at approximately a hundred million people (about a fifth of what it is today). Out of this total, ten million may have been subjects of the Tsar. At that time the density of population in Russia and the Ukraine may have been five inhabitants per square kilometre, while at the other end of the table the density of population in the Dutch Republic (or United Netherlands), then the most prosperous country in the Western world, was fifty per

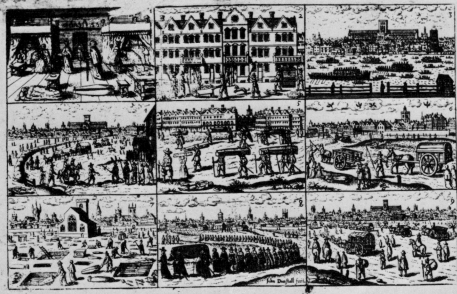

for the City of LONDON, And Parishes Adjacent:
1665. being a true Account how many Persons died Weekly in every of those Years, also how many ... Figures of the Greatness of the CALAMITY, and the Violence of the Distemper in the Last Year, 1665.

A A Last Great Years of Past every Parish in the said Ye...

Parishes Names	1625 Bu.	1625 Pl.	1636 Bu.	1636 Pl.	1665 Bu.	1665 Pl.
Albans Woodstr.	188	78	42	13	200	121
Albertsons Bark.	397	263	142	32	514	310
Alhallows Breadstr.	34	14	14	2	35	16
Alhallows the Great	455	302	123	41	455	426
Alhallows Barking	18	8	3	0	10	5
Alhallows the lesse	259	205	47	8	239	175
Alhallows Lumb. str.	86	44	22	2	90	62
Alhallows Staining	183	138	28	5	185	112
Alhallows the Wall	301	155	111	40	500	356
Alphage	240	150	62	11	271	115
Andrew Hubbard	146	101	26	10	71	25
Andrew Vndsh. East	219	147	44	12	189	83

Buried within the 97 Parishes within the Walls of all Diseases in the Year 1625, 14330, whereof of the Plague 9197, and in the Year 1636 of all Diseases 4108, whereof of the Plague 1100, and in the Year 1665, 15207, were of the Plague 9904.

Buried in the 16 out Parishes and at the Pesthouse 26771 of all Diseases, whereof of the Plague 17115, in the Year 1625; and in the Year 1636 there died of all Diseases 12880 of all Diseases, whereof of the Plague 9959, and in the Year 1665 there died of all Diseases 41701, whereof of the Plague 28198.

Buried in the Nine out Parishes in Middlesex and Surrey of all Diseases in the Year 1625, 12953, whereof of the Plague 9067, and in the Year 1636, 6454, whereof of the Plague 6761.

Buried in these 8 Parishes and at the Pesthouse in the Year 1665, 17174, whereof of the Plague 12218.

Collected by John Seller.

square kilometre. During the sixteenth century a population explosion had taken place which partly explained the astonishing rise in prices that continued, though at a diminishing rate, until the third decade of the seventeenth century. Thus, quite understandably, there was much talk of overpopulation and the emigration of the poor and ambitious to the New World was approved. But in the second half of the century the European population as a whole tended to be stagnant or even to decline so that underpopulation became the concern of governments and publicists.

What were the causes of this decline in population? Various suggestions have been put forward, not all of them entirely convincing. First, it is said that the toll of life taken by plagues and epidemics was particularly heavy in the middle of the seventeenth century. The plague hit most parts of Europe during the thirty years that succeeded the ending of the long war in Germany. Virtually every place was affected by epidemics, from southern Spain to Copenhagen and from Genoa to Amsterdam. The most spectacular visitations of the plague took place in Naples in 1656 and London in 1665, though both the capital and other towns of England had suffered from earlier outbreaks. Not only great cities but also the countryside were ravaged. Mortality was actually higher in the country because of the insanitary conditions in which the cottager dwelt. The belief that warfare was a direct cause of the reduction of populations no longer prevails: indeed armies syphoned off surplus men, while good generals, like George Monck and Marshal Turenne, took care to see that their soldiers were adequately fed and clothed and that their lives were not unduly risked. Though parts of Germany were undoubtedly damaged in the course of the Thirty Years' War – the population of Munich, for example, is said to have been halved by it – the idea, once widely held, that Germany and Austria as a whole were depopulated appears to have been an illusion. While many rural areas and some towns, such as Magdeburg, were largely deserted, population increased in north-west Germany, in Austria, in the Tyrol and in Switzerland. Still, war did have secondary demographical effects beyond the numbers it killed in the fighting; it contributed to the spreading of illnesses like syphilis, to destroying means of livelihood, and to malnutrition.

Outside Germany, the population of southern Europe was falling, particularly in Spain and in Italy, both of which were experiencing an economic depression. Commerce was shifting away from the Mediterranean which had been the focus of Western

Opposite Table of the parishes of the City of London, giving the number of people who died from the plague in each during the terrible outbreak of 1665. In the illustrations above are shown the emergency measures employed for burying the victims of the epidemic.

civilization for a period of some fifteen hundred years. The Spanish empire, to some extent seduced by the flow of silver from the New World, had neglected its opportunities to build up real wealth, while the industries of northern Italy, such as silk manufacture, had been damaged by competition and by the movement of principal trade routes to the north and the west. While southern Europe and central Germany had undergone depopulation, a modest expansion had taken place in northern Europe. The United Netherlands, which had flourished even during its eighty years' struggle for independence against Spain, retained, it has been claimed, 'a practical monopoly of transport' and an intact commercial position for nearly another century. England was also economically viable; its foreign trade was growing; and although it did not break the Dutch supremacy in shipping services English vessels carried most English goods outside the Baltic. The population of London doubled between the beginning and end of the century. France, however, was the country with the largest population in Europe, a population which may have reached twenty million by the middle of the century. Thus the Bourbon monarchy was able to maintain an army that expanded in size from a hundred thousand to two hundred and fifty thousand men during the height of Louis XIV's wars. It has even been suggested that the pressure of population on the means of subsistence was a fundamental cause of the French monarchy's aggressive and expansionist policies.

Another significant factor affecting population was the weather. A bad harvest could cause malnutrition or even starvation. But of course population and prices reacted upon one another. A reduction in demand would make prices fall and in fact prices did fall in the second half of the century, a period which has been described by a distinguished Dutch historian of agriculture as one of unusually prolonged depression in western Europe interrupted by violent fluctuations. A German farmer is quoted as having stated in 1658 that the price of grain had dropped so low that he had either to barter it or give it away. These falling food prices, however, cut both ways; they improved the real wages of all those in work who had to buy their own food and they stimulated in the more advanced countries a diversification of economic activities, for instance by encouraging manufacturing industries and extending pastoral farming. Finally, it may have been (as has been argued by some younger historians) that contraception was being practised not only in sophisticated Italy but even in English villages.

If Europe had a population of about a hundred million in the mid-seventeenth century what was the population of the growing Western world outside Europe? No precise figures are available (any more than there are for Europe itself where censuses were not yet being undertaken and where parish registers are incomplete or even misleading as statistical sources), but intelligent guesses are possible. In North America there were nearly a hundred thousand English settlers, concentrated in New England, Virginia and Maryland, who had to cope with about two hundred thousand native Indians whom they sometimes converted or attempted to convert to Christianity but more often massacred. Possibly another fifty thousand English dwelt in the West Indies and the Bermudas. By contrast Canada contained only twenty thousand Frenchmen, while a handful of Dutchmen occupied what was to become New York State. The American Indians lived by hunting and fishing and expected their women to toil in the fields. Understandably they resented the European intrusion. The Indian chief Powhatan said to the English: 'You have come here not to trade but to invade my people and possess my land.' The healthy climate and natural resources of North America, comprising wild fowl, fruit and fish for the taking, in fact encouraged dynamic English colonists to settle; thus the population was soon to advance by leaps and bounds.

The population of New Portugal (Brazil) was also considerable. The population of Portugal itself may have reached two million and it has been suggested that it was because of their need to expand that the Portuguese had sought in 1640 to throw off their allegiance to the deteriorating Spanish Habsburgs (who had acquired the Portuguese kingship in 1580). The Portuguese were resentful at the way in which the Spaniards had allowed the Dutch to acquire control of their prized possession of Brazil. But the Dutch were never very successful colonists, whereas thousands of Portuguese had settled along the Brazilian littoral. When the native Indians refused to work for them the Portuguese imported Negro slaves from Angola in Portuguese West Africa and in due course Buenos Aires became a slave market for Spanish Peru since the Spaniards had no direct access to African Negroes. The estimated population of Brazil after it had been wrested back from the Dutch was about thirty thousand whites and a hundred and twenty thousand slaves.

In Peru, conquered by Francisco Pizarro in 1530, and in Mexico, conquered by Fernando Cortez in 1521, each with a handful of

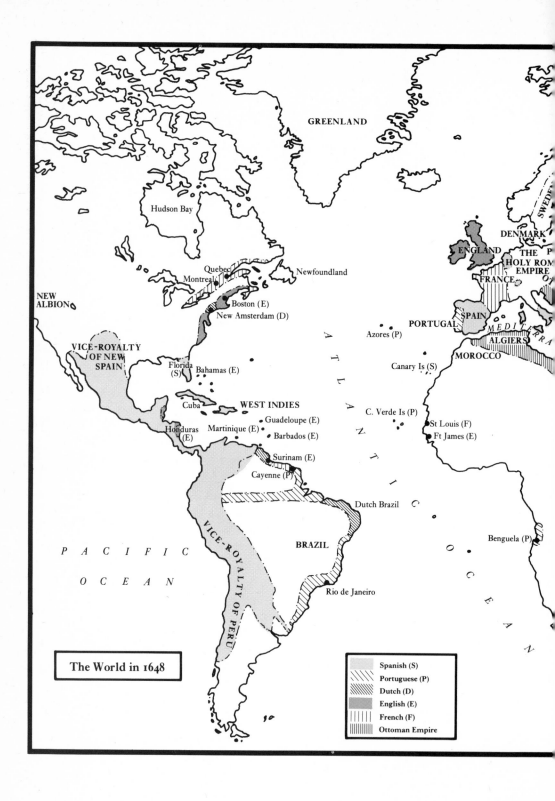

GREENLAND

Hudson Bay

NEW
ALBION

Quebec
Montreal
Newfoundland

Boston (E)
New Amsterdam (D)

VICE-ROYALTY
OF NEW
SPAIN

Florida
(S)
Bahamas (E)

Cuba

WEST INDIES

Honduras
(E)
Martinique (E)
Guadeloupe (E)
Barbados (E)

Surinam (E)
Cayenne (P)

Dutch Brazil

BRAZIL

Rio de Janeiro

VICE-ROYALTY OF PERU

PACIFIC

OCEAN

SWEDE

DENMARK
ENGLAND
THE P
HOLY ROM
EMPIRE
FRANCE
PORTUGAL
SPAIN
Azores (P)
MEDITERRA
ALGIERS
MOROCCO
Canary Is (S)

C. Verde Is (P)
St Louis (F)
Ft James (E)

Benguela (P)

ATLANTIC

OCEAN

The World in 1648

	Spanish (S)
	Portuguese (P)
	Dutch (D)
	English (E)
	French (F)
	Ottoman Empire

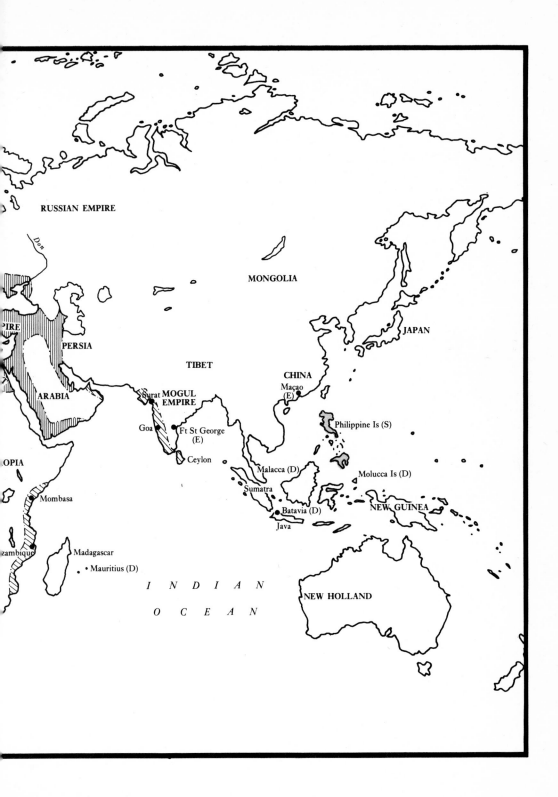

RUSSIAN EMPIRE

Don

MONGOLIA

EMPIRE

PERSIA

JAPAN

TIBET

CHINA

Macao
(E)

Surat MOGUL
EMPIRE

ARABIA

Goa

Ft St George
(E)

Philippine Is (S)

OPIA

Ceylon

Malacca (D)

Molucca Is (D)

Mombasa

Sumatra

NEW GUINEA

Batavia (D)

zambique

Madagascar

Java

Mauritius (D)

I N D I A N

O C E A N

NEW HOLLAND

Festivities in a Mexican village, *c.* 1650, from a painting on a screen.

soldiers, the Spaniards made a genuine attempt to convert the aborigines to Christianity. First, the Dominican and Franciscan friars obtained remarkable successes in Mexico where new churches replaced pagan temples and later the Jesuits swarmed all over South America. But the missionaries achieved less in Peru than in Mexico and the work of the friars was resented by the settlers who did not wish to engage in hard work themselves – as most English colonists did – and disliked Christianization because it might undermine their control over native labour. In fact the size of the native population, originally estimated at twenty-five million, fell catastrophically through pestilence, starvation and ill treatment. By the seventeenth century the population of New Spain (Mexico) was believed to be a hundred and twenty-five thousand white men and a million and a quarter Indians. The white population, known as Creoles, who were descendants of European settlers born in the American colonies, was to be found not merely in New Spain proper but scattered over what was to become Guatemala, Panama, Ecuador, Colombia and Peru. Spaniards, Portuguese, French, Dutch, as well as English were also to be found in the West Indian islands, that is to say the Greater Antilles, consisting of Cuba, Hispaniola (modern Haiti and the Dominican Republic) and Jamaica, and also the Lesser Antilles, which were to be fought over for at least a century by Europeans who found the growing of sugar and tobacco exceedingly profitable. The Spaniards in America were enriched by silver mining and the Portuguese later by discoveries of gold. All in all, one may hazard the guess that there were already by the middle of the seventeenth century nearly half a million Europeans in the New World, apart from the Indians and Negroes whom they subjugated and enslaved.

To return to Europe after the conclusion of the peace of Westphalia in 1648: in middle Europe 'the Holy Roman Emperor of the German nation', who had long ceased to be the most powerful secular ruler in the Western world, had been obliged to make three concessions. First, the Swedes were allowed to acquire western Pomerania and other parts of the Empire. On the basis of this Sweden substantially increased its population and became a considerable power in the Baltic. Secondly, the Habsburg Emperor had been compelled to recognize Calvinism alongside Lutheranism as a religion which could be imposed by German rulers upon their subjects, thus acknowledging the final failure of the Counter-Reformation. Lastly, he had been virtually obliged to concede to the three hundred and fifty German princes a substantial measure of independence; for example, they were now allowed to pursue their own foreign policies as long as they were not directed against the Emperor, who remained, at least in name, their suzerain. But henceforward it became difficult for the government at Vienna to invoke the military support of the whole of Germany against its enemies either in France or in the Ottoman empire. In effect, if not in name, the German Habsburg empire had shrunk, yet at the same time it had become more compact. For the Imperial Government, besides ruling over Austria and neighbouring territories, comprised both the kingdom of Bohemia and the kingdom of Hungary. By the end of the century the German Habsburgs were pursuing an expansionist policy both eastward and westward.

The Spanish Habsburgs were much more seriously damaged in

their imperial position after the ending of the Thirty Years' War. In the treaty of Münster they had recognized the independence of the Dutch Republic. Also, though this was not to be finalized for another twenty years, they were compelled to realize that Portugal might again become an independent kingdom if it could not be held down by force. Lastly, the war with France which had begun in 1635 was not brought to an end by the treaties of 1648. Though the Spaniards had come to the assistance of the Habsburg Emperor at the very beginning of the Thirty Years' War, they forfeited, at any rate for the time being, any claim upon an alliance with Vienna. The Spaniards, a declining imperial force, had hence forward to face the French alone, above all in the southern Netherlands and along the northern frontier of the Iberian peninsula. Moreover they were subjected to widespread attacks by their enemies upon sea as well as upon land.

One consequence of the ending of the war in Germany was the stimulation of political and social unrest throughout much of the Western world. In France, which, with Sweden, was the main beneficiary of the peace – it had, for example, obtained recognition of its sovereignty over the bishoprics of Metz, Verdun and Toul and gained a large part of Alsace, thus strengthening its vulnerable eastern frontier – the princes of the blood, led by the ambitious Louis de Bourbon, Prince de Condé, had rebelled against the Regency which governed the kingdom after the death of Louis XIII in 1643. This 'second Fronde', as it was called, invoked no real principles as standards of revolt. The Frondeurs had secured Spanish aid, but by 1652 Cardinal Mazarin, who was the close friend and confident of the Queen Regent (Anne of Austria), brought the trouble to an end and reasserted the strength and unity of the French kingdom. In England Charles I of the Stuart dynasty, who had vainly sought foreign aid to suppress a rebellion by the Parliamentarians, had, following defeats in the civil wars, met his death upon the scaffold as the result of a public trial in which he had been condemned as a tyrant. Charles I's son, Charles II, landed in Scotland in 1650, and invaded England the following year, only to be defeated by Oliver Cromwell, the Commonwealth Captain-General, at the battle of Worcester. Two years later Cromwell, by birth a modest country gentleman and Member of Parliament for the borough of Cambridge, was appointed Lord Protector of the Commonwealth of England, Scotland and Ireland and four years after that was offered the crown by Parliament. Cromwell, with an army of over forty thousand men on his hands, victorious

in three civil wars, and with a first-class navy, which in 1652–4 inflicted a resounding defeat upon the Dutch, who were fellow republicans, elected to attack Spain mainly with the aim of expanding British power 'beyond the line' into the New World. When the Spaniards retorted by declaring war on the Commonwealth the French and English entered into an offensive alliance against Spain, while the Dutch, once more at peace, took the opportunity to fortify their commercial and shipping position still further. In 1655 an expedition, dispatched by Cromwell, captured the Spanish island of Jamaica and thus gained a valuable base in the Caribbean from which Spanish sea routes between the New and Old Worlds could

The peace of Münster signed in 1648. This peace brought to an end the Thirty Years' War and recognized the independence of the Dutch Republic. Engraving of a painting by Ter Borch.

25

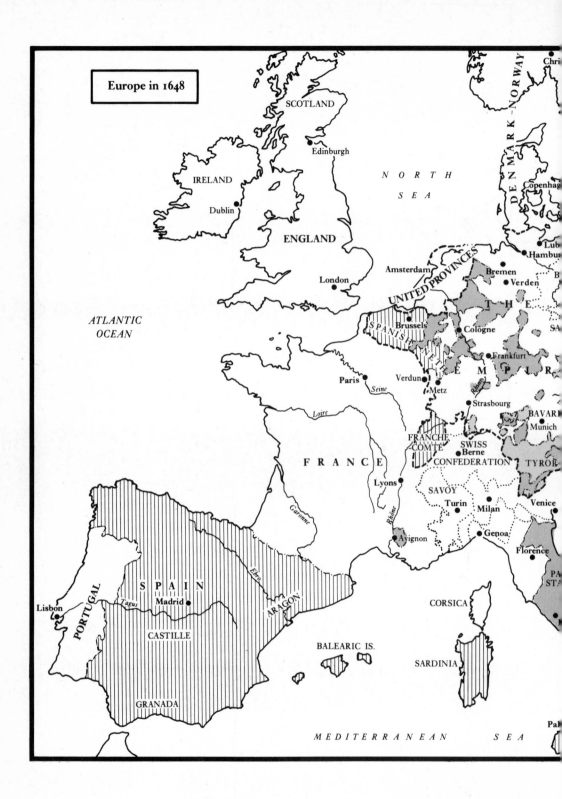

Europe in 1648

Stockholm

ESTONIA

Novgorod

LIVONIA

Riga

COURLAND

BALTIC SEA

Danzig

DUCHY OF
PRUSSIA

Vistula

LITHUANIA

RUSSIA

Don

Warsaw

P O L A N D

VOLHYNIA

SILESIA

Odra

Cracow

GALICIA

PODOLIA

Dneiper

UKRAINE

MORAVIA

HUNGARY

Vienna

Buda Pest

TRANSYLVANIA

IMPERIAL

H U N G A R Y

MOLDAVIA

BESSARABIA

Belgrade

WALLACHIA

Bucharest

B L A C K   S E A

BOSNIA

SERVIA

Danube

HERZE-
GOVINA

MONTENEGRO

O T T O M A N

BULGARIA

Sofia

Constantinople

ALBANIA

RUMELIA

E M P I R E

A N A T O L I A

AEGEAN SEA

Athens

- - -	Boundary of Holy Roman Empire
	Church lands
	Lands of House of Habsburg (Austrian Branch)
‖‖‖	Spanish lands

be attacked. Though Cromwell was at first disappointed with this conquest, before he died he and the English had ensured their ability to keep and rule Jamaica. In 1658 the French and English allies took the Spanish port of Dunkirk, which was reluctantly handed over by the French to the English, who thus acquired for the first time since the reign of 'Bloody Mary' a foothold on the European mainland. After the Cromwellian Protectorate, of which the ruling classes had tired, had been brought to an ignominious end, and Charles II had been restored to his father's throne in 1660, the decision was taken to sell Dunkirk to the French and to retain Jamaica despite Spanish protests. Thus the English began turning their faces towards the Americas rather than 're-entering' Europe.

One consequence of the Anglo-French alliance was that Portuguese independence was secured. The French were not allowed by the terms of the treaty of the Pyrenees in 1659 (through which they gained Spanish territory stretching across the Pyrenees as well as a number of towns in Flanders) to give open aid to the Portuguese still at war with Spain. But the French hoped that the English, who had concluded a treaty of amity with the Portuguese when Oliver Cromwell was Protector, would be induced by economic and financial considerations to furnish assistance to the Portuguese rebels. That in fact was what happened. For Charles II in 1662 married a Portuguese princess (the Infanta Catherine of Braganza) who brought as her dowry the fort of Tangier in the Mediterranean and the trading town of Bombay in India as well as a handsome gift of money. In return the Portuguese were allowed to recruit mercenaries in England who fought for Portuguese independence. For many years Portugal was known as England's 'oldest ally'.

Although the peace of the Pyrenees did not help the Spanish empire to retain Portugal, it did confirm the claim of Madrid to govern Catalonia, the province which had once been the brightest jewel in the crown of Aragon. The French had invaded Catalonia in 1639 and although they were driven out, the Catalans themselves revolted against the Spanish king in 1640, on the ground that their ancient privileges were being violated; they declared their country a republic under the protection of France. The Catalans maintained their independence for three years after the Dutch had finally shaken off the rule of the Spanish Habsburgs, but in 1652 Barcelona, the capital of Catalonia, surrendered to an army sent from Castile. So although Portugal and the United Netherlands were finally lost to Spain in the second half of the seventeenth century, Catalonia, the most enterprising and prosperous part of Spain both commercially and industrially, remained subject to the Spanish government and has continued to do so, in spite of more than one revolt, until the present day. The Spaniards moreover still ruled Central and South America (except Brazil), much of the West Indies (including Cuba), a large part of Italy and the southern Netherlands as well as the neighbouring provinces of Artois and Franche-Comté (the former free county of Burgundy). But the prolonged war against France (1635–59), the struggle with Cromwellian England, the contests with the Dutch, the Catalans and the Portuguese, and the drying up of the imports of treasure from the New World after the 1630s left the Spanish empire enfeebled and exhausted. Its ablest statesman, Gaspar de Guzman, Count of Olivares, died in 1645 and his master Philip IV, who had dismissed him from office in 1643, himself died in 1665 three months after the battle of Villaviciosa which finally ensured Portuguese independence. Philip IV was succeeded by a minor, Carlos II. For the next thirty years Spain played a secondary role in the history of the Western world.

The Habsburg giants were thus left temporarily to lick their wounds. The sprawling state of Poland-Lithuania, the second largest land area after Russia but with about the same number of inhabitants, that is to say ten million, began its long period of decline which was to culminate in its disappearance from the map at the end of the eighteenth century. Poland's kings were elective and the last Vasa monarch (the Vasas were also the Swedish royal family), John Casimir, came to the throne in 1648, chosen by the Diet, which consisted solely of the nobility. During John Casimir's reign the extraordinary procedure of the *liberum veto* was reestablished; this meant that a single deputy could veto a decision and break up the Diet. Thus the road to anarchy was opened.

Poland's neighbours, Sweden and Brandenburg-Prussia, flourished after the ending of the Thirty Years' War. The conquering King Gustavus Adolphus of Sweden had been succeeded by his daughter Christina, an extremely odd character. She was a bluestocking and possibly a lesbian. What she appears to have sought, above all, was her own freedom. She once said: 'All women in search of pleasure wish to have a man as a pretext.' This was a pretext of which she did not approve. She therefore refused to tie herself to any man, even to her cousin, Charles Augustus, whom she had loved when a young girl. In 1654 she resigned her throne in his favour and left Sweden for Italy, being converted to Roman Catholicism on her way. Charles x ruled Sweden for only six years but showed himself a warrior after the pattern of his uncle. Sweden dominated the Baltic ocean from the territorial point of view though not commercially, since it was always full of Dutch merchant ships. To preserve his inheritance Charles x had to fight the Poles, the Russians and the Danes. Peace was made with the Danes at Copenhagen in February 1660, with the Poles at Oliva in May 1660, and (after his death) with the Russians at Kardis in June 1661. The signing of these treaties, which did not detract from the Swedish empire in the Baltic, marked the peak of Swedish power, but the royal government was given only a decade to digest its conquests in peace. The Danes were envious of their neighbour's achievement. The political history of these two countries, Sweden-Finland and Denmark-Norway, during the next seventy years was to be a search for allies with whose aid to outmanœuvre each other. Meanwhile Brandenburg-Prussia, whose able Elector, Frederick William, had come to power in 1640, waited in the wings, as it were, building up his army and his finances, in the hope of profiting from any misfortunes suffered by his neighbours, Sweden and Poland.

Such, broadly, was the situation in the Western world in the twelve years after the peace of Westphalia. Nearly everywhere a quest for stability followed the long European wars and the disturbances caused by revolutions or attempted revolutions, ranging from Portugal to the Ukraine. After the failure of most of these revolutions in which many countries were involved, it was to be a world dominated by absolutism: the notable exceptions were the Dutch Republic, the kingdom of England and the English colonies in North America. Economically it was still an agricultural world. The countryside dominated the lives of the vast majority of people, whether they were the free farmers of New England, the smallholders in England and the Dutch Republic or the serfs of Poland and Russia. The historian Henry Kamen observes everywhere 'an impression of immense loneliness'. Mortality was high and the expectation of life was short.

Only two modifications of this general picture need be emphasized. The first is that from the very beginning of the century philosophical and scientific progress is to be detected in western Europe. The second is that the more advanced countries, the Dutch Republic, England and France, were seeking to diversify their economies and ways of life by the stimulation of commerce and industry. In 1660 the restored Charles II might look forward, if he wished, to an era of peace and prosperity during which England's trade and shipping could continue to grow. In France Louis XIV, who had assumed full authority in 1661 after the death of Cardinal Mazarin, had in effect a choice between military glory and economic growth, based upon a large hard-working population and a fertile soil. But it was only the Dutch burghers who deliberately attempted to opt for permanent peace during which to maximize national welfare. Reluctantly they were twice dragged into naval wars with their English rivals at sea and into a land-war with the French. In the English case they concluded peace as speedily as possible. The influential Regents of Amsterdam, the richest town in the Western world, sought greatness not by war but by commerce, finance and industry. Theirs was a unique contribution to Western civilization.

2 The Golden Age of the Dutch Republic

'The second half of the seventeenth century', a Dutch historian has written, 'was the most glorious period in Netherlands history.' Having thrown off the yoke of Spain – which they had succeeded in doing in 1609, although they did not do so *de jure* until 1648 – the Dutch attained an astonishing state of prosperity. The contemporary English diplomatist, Sir William Temple, who knew the Dutch extremely well, observed that they were 'the Envy of some, the Fear of others and the Wonder of all their neighbours'. They still had to undergo an ordeal by fire, for they were attacked at sea by the English and on land by the French. Nevertheless they survived and flourished.

The structure of their government was remarkable, but it was the product of their earlier history. Originally the seven provinces, of which Holland and Zeeland with their coasts on the North Sea were the richest, had banded together in a loose alliance to resist Spanish domination. Each province looked after its own affairs and merely sent a delegation to the States-General, which met at The Hague, to direct foreign policy. Even then unanimity had to be reached about this policy, though the States-General appointed ambassadors, dealt with diplomatic correspondence and received representatives from abroad. The only other function of the States-General was to govern 'the Generality' consisting of lands that had been conquered from the Spaniards after the original Union of Utrecht. Another common source of authority was the Stadholderate. Stadholders had been appointed by the king of Spain as royal representatives. Prince William 1 of Orange, the first hero of the war against Spain, had been Stadholder of three provinces and by his personality as much as his office had exerted considerable if indirect influence. William 1 of Orange was also Captain-General of the forces. In 1647 the second William of Orange – the fourth Captain-General of the Republic – had been critical of the foreign policy of the States-General and appears to have aspired to monarchy. But he died when he was still a young man in 1650; and the Dutch were not to be subjected to a monarch

who was a prince of the House of Orange until 1814.

The nature of government varied from province to province. But it differed from that of practically every other country in the Western world except New England because it possessed no large and powerful landed gentry. A Dutch nobility existed but it played a minor role in the government, though its members often married into the merchant class. Basically the Dutch government was directed by a class, known as the Regents, which has been called 'an urban patriciate'. The Regents were changing their character after the end of the eighty years' war with Spain in 1648. Previously they had been mainly active merchants and business men. Now so wealthy had the mercantile class become that it could provide administrators who were either retired merchants living on their investments or merchants who spent only a small part of their time on their own private affairs. But if therefore, in Temple's words, the Dutch Republic on the surface consisted of 'a Confederacy of Seven Sovereign Provinces', it was Holland which paid nearly sixty per cent of the taxes of the entire nation, furnished the equipment of the fleet, and provided most of the weapons of war. Its leading town was Amsterdam, where a population of a hundred thousand had doubled in the

The wealthy merchant class of the Dutch Republic, epitomized in this portrait by Rembrandt of the sampling officers of the Draper's Guild of Amsterdam.

33

course of the seventeenth century, and it took the place in the Western world which New York was to occupy three hundred years later. Thus Holland could exert pressure in the shaping of foreign policy. That was what William II resented; and he actually laid siege to Amsterdam before he was struck dead by smallpox.

The Dutch were therefore governed by about ten thousand members of an upper middle class. Besides the landed nobility and the wealthy merchants, society included what has been called a 'middling' middle class, shopkeepers and the like, a lower middle class – for example, artisans – a more or less orderly proletariat which participated in the general prosperity (though it was not highly paid and occasionally engaged in strikes) and a rabble that sometimes broke loose in the towns and sea ports.

After the death of William II the chief Dutch republicans decided to rid themselves of the monarchical pretensions of the House of Orange. This was relatively easily done since William II's only son, whose mother was an English princess, daughter of the unfortunate Charles I, was born posthumously. On the initiative of Holland, a Grand Assembly was summoned to The Hague which agreed to abolish the office of Captain-General and to decentralize control of the army and navy. Henceforward the close and more or less exclusive urban oligarchy reigned supreme. Jacob Cats, the Grand Pensionary or chief officer of the province of Holland, observed that Prince William II had been 'a large candelabrum which used to give much light and ornament', but, he added, 'the loss of this candelabrum can easily be remedied, since the pillars of the State have been preserved, and they will have to provide the candelabra as well as the candles'.

Two years later John de Witt, a former Pensionary of Utrecht, became Grand Pensionary of Holland. He belonged to the Regent class, was educated at the University of Leyden, had practised law and travelled on a grand tour of western Europe. He was an assiduous worker, a statesman of ability and a convinced believer in republicanism. Nevertheless throughout the first Stadholderless period, as it is called by Dutch historians, the Orangist party was by no means wiped out. Its members resented the fact that De Witt made a secret agreement with Oliver Cromwell (which soon leaked out) to exclude their leaders from all power in Holland; for Cromwell feared that the Orangists would continue to support the exiled House of Stuart with which they were intermarried. The Orangists also had adherents among the strict Calvinist clergy or Counter-Remonstrants who were unsullied predestinarians. The second Stadholder, Count John Maurice of Nassau, Prince of Orange, had actually managed to put to death a former Grand Pensionary merely because, in the words of Voltaire, he had believed that Christians could 'save themselves by good works as well as by faith'. During the Stadholderless period, as will be seen, De Witt pursued a pro-French policy since the French, like the Dutch, were the traditional foes of Spain. This ended in disaster and the House of Orange was called back to office.

The Dutch Republic was a notable example of what Arnold Toynbee has called 'challenge and response'. The United Netherlands possessed few natural advantages other than easy access to the sea with good harbours and river estuaries. Much of the land was waterlogged or in other ways unfertile. The country was over-crowded by the standards of the day and had no natural frontiers to the south or east to protect it against attack from France, Spain or Germany. What then was the explanation of the extraordinary deeds of the Dutch in war and peace? How did this small Republic become the leading country in the Western world not only in commerce and shipping but also in finance and industry?

In the first place it may be conceded that Toynbee's analysis is correct. As Temple wrote, 'No state was ever born with stranger Throes or nurst up with harder Fare, or inur'd to greater Labours or Dangers in the whole course of its Youth'. In search of food the Dutch looked to the sea and created a flourishing fishing industry. Dutch fishing boats were adapted out of season as mobile carriers. This in turn led to their sailing the seven seas, to the building of light vessels (*fluitschips* or 'flyboats') for trading in the Baltic, from which timber was fetched, and to the development of a major shipbuilding industry. Then, when the mercantile marine brought in unfinished goods from abroad, Amsterdam and Rotterdam and other ports became not only entrepôts for re-exports but centres of manufacture, for example in dyeing textiles or brewing beer.

Secondly, and this has been widely held to have been the real secret of Dutch progress, a secret which is fully realized in the twentieth century, the Dutch invested capital in industrial and commercial undertakings on a scale known nowhere else in the Western world. The rate of interest was kept low; interest on the national debt fell from six to four per cent seven years after the Spanish war ended and money could sometimes be borrowed for as little as two per cent. It has been suggested that one explanation for the availability of capital for investment was that in the Dutch Republic, unlike most other countries, investors were not

A seventeenth-century Dutch shipyard.

tempted to buy land. In England, for example, anyone who made money out of public employment or commerce rushed to buy landed estates if it were only to heighten his prestige. It was also emphasized by most contemporaries that the majority of the Dutch people were extremely frugal. They had no glittering Court or aristocratic hangers-on. Thus money bred money. 'Profit', remarked Temple acidly, was 'more in quest than honour'. The Dutch invested their gains from trade in capital enterprises. Drainage schemes added to the extent of arable land. Industry was expanded, particularly printing, textiles and shipbuilding. Canals were constructed. The Dutch East India Company had six million guilders in capital, much more than rival companies. Moreover Dutch financiers were not afraid to invest abroad. King Gustavus Adolphus had been backed by Dutch capital and Dutch experts had stimulated Swedish industries. Bullion was exported to finance trade in India and the East Indies. Investments were made in the slave trade. Dutch agents obtained a controlling interest in the French wine trade. It is estimated that in 1666 three-quarters of the capital employed in Baltic commerce was Dutch. Finally, the Dutch filled their houses with furniture and pictures, not only for their cultural satisfaction but also as a sensible investment.

Although the Bank of Amsterdam, founded in 1609, did not itself engage in much investment – it was essentially a bank of deposit and exchange – its very existence lent an impressive background to the numerous enterprises of Amsterdam, the bullion market, the world centre of marine insurance, the commodity markets, the stock market and in general an emporium where merchants obtained a quick return. The Bank, wrote Temple, 'is the greatest Treasure either real or imaginary that is known anywhere in the World'. ''Tis certain', he added, 'that whoever is carried to see the Bank, shall never fail to find an Appearance of a mighty real Treasure, in Bars of Gold and Silver, Plate and infinite Bags of Metals, which are supposed to be all Gold and Silver, and may be so for aught I know.' Through their investment and enterprise the Dutch created a trading empire with commercial outposts scattered from Archangel to Recife and from New Amsterdam to Nagasaki. But the merchants of Amsterdam were not enthusiasts for colonial settlement and Dutch women preferred to stay at home. Indeed, when in 1661 the Portuguese overthrew the Dutch in Brazil and the Chinese thrust the Dutch from Formosa, while later the English conquered New Amsterdam, the Dutch revealed their essential weakness as colonial conquerors and settled instead for an empire of trade.

Not only did the Dutch discount the value of colonial settlements as such, but in general the rulers of Amsterdam preferred peace to war. It is true that the Dutch had a big navy, though its warships were not as well gunned as the English, but it was intended primarily to protect their huge and widespread mercantile marine against pirates, privateers and freebooters. Another factor which contributed to Dutch economic progress was religious toleration. Admittedly the Counter-Remonstrants or strict Calvinists, who manned the State Church, were not remarkably liberal and certainly tried from time to time to reduce the liberties enjoyed by other religions; their ministers advocated the suppression of Roman Catholicism and strict control over dissenters; but, as Professor Kenneth Haley has noted, 'there were no tithes or church rates for non-members of the official church, and civil marriage at the town hall was valid for all'. A substantial Roman Catholic minority, who were survivors from the days of Spanish

rule, still existed, and perhaps a third of the population consisted of dissenters, apart from the Calvinist Remonstrants who believed in free will. The Jews were active, particularly in Amsterdam. The great philosopher Benedict Spinoza worked in Amsterdam and The Hague as a lens polisher. Prince Maurice of Orange had invoked the help of the Jews in trying to save Brazil from re-conquest by the Portuguese. The idea, once widely accepted, that Calvinism and economic enterprise went hand-in-hand has now been largely abandoned by historians. On the contrary, it was liberty of conscience for all that made for free enterprise. Yet religious duties were treated seriously. Large, if austere, churches were built. Industrial workers were not very well paid and un-employment at times prevailed, but the Dutch middle classes did not neglect their charitable obligations to the poor. It has justly been said that 'the warp of Dutch life was economic and its woof religious'.

The philosophy of the Regents who governed the Dutch Republic for over twenty years was expounded in Peter de la Court's book *The Interest of Holland* (1662) which was read in manuscript and amplified by John de Witt. De la Court argued that the pursuit of trade was necessary to Dutch prosperity and that commercial activities should be freed from state interference. He believed that religious freedom, low taxation and the protection of a navy were

PLATTE GROND DES KERKS

A seventeenth-century
print of the Jewish
quarter in Amsterdam.

essential, while the masses should be kept in their place. Further-more he asserted that 'Holland's interest is to seek after peace, not war.' This book, however, was concerned solely with the province of Holland and was directed against the militaristic policy of William II and the House of Orange.

It has to be remembered that the economy of Holland was not typical of the whole of the United Netherlands. In fact outside Holland and Zeeland the Dutch were, like the rest of the Western world, agriculturalists. A critic of de la Court argued that even Holland could be made self-supporting apart from its commerce, finance and industry. Its milk, butter, cheese and fish, he claimed, were the best to be found anywhere. Dutch cows were celebrated throughout Europe and are still familiar to us today from the canvases of Albert Cuyp (1620–91). The Dutch were often jeered at as 'cheese-mongers'. The large urban areas of Holland offered a ready market to the rural provinces away from the sea. Land was reclaimed and drained; Dutch farmers eliminated the fallow year from their rotation of crops; they were probably the first to introduce root crops, such as turnips, which enabled them to keep a greater number of cattle alive throughout the winter. They specialized in crops that they found profitable – such as barley and hops for making ale and beer – and they were splendid market gardeners. Dutch tulips became famous throughout the Western world. Moreover the extent of the Dutch export trade enabled the Republic to buy grain from northern and eastern Europe so that their peasants never starved, however bad the weather.

Dutch civilization was therefore the most advanced in Europe. The advantages of laissez-faire and religious toleration were recognized and advocated. Dutch towns were clean and hygienic. 'Thirty or forty pails of water', Professor Renier wrote, 'were carried into most houses every day. Many housewives brushed and scrubbed from morning till night. . . .' Excellent systems of sanitation existed and Dutch engineers of all kinds were in demand throughout the world.

Dutch education and culture were also on a high level. The University of Leyden was celebrated for its scientific, medical and linguistic studies as well as its theology. It offered high salaries and good conditions to its professors and it practised religious freedom. Because the Dutch were such skilled printers many books were produced, some for sale abroad. English and French critics of their respective establishments found printers in Holland. In the arts the Dutch were advanced though not outstanding. The great age

39

One of Albert Cuyp's celebrated paintings of cattle.

of Dutch literature had largely passed away by the middle of the seventeenth century. The versatile Hugo Grotius died in 1647. Jacob Cats, who was not only a good administrator but a poet who produced an amazing outflow of verse, died in 1660 at the age of eighty-two. Peter Hooft, like Grotius, a versatile writer and also a poet, died in 1647. Only Vondel, the poet and dramatist, survived until 1679. Dutch architecture of the seventeenth century, much of which is still extant, has sometimes been underestimated. It is true that the Republic could boast no vast palaces or huge country houses. But the churches, town halls and houses of wealthy merchants, which still line the banks of the Amsterdam canals, are beautiful. The Dutch classical style can be observed in the Maurits-huis at The Hague and in the Amsterdam Town Hall. Sculpture, however, was in little demand except for memorials to heroes. Few statues are to be found and sculptors, when needed, had to be imported.

The glory of Dutch culture was of course painting, of which Rembrandt van Rijn (1606–69) was the most gifted master, though hundreds of other wonderful painters flourished chiefly in the first half of the century. The Dutch middle classes were avid buyers of paintings to adorn their homes, though it has been disputed whether this derived from a desire for prestige, for investment or from love of beauty. Puritanism, however, in the Dutch Republic as elsewhere exerted a baleful influence upon art. Organ music was frowned upon by the Calvinists, while Grotius had been forced into exile and Spinoza's works were to be banned.

Dutch civilization, culture and, above all, prosperity were the envy of the rest of the Western world in the middle of the seventeenth century. But at the same time this made them many enemies and they were extremely vulnerable to attack. Moreover the neighbouring southern Netherlands was to become the cockpit of Europe. The first war in which the Dutch were involved after 1648, however, was at sea. Admittedly they had a sizeable navy but it was chiefly needed to protect their extensive trade routes. Thus the Dutch merchant fleet and trading posts were tempting targets for the English who possessed the second largest fleet in the Western world and were at the same time the principal commercial rivals of the Dutch. In his *Interest of Holland* Peter de la Court wrote: 'Above all things war, and chiefly by sea, is the most prejudicial (and peace very beneficial) for Holland.' Thomas Mun, an English East India merchant, whose book, *England's Treasure by Foreign Trade*, was published two years after de la Court's though it was written many years earlier, included the observation that Dutch wealth 'rests on an infinite number of weak ships'. Both these quotations might have been texts based on the lessons learned from the first Anglo-Dutch war.

The causes of the war were not essentially economic, though its conditions were. One of the grievances of the English Republic was the protection that had been afforded by the Dutch to the exiled Royalists. For example, it was common knowledge that Charles II's expedition to Scotland in 1650 and the subsequent planning of revolts in that country were mainly engineered from Holland. Secondly, there were clashes at sea between the two navies. The English insisted that Dutch captains should lower their flags on encounter and that it was right to search Dutch vessels carrying the goods of their enemies although the Dutch were neutrals. Colonial rivalries in the East Indies also led to conflicts, the English claiming the small island of Pulo Run. The Dutch, for their part, resented the passing of the Act of Navigation by the English Parliament in 1651, which confined imports into England and the English

Rembrandt's portrait of himself as an old man, painted in 1657.

plantations to English ships or ships of European countries in which the goods were produced or manufactured. The Act was obviously aimed at the Dutch transport trade, though modern research suggests that the number of Dutch ships calling at English ports had already fallen off drastically before the Act was passed.

The English Commonwealth's leaders, Oliver Cromwell and his friends such as Oliver St John, were anxious to avoid a war with the Dutch: indeed they wanted to conclude a close alliance with their fellow Calvinist republicans. But negotiations broke down and to some extent the war in 1652 came about accidentally. The strategies of the two sides were different. The Dutch admirals, eager to win the war as quickly as possible, aimed at destroying the English fleets. The English policy, on the other hand, was to cut off Dutch trade and starve the Dutch into surrender by blockade. A Dutch

Grand Pensionary summed the matter up in a famous phrase: 'The English,' he said, 'are about to attack a mountain of gold; we are about to attack a mountain of iron.'

Both sides had excellent admirals. Early in 1653 Robert Blake twice repulsed Cornelis Tromp in the English Channel. That was a grave blow to the Dutch because if their merchant ships could not sail through the Channel into the Atlantic they would have to be diverted to the north of Scotland. After Tromp had been defeated and was killed in a battle off the English coast, the English blockaded the Dutch coast and harassed Dutch fishermen on whom much of the Republic's food and some of its exports depended. In the spring of 1654 the Dutch agreed to peace on English terms. Cromwell let them off lightly (apart from his insistence that all members of the House of Orange should be excluded from the Stadholdership) and most of the quarrels over which the war was fought were left unresolved. The Dutch said they would give up Pulo Run.

Between 1654 and 1660 two hundred ships were added to the British navy. It was symptomatic of the way in which the basic tenets of a country's foreign policy usually alter little with a change of government, that Charles II came in fact to pursue a foreign policy similar to that of Cromwell, though much less successfully. Charles was dragged by Parliament into a second naval war against the Dutch though he himself was opposed to it. At the same time, like Cromwell, Charles was to conclude an offensive alliance with France, but he was unable to do this until after the Dutch war ended because in 1662 the French monarchy had agreed to a defensive alliance with the Dutch. The causes of the second Anglo-Dutch war were much more specifically economic than those of the first; indeed it has been called the first purely trade war in modern history. Among its causes was rivalry for the lucrative slave trade.

Originally the export of Negroes from west Africa to the West Indies and elsewhere had been chiefly in the hands of the Dutch. The Royal Africa Company, founded in 1662, in which Charles II and his brother held shares, began to injure the Dutch monopoly. An English admiral had been sent to lay hold of parts of west Africa, compelling the Dutch to surrender their forts. Another admiral had been dispatched to attack the Dutch settlements in North America which were sandwiched between English colonies and were highly vulnerable. These specific sources of conflict were exacerbated by trouble in India and the East Indies where the Dutch had failed to surrender Pulo Run.

The conditions of the war were much the same as before. England was at a disadvantage in only two respects: first, the coal ships which carried supplies from the Newcastle area to London could be halted by Dutch warships; secondly, an invasion of the east coast of England was always a possibility. To begin with the English navy again warded off direct assaults. But the Dutch had the better of a four-day battle in June 1666 and when in the spring of the following year a bold raid was made on English warships lying at anchor near Chatham, the English government was deeply humiliated. It has been argued that the military significance of the raid on Chatham was exaggerated, but it was a blow to English prestige. If there had been an English fleet in the North Sea at the time, such a raid would have been difficult if not impossible. As it was, Charles II's government had been compelled to lay up its larger warships for lack of means to pay for them, even though the English Parliament had voted the King a substantial sum of money for the war.

The treaty of Breda, which concluded the war in July 1667, produced gains for both sides. The Dutch won their way over the right of search: the English agreed that the flag covered enemy goods carried by neutrals at sea and accepted a narrow definition of contraband. The Dutch also retained Pulo Run and obtained some modification in the comprehensive Navigation Act which had been passed by Charles II's first Parliament in an attempt to wrest away from the Dutch the carrying trade to and from the West Indies, North America and the Baltic. The English, for their part, were confirmed in their possession of New Amsterdam, renamed New York, and Delaware, thus extending the number of English settlements across the Atlantic, and so made an early contribution to the idea that North America should become a melting pot of western peoples. The *status quo* in west Africa and the West Indies was accepted and the English kept a profitable share in the slave trade. The treaty of Breda was therefore a meaningful milestone in the history of the Western world. Dutch commercial supremacy had been challenged – for the rest of his reign Charles II himself regarded the Dutch as England's chief rivals; an English overseas empire, the core of the first British Empire, which had to be sustained by force, was in the process of being established; and the Dutch people, weakened by two naval wars, had now to face a major war on land in which the English were the willing partners of the French.

3 Threats to Peace 1661-88

Because the Dutch and English were distracted by the second Anglo-Dutch war of 1665–7, Louis XIV took the opportunity in 1667 to launch the first of his many acts of aggression in the Western world. Louis, who had taken over the full direction of the government when his foster father, Cardinal Mazarin, died in March 1661, was still in his twenties and full of ambition for his dynasty, the Bourbons, and his kingdom, which he identified with himself. The precise reasons why he decided upon a campaign in the Spanish Netherlands (modern Belgium) have been disputed. The excuse for the attack was that Louis's Queen, Maria Teresa, daughter of King Philip IV of Spain, had a claim, according to the local law of Brabant, to inherit the southern Netherlands in preference to Philip IV's son, Carlos II, because she was the daughter of Philip's first wife, while Carlos, her half-brother, was the son of the second wife. In actual fact when Maria Teresa married in 1660 she had renounced all rights to the Spanish inheritance: but it was argued by the French, first, that this renunciation was dependent on a dowry which had not been paid; and, secondly, that no treaty nor contract could overrule rights which had been conferred on princesses by God.

Philip IV had died in September 1665 but the French government, which was recovering from many years of war against Spain and in Germany, needed a breathing space. Michel Le Tellier who was one of the three very experienced ministers that Louis XIV had inherited from Cardinal Mazarin, had in his capacity as Secretary for War unified and reinforced the French army. Free companies raised by provinces and cities were disbanded; the Crown assumed a larger part in the commissioning of officers such as lieutenant-colonels and majors, while the position of captains and lieutenants was improved. Furthermore a treaty concluded with the Swiss by Hugues de Lionne, the Foreign Secretary, provided for a narrow corridor between Franche-Comté, belonging to Spain, and Savoy, belonging to the Duke of Piedmont, through which Swiss volunteer soldiers, possibly the finest soldiers in western Europe, could enter France to serve in the army of Louis XIV; twenty thousand of them took part in his first war.

The frontier of the Spanish Netherlands was uncomfortably near to Paris, as the French Regency had learned to its cost during the recent war with Spain, and it had long been on the agenda of French rulers to push back this frontier as well as other frontiers farther south; for example, if they could acquire Franche-Comté then their frontier would meet Switzerland. When therefore the resolution was taken to begin the war of the Queen's Rights (it was also called the war of Devolution), it could be carried out by a strong army at a time when Stuart England and the Dutch Republic, the two so-called maritime powers, whose common concern it was to preserve the Spanish Netherlands as a buffer state against possible attack by the virile and populous French kingdom, were occupied in fighting one another. It was indeed partly the knowledge that Louis XIV was preparing to assert his right to take over the Spanish Netherlands in his Queen's name that induced these two countries to make peace.

Louis XIV perceived no other obstacles in his path. The Spanish Regency, governing in the name of Carlos II, who was a sickly young child, had internal difficulties and the Emperor Leopold I, who had been elected only in 1658, found many problems on his hands in eastern Europe, while both Spain and Germany were still licking their wounds after prolonged wars. The French King thrust no fewer than three armies into the Spanish Netherlands. 'Since I knew that the Spaniards lacked ... soldiers,' he explained, 'I decided to terrorize them from all sides at once to oblige them to divide the few troops they did have into a number of garrisons.' The campaign met with comparatively little resistance. During the initial invasion Louis XIV accompanied the central army under the veteran Marshal Turenne; all having gone according to plan, he went home and fetched 'the three queens', as they were called, his declining but devoted mistress, his rising and flamboyant mistress and his unfortunate wife, a small and ill-educated princess, who had only blue eyes and a white skin to attract her husband. The King also brought all the comforts of Paris along with him and soon he was able to order Te Deums to be sung in honour of hollow victories. He wrote to the Archbishop of Paris saying that he wished to give thanks to God for his divine bounty.

However, it was not all easy money. Some Spanish garrisons had the impertinence to resist; and Louis recognized that campaigns could not be fought without spilling blood. His military

LE MANIFIQVE FESTIN
du Roy de France et du Roy
d'Espagne qui fut fait aprés le
Mariage à Sainct Iean de Luc
a Compagné de prince et
Seigneur de france et despagne

The feast held to celebrate the marriage in 1660 of Louis XIV, the young King of France, to Maria Teresa, daughter of Philip IV of Spain.

Opposite: In the summer of 1667, the Dutch fleet crossed the Channel and broke past the chain in the Medway which guarded Chatham. To the humiliation of the English fleet, they captured the flagship *The Royal Charles*, and towed it back with them across the open sea. This painting shows the havoc wreaked by the Dutch in their passage down the Medway.

Carlos II, the last Habsburg King of Spain. He succeeded to the throne at the age of four in 1665, but he was not expected to live long. He defied all the calculations of Europe for thirty years, until his death in 1700 sparked off the war of the Spanish Succession.

advisers, headed by Marshal Turenne, wanted to push on and occupy the entire Spanish Netherlands. But his diplomatic advisers, led by Lionne and Le Tellier, argued that he should not fritter away his resources on a war that had been so expeditiously won. If he failed to negotiate an agreement with the Spanish government reasonably quickly, then the Germans, the Dutch, the Swedes and the English might attempt to intervene. In fact on 23 January 1668, England, the Dutch Republic and Sweden had concluded a Triple Alliance with the aim of ending the war, a secret clause providing that if the French King did not restore peace in response to their mediation, they would take action against him. Meanwhile, during the winter, Louis had sent another well-qualified general, Louis, Prince de Condé, to seize Franche-Comté and this he accomplished without difficulty. The Dutch, who had been the allies of France since 1662, and the English, whose king was eager for a French alliance, hastened to assure Louis XIV that all they intended was to support him in securing the very terms from the Spaniards for which he himself had been asking: that is to say either the acquisition of Franche-Comté or the occupation of fortresses beyond the north-eastern frontier of France in the Spanish Netherlands. The Emperor Leopold was also prepared to accept a French victory over his Habsburg cousins in Madrid provided that if the infant Carlos II should meet an untimely death, the entire Spanish empire should be partitioned between him and the Bourbons.

Historians have disputed whether or not the formation of the Triple Alliance seriously influenced Louis XIV's decision to make peace, which he did in May 1668 at Aix-la-Chapelle. One thing is certain: the King soon learned of the secret clause in the Triple Alliance treaty and was angered by it. All that in fact he gained territorially from the settlement of Aix-la-Chapelle was a highly irrational frontier in which French and Spanish fortifications were inextricably mixed. He abandoned for the time being his demand for Franche-Comté. Nevertheless the treaty had significant results. It meant that the Spanish government recognized the French Queen's hereditary rights despite her earlier renunciation of them. Thus both the French King and the Holy Roman Emperor – who also had a Spanish wife – could hopefully await the death of Carlos II so as to split up the huge if decadent Spanish empire between them. Unfortunately for their calculations Carlos was to marry two wives and to live for another thirty years. Meanwhile Louis XIV's pretensions and excursions had alarmed much of the

Western world. Henceforward the princes of Europe would have to be either his clients or his enemies.

The treaty of Aix-la-Chapelle proved to be no more than a truce. Louis XIV was deeply resentful of the interference by the Dutch, whom he regarded as the architects of the Triple Alliance. He thought of them as ungrateful heretics who had spurned his friendship; he even described them as *magots*, hairy apes. It is sometimes argued that the French King's annoyance was not a major cause of the war against the Dutch for which preparations went on during the years between 1668 and 1672. Undoubtedly more solid reasons existed. Louvois, the French Minister of War, and the French generals were convinced that the occupation of the whole of the Spanish Netherlands was essential to the security of France. Louvois told the Prince de Condé in 1671 that 'the only means of achieving the conquest of the Spanish Netherlands is to subdue the Dutch and if possible to annihilate them'. Indeed it was the opinion of many of Louis XIV's most influential subjects that the treaty of Aix-la-Chapelle was a disappointment and even a humiliation.

Jean Baptiste Colbert, the French Superintendent of Finance, had a somewhat different point of view. He thought it was to the interest of the French economy to destroy the Dutch Republic. He had already aimed to injure Dutch trade by imposing severe tariffs on imports from the United Netherlands into France in both 1664 and 1667. He was anxious to expand French commerce and the French navy. 'Just as we have annihilated the Spanish on land,' he wrote, 'so it is necessary to destroy the Dutch at sea. The Dutch have no right to usurp all commerce, the basis on which they have established their State.' He believed that if they were not resisted, they would be able to dominate Europe and 'overthrow kings'. He also considered that if Antwerp (whose position as a port had been skilfully undermined by the Dutch) became a French port, it would be possible to damage Dutch commerce and build up that of France.

Unlike Oliver Cromwell who told the Dutch that there was room in the world for the trade of both England and Holland, Charles II, like Colbert, was convinced that the amount of wealth in the world was limited and that one country's gain was another's loss. Charles also felt resentful towards the Dutch; first on account of the way in which they had treated him and his relatives (William III of Orange was his nephew); secondly, because he realized that England had been disgraced in the second Dutch war. Charles's

Opposite: Detail of Jacob from Rembrandt's painting of the *Blessing of the Sons of Joseph*, executed in 1656.

51

consistent policy was therefore to reduce the competitive power of the Dutch and he relied upon patriotic sentiment to induce his Parliament and people to follow him in this policy. The Triple Alliance had not been received enthusiastically by his Parliament while the obscure island of Pulo Run still appeared to be a desirable objective. It therefore came about that French diplomacy was able to destroy the Triple Alliance without much difficulty. It was not so much the promise of French money that broke it up, for the rulers of both England and Sweden were envious of the Dutch. The English undertook by the secret offensive treaty of Dover, signed in May 1670, to attack the Dutch at sea while the French were invading the United Netherlands by land. In return Charles II was promised valuable territorial gains. The Swedes were annoyed that the subsidies promised them for their entry into the Triple Alliance had not been paid; and they were also aware that the Dutch were the traditional allies of their rivals, the Danes, while although the Baltic was more or less a Swedish lake, it was Dutch merchant ships plying a highly profitable business that filled it. French diplomacy completed the arrangements for the agreed war against the Dutch by concluding treaties with various German princes, including the Electors of Brandenburg, Bavaria and Cologne, and by obtaining a promise of neutrality from the Emperor Leopold I.

The Dutch, headed by John de Witt, found it hard to believe that their former allies would attack them without warning. What was the motive? After all, the French had solemnly promised in the treaty of Aix-la-Chapelle to respect the neutrality of the Spanish Netherlands. Thus the Dutch were scarcely ready for war. Their army had been reduced in size and decentralized since the death of William II, while the navy was also deprived of a central command. How could they be expected to withstand the assault of a large French army, which had been highly trained and reinforced with foreign mercenaries? How could they hope to resist the combined navies of France and England? And yet they did both.

In the opening campaign of 1672 the Dutch garrisons manning the frontier fortresses at once surrendered to the French; led by Turenne, the French forces bypassed the Dutch-held fortress of Maastricht on the Meuse and marched north into the United Netherlands. Farther west the Prince de Condé thrust his way across the Rhine near its estuary and soon three of the seven Dutch provinces were occupied. But the Dutch navy had defeated the

Anglo-French fleet at the end of May and therefore an attack on the Dutch from their rear was warded off. By cutting the dikes and flooding the polders the Dutch were able to convert Amsterdam and the surrounding country into a small island, protected on all sides by the waters. Nevertheless the Dutch, particularly the beleaguered citizens of Amsterdam, were eager for peace. The States-General therefore offered to surrender to the French all the territories that they ruled outside the seven provinces, to give up the commanding fortress of Maastricht, to pay an indemnity, and in effect to withdraw their opposition to the French absorption of the Spanish Netherlands. But the French unwisely demanded much more: they wanted the possession of towns inside the Republic including Nymegen, the reduction of Dutch tariffs imposed upon French exports, and the humiliation of the Dutch people before their conqueror. These terms were refused and the Dutch fought on. The pro-French John de Witt and his brother, having been dragged out of prison in The Hague, were murdered by a mob on 27 August, and the twenty-one-year-old William III

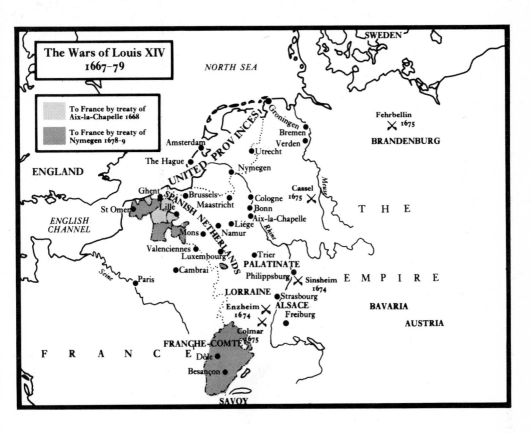

of Orange was appointed Stadholder of Holland as well as Captain-General of the Republic in the hope that he would emulate the feats of his ancestors, though this time the enemy were the French and not the Spaniards.

Dutch resistance put an end to the *Blitzkrieg* and resulted in the break-up of the French alliances. By 1673 troops had been withdrawn from their forward positions in the United Netherlands and Louis XIV concentrated on the siege of Maastricht, which surrendered in July. Afterwards he moved forces into Alsace and Lorraine, thus creating alarm in Germany. The volatile Elector of Brandenburg was the first to change sides. A coalition, known as the Grand Alliance of The Hague, which included the Emperor Leopold, the Spanish Habsburg government and the Duke of Lorraine as well as the Dutch, obliged the French to withdraw from the line of the Meuse. Early in 1674 the English were compelled to retire from the war since the French subsidies were entirely insufficient to keep their ships at sea; indeed the English

Engraving showing the cruelties inflicted upon the Dutch by French soldiers in their invasion campaigns of 1672.

On 27 August 1672, Cornelis and John de Witt were dragged out of prison in The Hague and were murdered by the mob. This broadsheet shows the fearful treatment meted out to their corpses.

government had only with difficulty been able to pay for two campaigns by withholding the interest on the government's debt to the London bankers. Although in 1674 and 1675 the French continued to make slow progress in their war against the Grand Alliance, their troops again occupying Franche-Comté and Turenne thrusting German troops back across the Rhine, they were to meet with serious setbacks outside the Spanish Netherlands. In 1675 Turenne was killed in Alsace and Marshal de Crequi was defeated on the Moselle. The Prince de Condé, who replaced Turenne on the Alsatian frontier, withdrew and then retired. In the same year the Swedes, fighting on the French side, invaded Brandenburg-Prussia and suffered their first defeat from a native German princely power (Brandenburg) at Fehrbellin near Berlin. By 1676 Louis XIV had agreed to send representatives to discuss peace at Nymegen. Meanwhile Sébastien Le Prestre de Vauban, the able officer who had been responsible for the swift fall of Maastricht in 1673, was obliged to occupy himself strengthening the defences on the north-east frontier of France lest his homeland should be invaded.

Three considerations induced Louis XIV to seek peace. The first was that a military stalemate had developed. The invasion of the United Netherlands was no longer a possibility and William of Orange had counter-attacked by besieging Maastricht in 1676, though without success. The second consideration was that the

55

The death of Turenne in Alsace in July 1675. He was directing the field of battle at Sassbach when a cannon ball struck him dead.

Grand Alliance, which had been built up to stem French aggression, was unlikely to fall apart unless peace were made. Finally in 1677 Charles II had permitted Prince William of Orange to marry his niece, Princess Mary, who was in the line of succession to the English throne. Although Charles excused himself to Louis XIV, this diplomatic marriage clearly signified that the Dutch were hoping for at least benevolent neutrality from England where Parliament was showing itself more and more anti-French. The conclusion of the peace of Nymegen was hastened by a series of French successes in the Spanish Netherlands culminating in the capture of the important town of Ghent. The terms of the treaty included the construction of a rational frontier between the southern Netherlands and France and the final secession by Spain to France of Franche-Comté. The Dutch for their part lost nothing by the war (except that the English had taken the opportunity to improve their international trading position). The French

56

surrendered Maastricht and undertook to lower their tariffs on Dutch goods. This last decision was a severe blow to Colbert, who had hoped by his tariff war as well as by the real war to destroy Dutch commercial supremacy and enhance that of his own country. Outside the Netherlands the French gave up Messina in the island of Sicily which they had captured from the Spaniards, and Leopold I reluctantly allowed the French to retain the strategic town of Freiburg east of the Rhine which was a shield to Alsace, in return for the French surrender of Philippsburg farther north.

It is now generally accepted that the conclusion of the peace of Nymegen marked the height of French power in the seventeenth century, though inevitably it created enemies for Louis XIV. English public opinion was alienated from France by the incursions into the Spanish Netherlands. The Earl of Danby, who had become Charles II's principal minister in 1674, was anti-French in his outlook and in fact Charles himself, though more or less pro-French, had been driven almost to the verge of war against France in 1678. The Germans were made fearful by French progress in Alsace and Lorraine as well as by the acquisition of Franche-Comté. The Emperor Leopold, while distracted by his problems in eastern Europe, recognized that the French were now his enemies. So French influence in Germany which had been considerable when France was ruled by Richelieu and Mazarin began to wane. The Grand Alliance formed against France in 1673 was the pattern for future coalitions formed to resist French ambition.

But Louis XIV's appetite grew with eating. He took the view that after he had consolidated his north-east frontier with Spain he could in a similar way extend and strengthen his frontier farther south with Germany. The method of doing so appears to have originated with the French Foreign Minister, Colbert de Croissy, and the War Minister, Louvois. After obtaining favourable interpretations of vague territorial clauses in the treaties of Westphalia and Nymegen from the local tribunals, Louis XIV sent troops to gain control of the whole of Alsace except for Strasbourg, which was a free imperial city, and of the county of Montbeliard, which lay between Franche-Comté and Alsace. The King may have persuaded himself or been persuaded by others that such annexations were lawful, but it was plain that they would never have been accomplished if they had not been backed by the strongest army in the Western world. These reunions, as they were called, provoked many Germans, who were further exacerbated when in 1681 the French seized hold of Strasbourg, the gateway between France and the Empire. Louis XIV made Prince William of Orange even more of an enemy when he took over his principality, though it was admittedly an enclave within the kingdom of France, which gave the Prince his territorial title. The fortifications of the city were dismantled and an attempt was made to compel the citizens, who were mainly French Calvinists or Huguenots, to become Roman Catholics.

In addition to the free city of Strasbourg French forces had in September 1681 seized the county of Chiny, a valuable fief of Luxembourg, which was under the sovereignty of Spain, and then in 1682 they laid siege to Luxembourg itself. In Italy the French purchased the strategic town of Casale on the river Po from the Duke of Mantua, who needed the money, and installed a garrison there. It is doubtful if France would have attained such a position of military supremacy by 1681 if it had not been for the fact that Spain was enfeebled, that Charles II of England was a French protégé (he relied on French arms, if necessary, to preserve his own authority) and that the Emperor Leopold I was distracted by the troubles to his east. Let us examine what these were.

During the middle of the seventeenth century two considerable empires in eastern Europe, the confederation of Poland-Lithuania and the Ottoman empire, had undergone decline for both internal and external reasons. A rebellion of the Ukrainians, led by the Cossack officer Bogdan Chmielnicki, against the Poles, had threatened the stability of Poland as severely as any of the revolutions in the west had endangered the governments of France and Spain. Although King John Casimir had defeated Chmielnicki in 1651 three years later the Cossack hetman was able by an act of submission to form a military alliance with the Tsar of Russia. At the same time Charles X of Sweden attacked Poland from the north and west and thus the Poles were menaced upon all sides. However, John Casimir was a capable general and the far-reaching ambitions of Charles X aroused a coalition against him. Though they took Warsaw and Cracow, the Swedes were driven out of Poland with the aid of Austrians. The treaty of Oliva, which ended the Polish-Swedish war in 1660, involved no loss of territory to Poland. But by the treaty of Andrussovo in 1667 the Poles surrendered Smolensk and Kiev to the Russians, a surrender which marked the beginning of Russian expansion westwards into

Europe. In the following year John Casimir, as the last Catholic Vasa King of Poland, abdicated and retired to France, to be succeeded by a wealthy but indolent Pole, Michael Wisnowiecki, who had none of his predecessor's abilities. Poland was left exhausted by these wars. Its population declined and its foreign trade fell off. The peasants were hit by taxation and feudal dues; the large Protestant minority was persecuted by the Roman Catholics; John Casimir, faced with conspiracies and with the almost republican liberties of the Polish nobility in their constitutional courts and assemblies, had been unable to make the monarchy hereditary. So anarchy continued to prevail.

In the Ottoman empire the mid-century was also a time of anarchy and defeat. A succession of incompetent Grand Vizirs proved incapable of managing the government. In 1648 a mad Sultan was deposed and succeeded by a child. Meanwhile the long war against the Venetian Republic, which had begun in 1645 and aimed at the occupation of Crete by the Turks, dragged on until 1664. The Turkish fleet suffered defeats at the hands of the Venetians, while the Turkish soldiers mutinied because of lack of pay and a debased currency. To begin to cope with these defeats, an aged Albanian, Mehmed Pasha Koprülü, was eventually in 1656 appointed Grand Vizir and by resolute action succeeded in restoring political stability and mending the government's finances.

By 1660 therefore, as John Stoye observes, 'everything tended to simmer down again after an immense wastage of human energy' in eastern Europe. Although the Polish government continued to be disturbed by Ukrainian Cossacks under a new leader named Peter Dorosenko, and by restless Crimean Tartars under the new king, John Sobieski, who proved himself a great military commander and who was elected with acclamation in 1674, Poland became more united for a time. The principal difficulties were created by the ambitions of a revived Ottoman empire, which was in effect ruled by members of the Koprülü family; Mehmed's son, Fazir Ahmed Pasha, followed his father as Grand Vizir and retained power for fifteen years; then he in turn was succeeded by his brother-in-law, Kara Mustafa, who planned a mighty offensive in the West, while his Sultan contented himself with perpetual hunting.

Once again the Western world became conscious of the dangers from a belligerent Ottoman empire, served by huge armies of fanatical soldiers. In 1664 an army of Poles and Austrians, supported by six thousand French 'volunteers', had stemmed a Turk-

John Sobieski, who was elected king of Poland in 1674. Nine years later, he led a Polish force to the relief of Vienna, and helped to drive back the Turks who were threatening the very heart of the Habsburg empire.

ish onslaught in western Hungary at the battle of St Gotthard, fifty miles south of Vienna. This was followed by the truce of Vasvar which let off the Turks lightly. In 1669 the Turks finally defeated the Venetians and occupied Crete. In the same year the Ukrainians, again shifting their allegiance, acknowledged Turkish suzerainty. In 1671 they raided Poland proper and a year afterwards the Turks followed with a heavy attack. Although in 1673 John Sobieski inflicted a crushing defeat on the Turks at the battle of Chotin in Podolia (in south-east Poland), which earned him the Polish crown, the Poles were obliged to cede Podolia to the Turks. Turning their arms against the Tsar, the Turks defeated a Russian army at Chigirin in the Ukraine. By the treaty of Radzyn in 1681 the Dnieper was fixed as the frontier line between the empires of

60

the Ottoman Turks and of the Muscovites while the suzerainty of the Ukraine was divided between them. After thus winning concessions from both the Poles and the Russians, the insatiable Turks, directed by Kara Mustafa, concluded a treaty with the western Hungarians, who had become restless under Habsburg rule, and prepared an offensive aimed at Vienna itself. Thus reluctantly the Emperor Leopold was forced to turn his attention from the aggressions of the French in western Germany to confront the menace from the east. For the last time in the history of the Western world the Pope (Innocent XI) inspired a crusade to protect Christendom against the infidels.

The immediate objectives of the vast army which the Turks assembled at Belgrade in the spring of 1683 are not entirely clear. It may well have been that the first intention was simply to overrun the whole of Hungary and extend Turkish power to within close reach of Vienna. The Turks recognized the rebel Thokoly as king of West Hungary and they called upon their allies or dependants to create a huge and formidable military machine. The Transylvanians and the Tartars from the Crimea, the princes of Moldavia and Wallachia, the Beys from Africa and the Pashas from Asia all answered the summons. Troops reached Belgrade from Adrianople via Sofia and from Salonika via Nish. Moving forward the Grand Vizir took the decision at Osijek on the Drava river (in modern Yugoslavia) to push straight on and assault Vienna. The Sultan had presented Kara Mustafa with the flag of the prophet in Belgrade before himself retiring to resume his usual hunting. The King of West Hungary joined Kara Mustafa at Osijek, but it was not until 14 July that the main Ottoman army encamped outside Vienna, from which the Emperor Leopold had wisely removed himself.

Three questions arise about the political meaning of this remarkable expedition. The first is what was the Turkish aim? The second is how did the French monarch, the most Christian king, view the assault by the infidels? And lastly what were the initial reactions of the Emperor? As to the Turks, it is arguable that to fight was their habitual occupation and that political trouble was likely to arise if the janissaries or infantry and the spahis or cavalry were allowed to kick their heels around the teeming capital of Istanbul. 'The assault on Vienna', writes John Stoye, who had studied the question closely, 'was only one of a long series of campaigns all caused in part by the special character of Ottoman court politics.' In fact the security of both the Sultan and the Grand Vizir required

61

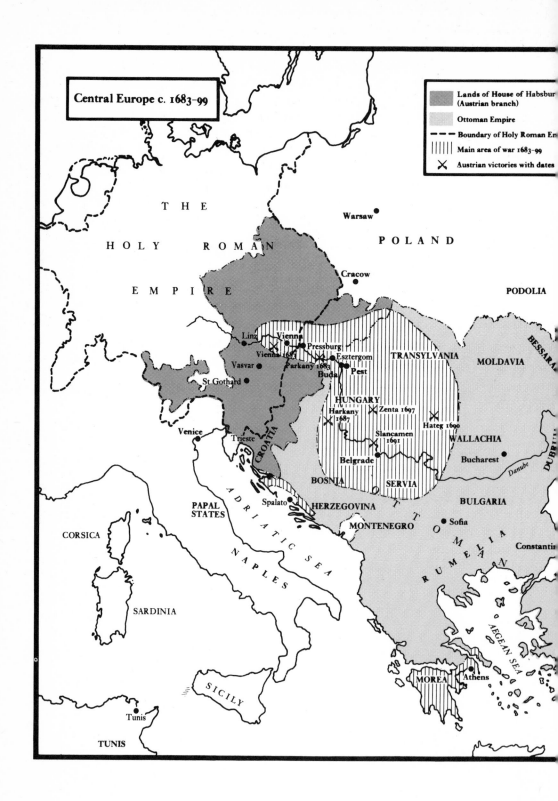

Central Europe c. 1683–99

Lands of House of Habsburg (Austrian branch)

Ottoman Empire

Boundary of Holy Roman Empire

Main area of war 1683–99

Austrian victories with dates

Warsaw

POLAND

THE

HOLY   ROMAN

EMPIRE

Cracow

PODOLIA

BESSARA

Linz

Vienna

Pressburg

Esztergom

TRANSYLVANIA

MOLDAVIA

Vienna 1683

Vasvar

Parkany 1683

Pest

St Gothard

Buda

HUNGARY

Harkany   Zenta 1697

1687

Hateg 1690

Venice

Slancamen

1691

WALLACHIA

Trieste

Bucharest

Belgrade

Danube

DUBRIII

CROATIA

BOSNIA

SERVIA

BULGARIA

Spalato

HERZEGOVINA

PAPAL
STATES

MONTENEGRO

Sofia

CORSICA

Constantii

ADRIATIC SEA

NAPLES

RUMELIA

SARDINIA

AEGEAN SEA

SICILY

MOREA   Athens

Tunis

TUNIS

military victory. What could be more glorious than the conquest of the greatest outpost of Christian civilization?

As to the French King, it is tolerably certain that without prejudicing his own position, he was pleased that the Emperor was thus distracted from the affairs of northern Germany. It is true that some twenty years earlier he had allowed French volunteers to fight against the Turks, but now he sent assurances to Istanbul that he had no intention of engaging in a religious war, which he regarded as being out of date. How far he was sincere in giving such assurances is open to question. It is possible that if Vienna had fallen, Louis XIV would have donned the armour of a crusader, used his own armies to push back the Turks, and sought the crown of the Holy Roman Empire for himself. Lastly the Emperor knew that he had not the resources to fight a war on two fronts. In fact he had vainly attempted to renew a twenty-year truce which he had concluded with the Turks after the victory of St Gotthard. In 1681 he had appealed to the Diet of Ratisbon to furnish him with an imperial army of a hundred thousand men but had only procured the promise of forty thousand. With such an imperial army he would have preferred to resist the French rather than the Turks whom he believed could always be thrust back into Hungary, while the French threat to Germany as a whole was more dangerous. In fact the Emperor was correct in his analysis of the situation. For all its size and all its banners the Ottoman army was a hollow ogre. It lacked sufficient guns and mortars and it lagged behind Western armies in its training. An Austrian envoy, who was at Belgrade in the spring of 1683, stressed the 'weakness, disorder and almost ludicrous armament' of the Turks and thought that they had only twenty thousand good fighting men in the whole army. Their communications were stretched over hundreds of miles and most of their allies were undisciplined. The disparity between the Turks and the French was emphasized in all the advice given to the Emperor. But when, bypassing the fortresses on the Danube, the Ottoman army, preceded by raiding Tartars, penetrated into Austria and surrounded the capital the Emperor had no alternative but to fight them. In spite of French intrigues John Sobieski with a Polish army joined Duke Charles V of Lorraine, the Emperor's own brother-in-law, with an Austrian army outside Vienna, while the garrison of the capital put up sterling resistance with cannonades and countermining. The fate of the inadequate Turkish army was therefore sealed. The Christians attacked from the north-west and in a confused battle on

12 September 1683 the Turks were defeated and began a long retreat across Hungary.

Once again the Emperor was faced with a difficult decision. Should he leave the Ottoman army to disintegrate and rally the German princes (some of whom were to join a defensive league concluded at Augsburg in 1686) to make war on Louis XIV? Or should he seek a truce with the French and chase the Turks out of

The raising of the siege of Vienna on 12 September 1683. King John Sobieski and his Poles joined forces with Duke Charles V of Lorraine, and together they shattered the Turkish army.

64

the Balkans? The temptation to deal with the demoralized army of infidels was too potent. The Pope gave his blessing. In August 1684 the Imperial Diet at Ratisbon agreed to a twenty-year truce with the French, which was also reluctantly adhered to by the Dutch. Charles II of England, who was to die in the following year, was delighted at the success of his protector, the French monarch, and thought that the Spaniards were foolish when they tried to resist him.

What happened after the siege of Vienna was that the French attempted to take advantage of the situation by imposing fresh demands upon Germany. A claim was made for the Palatinate because the sister of the Elector, who died in 1688, was also the sister-in-law of the French King. Moreover Louis tried to support the claims of his protégé, Cardinal Fürstenberg, whom he had previously appointed Roman Catholic Bishop of captured Strasbourg, as future Elector of Cologne. In 1684, while the armies of Austria and Poland were advancing on Buda, the French launched another *Blitzkrieg*. Luxembourg was occupied; the Spanish Netherlands were invaded; and the Republic of Genoa, which had supplied the Spaniards with warships, was bombarded. The truce of Ratisbon had guaranteed to Louis XIV the possession of Strasbourg, Luxembourg and the other territories he had seized earlier. But the Emperor refused to transform the truce into a permanent peace which recognized the French conquests for all time. Louis's attempts to subject the Palatinate and Cologne to his influence failed; and while the main French army was stationed at Philippsburg in the Palatinate the Dutch Captain-General, William III of Orange, after obtaining an invitation from seven leading Englishmen, took the opportunity to invade England and, meeting no resistance, forced his Roman Catholic father-in-law into exile. The English political nation, which James II had vainly wooed in an effort to secure complete liberty of conscience and civic equality for his fellow religionists, accepted William as their king and his wife as queen, while her father was obliged to abandon his throne and flee for protection to Paris. By 1689 William had persuaded both the Dutch and the English to declare war on France. France had in effect declared war on the Emperor in the previous autumn. Thus Louis XIV's sudden attack had failed and he was compelled for the second time to fight a Grand Alliance which aimed to preserve the balance of power in the Western world.

4 The Glory of the French Monarchy

The second half of the seventeenth century is generally described as 'the age of Louis XIV'. But modern French historians tend to concentrate on the conditions of the peasantry in relation to the social structure of the kingdom and to be unemphatic about the role of the King himself, for he was a man and not a class. On the other hand, the numerous biographers of Louis XIV are mainly concerned with the King and his glittering Court while more or less ignoring the peasantry, who did not inhabit the palace of Versailles. No doubt the role of the King can be exaggerated, but it should not be ignored.

It would be difficult to show that any important changes of policy resulted when Cardinal Mazarin died in 1661 and Louis XIV, at the age of twenty-three, announced that henceforward he was going to be his own first minister. What was significant was that by then Louis had sown his wild oats and was prepared to become an industrious ruler. Mazarin had taught him most of the arts of government, while his Spanish mother had stressed the value of strict Court etiquette. He learned that it was necessary to think things out, to study the relevant information placed at his disposal before reaching a conclusion; thus when he was asked for even a small favour his custom was to reply 'I will see.' As to the Court, its elaborate ceremonial was intended to impress upon the world the King's supremacy. As Professor Goubert has written, 'since the greater part of the Court, the pulpit and the town of Paris proclaimed that he was the lieutenant of God upon earth, it prepared to cry out with Bossuet: "Oh kings, you are as gods" nothing of all this could surprise him'. Indeed it was to draw attention to his isolation far above ordinary mortals that the main changes after Mazarin's death were directed. Louis excluded not only the princes of the blood from his councils of state but also his mother, who had been Regent of the kingdom during the eighteen years since his father had died. His only brother was allowed no place in the government nor any political post and in later years his only son was also kept in his place. Nothing was allowed to

Opposite: Louis XIV, patron of the sciences – attending the establishment of the Academy of Sciences and the Foundation of the Observatory in 1667. Detail from a painting by Henri Testelin.

detract from the glory of the sun king. He employed the same three ministers who had served Mazarin, Le Tellier, who was responsible for the army, Lionne who was concerned with foreign policy, and Fouquet, the superintendant of finance. But the King expected to be consulted about everything. On Monday, Wednesday and Saturday he presided over the ministerial council, the *conseil d'en haut*; on Tuesdays and Thursdays he generally attended the council which dealt with financial matters; and Fridays were devoted to religious questions in collaboration with the Archbishop of Paris and other leaders of the Church. It is sometimes argued that all this was a façade, that the real work was done by others. The King himself would never have admitted as much. He did not like anything to be kept from him and believed that most problems could be solved by the application of commonsense. But it is probably true that his principal interest lay in foreign affairs. 'You will always', he wrote in instructing his son about his duties, 'see me dealing directly with foreign ambassadors, receiving dispatches from abroad and writing a large part of the replies to them, while giving to my secretaries the substance of the way in which others are to be answered.'

The period of peace which followed Louis XIV's accession to power enabled him to put his house in order. One should not underestimate the effect of the two Frondes upon his mind. During the second Fronde a Paris mob actually penetrated into his bedroom in the Palais Royale. It was because of the behaviour of the Prince de Condé and other princes during the second Fronde that the King excluded them from his councils, although he was later reconciled to Condé and employed him as a military commander. Because he had seen Frenchmen fighting one another it has been suggested that unity and consensus 'became a near-obsession with him in later years'. The decision that he ultimately took to remove himself and his Court from Paris to Versailles, where a royal château had been sufficiently enlarged to enable him to keep an eye upon most of the higher nobility, must have been partly motivated by memories of the Fronde.

Before he died Mazarin had recommended to the King the abilities of Colbert, who came from merchant stock and had looked after the personal financial affairs of the Cardinal. Colbert was a master of the skills of administration. On Louis XIV's initiative he ferreted out the peculations or at any rate the irregularities of the able and cultivated Nicolas Fouquet. Once the King was satisfied that Fouquet had benefited himself overmuch from the exercise of

Opposite above: Louis XIV, patron of the arts – visiting the state factory at Gobelins in October 1667. Detail from a tapestry designed by Charles Le Brun, who is shown presenting the craftsmen to the King.

Opposite below: Louis XIV looking upon Versailles – the palace created by Le Vau, the architect, Le Brun, the painter and Le Nôtre, the landscape gardener, as a suitable setting for '*Le Roi Soleil*'.

An episode from the second Fronde, one of the two civil wars which tore France during the minority of Louis XIV.

his office while neglecting the true needs of the country, he had him arrested and insisted that he should be imprisoned for life. Here again Louis was moved by memories of the Frondes, for he feared that a man as rich and successful as Fouquet might become a disruptive influence. He came to trust the less glamorous Colbert, who was in due course appointed Controller-General of Finance, Minister for the Navy, Minister for the Arts and director of the royal building programme, which, after war and sex, was the monarch's chief passion.

It used to be thought that Colbert's aim was to enrich the kingdom in peace and that he offered the King a choice between economic and military expansion, but that view is no longer accepted. What Colbert wanted to do was to take advantage of the period of peace to reorganize the royal revenues. The population included some fifteen million peasants on whom the main burden of taxation fell, at least directly. Colbert aimed to stimulate industry and trade so as to prevent the kingdom from being dependent solely on agriculture. A conscientious servant of the Crown and an indefatigable worker, Colbert chivied the rentiers and local officials, reduced borrowing, converted existing debts, tried to eliminate waste, extended the range of those liable to the *taille* or land tax (but did not trespass upon the exemptions of the privileged classes in the nobility and Church), subsidized industry, imposed tariffs to reduce imports, expanded the mercantile marine and regulated manufacture and agriculture. He tried to impress upon the King that ultimately the yield from taxation was determined by the state of the economy. But Colbert was no financial wizard with startlingly original ideas. He did not reform the financial machine; he believed that in international commerce one country's gain was another's loss, and he did not insist that peace was necessary for the national well-being. On the contrary, he simply aimed to fulfil his King's wishes, to take advantage of a unique opportunity to build up a war chest. He did this largely by restricting the scope of privilege and tightening up the collection of taxes. His achievement has sometimes been overrated: Colbert's chief gifts were obstinacy and energy.

What was the foreign policy for which Louis XIV needed an army, a navy and plenty of money? This has been the subject of violent debates and various explanations of his purposes have been offered. It has been suggested that he wanted to attain the 'natural frontiers of France', that is to say the Pyrenees, the Alps and the Rhine. But there is no evidence for this and in fact the Pyrenees had already been reached, after twenty-four years of war, before Mazarin died. Secondly, it is argued that the king subjected all other aims to that of winning the succession to the Spanish empire after Philip IV died and left a child and a weakling as his only direct heir. Another explanation is that he sought by dominating Germany to gain the imperial crown which had long been the monopoly of the Habsburg family. Again, it has been urged that he was guided by a desire for *gloire* which did not mean merely self-glorification but the glorification of his country as symbolically embodied in himself by God. Lastly, he has been pictured simply as a pragmatist who exploited his opportunities as they came his way. In fact, it does not seem that he had any steady purpose, but that he merely followed the same lines as the great Cardinals, Richelieu and Mazarin, who both wanted to drive back the Habsburgs and give France an independent role in Europe. Louis regarded the Habs-

Jean Baptiste Colbert, one of the leading ministers of Louis XIV's régime. Portrait by Claude Lefèbvre.

71

burgs of Spain and of Austria as his natural and hereditary enemies who had been able in the past to fasten a stranglehold on France. Once the Pyrenean frontier had been established, Louis laboured to push forward the French frontiers to the north-east and to the east as far as he could in Spanish Flanders, Alsace-Lorraine and northern Italy. Thus rational considerations were fed by his ambition. As Louis André wrote,

After 1663 Louis XIV ceased to be satisfied with the domains that he possessed and aimed to increase them at the expense of the Habsburgs. His pride and his desire for glory involved a wish to achieve success by arms, to make conquests beyond everything. Here again the King was in accord with the wishes of his subjects who also sought glory, above all since the treaty of the Pyrenees. Everyone thought that 'to be a conqueror is the most noble and most elevated of aims'.

Another ambition of Louis XIV was to justify his title of the most Christian king. He wished to emulate the most Catholic king of Spain and the Holy Roman Emperor. To begin with, Louis thought of becoming a crusader. As we have seen, he furnished six thousand men to fight against the Turks in 1664 and offered the Holy Roman Emperor twenty thousand men to help drive the Turks out of Europe. Later in his reign when the Turks attacked Vienna, he hoped that if the Austrian capital fell, he would be able to pose as the saviour of the West. During his reign he used his influence to protect Roman Catholic minorities, for example in England and the United Netherlands. He encouraged the Duke of Savoy to repress the Protestants. Logically therefore he had also to suppress the heretics and unbelievers in his own kingdom. Essentially, however, the driving force of his religious policy at home was his desire to ensure political unity. So while maintaining as far as he could liberty of action in relation to the Papacy, which at times he attempted to humiliate, he wanted to discipline the Jansenists, who were Roman Catholic ascetics advocating an austere life and upholding the doctrine of salvation through grace alone. Furthermore he embarked on the wholesale conversion of the French Protestants or Huguenots who had enjoyed privileges conferred upon them by the Edict of Nantes in the reign of Louis's grandfather. It has recently been argued with considerable plausibility that the King of France was not really aware of the drastic methods used to compel conversions by Louvois, who succeeded his father as Secretary of State for War in 1966. Louis thought that the conversions, achieved by force or bribery, were genuine and that

The revocation of the Edict of Nantes by Louis XIV on 18 October 1685.

the Edict of Nantes could be revoked because it had become superfluous. But in his early years he himself was not a *dévot*. He flaunted his mistresses, acknowledged their children, and laughed at clerical hypocrisy along with the great Molière (Jean-Baptiste Poquelin). His own conversion did not come until late in life. As Goubert writes, 'the Most Christian King thought only of glory, not yet of salvation'.

The move to Versailles took place in May 1682 before the reconstruction of the palace, which had originally been a hunting lodge of his father's, had been completed. The Duc de Saint-

73

Simon thought the move absurd and that Versailles (where a town as well as a palace was then being built) was 'the saddest of places without a view, without wood or water, only shifting sands and marshes where the air was bad'. It cost millions of pounds and killed thousands of workmen. Yet the grandeur of Versailles, and particularly of its gardens, has continued to impress visitors from all over the world even in the age of democracy. It is because of this that the French King and his ministers have earned a rather spurious reputation as patrons of the arts. It is true that Colbert aimed to glorify his King with buildings, sculpture and paintings and found the money to do it. He worked through Charles Le Brun, a versatile if uninspired artist, and through Nicolas Boileau, a critic known as 'the Lawgiver of Parnassus'. But it must be remembered that it was the disgraced Fouquet who had discovered most of the great writers and artists of the reign such as Molière and Jean de la Fontaine, just as Mazarin had found the ablest administrators. Versailles itself was not an architectural success; the wings added by François Mansart to Louis Le Vau's original design threw it completely out of proportion. The famous gallery of mirrors also spoilt the design of the exterior. The inside was embellished by the furniture and the tapestries produced by the state factory of the Gobelins, but there was no sort of blending of the different arts such as that which was characteristic of the baroque or rococo. When the celebrated baroque architect and sculptor, Giovanni Lorenzo Bernini, was invited to Paris to re-design the Louvre, his plans were rejected largely on the impulse of Colbert who thought them too costly. Le Brun saw to it that painting was flattering rather than original. In literature authors and playwrights enjoyed a freer hand because their livelihood depended upon a wider patronage than that supplied by the monarch and his Court alone. Yet Jean de La Bruyère, a penetrating essayist, stated that 'important topics are forbidden'. Before Colbert died the budget for the arts was reduced, for he could not support beauty as well as war on a large scale. Louvois, who became Colbert's successor as Minister of the Arts, was even less concerned and had poorer taste. The French classical style will be discussed in a later chapter.

The achievements of the monarchy were founded upon the unceasing labour of the peasantry who were allowed, if they put on their best clothes, to wander in the gardens of Versailles and to supply cannon fodder for the royal armies. The rise of the bourgeoisie had not yet diminished the agricultural basis of the economy

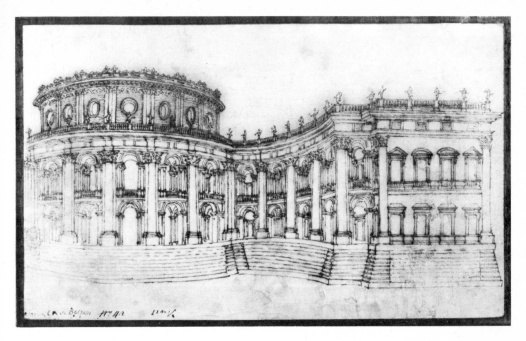

which was inherited from the Middle Ages. At the beginning of the seventeenth century fewer than a million out of fifteen million inhabitants of France lived in towns. The peasants owned less than half of the land. They had to pay taxes to the government, feudal dues to the bigger landowners and tithes to the Church. It has been estimated that the share extracted by the nobility and the Church from the peasants' output was of the order of thirty to forty per cent. Many different kinds of service had to be provided by them. They might be able to maintain a satisfactory standard of living when the weather was fine and the harvests were good, but in bad times they were ill-fed and not infrequently starved. It is one of the ironies of French agriculture that the peasants often grew insufficient grain to feed their own families and were forced to buy bread out of their earnings. Naturally the position varied from province to province and where the peasant was able to diversify his crops or supplement his farmwork by doing casual work of one kind or another or by fishing and poaching he was better off. But little progress in agricultural technology is recorded; traditional and old-fashioned methods were used. Books dealt with the art of gardening, the pursuit of hunting or how to make jam, not with the rotation of crops. Ploughing was tedious and wasteful, often producing poor yields. In one year out of two the grapes failed to ripen; in one year out of eight or ten the harvest

In 1665, when Louis XIV contemplated the restoration of the Louvre, the medieval palace of the Kings of France, he invited Bernini to Paris to produce designs. The drawing shows Bernini's first project for the east front. Although the King did not adopt his designs, he rewarded Bernini liberally, before sending him back to Rome.

75

The brothers Le Nain produced lively and realistic paintings of the poor people of France, which form a sharp contrast to the stiff formalized portraiture of the King and his court. Matthieu Le Nain here depicts a group of itinerant musicians.

was insufficient. Moreover industry and commerce contributed in only a small degree to the national income. The trading companies created by Colbert were unsuccessful: practising merchants refused to join these companies which were so strictly regimented by the government. France relied essentially upon its rich soil and its hard-working people.

Modern French historians in describing the difficulties under which the peasants laboured have perhaps given a somewhat exaggerated impression. When compared with the serfs of

76

parts of Germany, or of Poland, Hungary and Russia the French were fairly comfortable and were at least free to express their grievances without being whipped by their masters. There were undoubtedly many wealthy peasants who concealed their well-stocked barns from the view of the tax gatherers. Even compared with the Dutch and English tenantry (though feudalism came to an end earlier in England than in France) they cannot have been too badly off. After all, everywhere agriculture was dependent on the weather; nowhere except in the United Netherlands and in parts of eastern England was technological progress noticeable at this time. Nowhere were peasants more hard working or less adaptable than in France. If they had not been so, Louis XIV would never have been able to continue his wars as long as he did.

War was a costly business: it did not pay for itself. To achieve the King's ambitions the largest armies ever seen in western Europe were built up. When the French attacked the United Netherlands in 1672 an army of over a hundred thousand men was put into the field, of which about a third consisted of foreign mercenaries who had to be paid lest they deserted. Before the end of the reign the army had swollen to a quarter of a million. Colbert also devoted himself to expanding the royal navy so that victories might be won by fighting battles, not merely by preying upon the enemy's trade. Yet a naval tradition could not be established in a day and it was not until 1690 that the French won a notable victory at sea. Lastly the diplomatic machine was expensive. The French had more ambassadors and agents scattered around Europe than any other country. Indeed the idea of having permanent embassies in European capitals largely derives from the French example during the seventeenth century. But Louis XIV was not satisfied merely with this. He frequently made use of special envoys as well as resident ambassadors and he also used the services of rather strange characters such as astrologers, clergymen and men of letters. French gold was employed for a variety of purposes, mainly to bribe influential men such as English members of Parliament or Swedish senators. Finally, the French marshals were concerned with diplomatic intrigue as well as with spying. The French Foreign Office was large, containing experts at ciphers, propagandists and archivists. Nevertheless diplomacy was merely a preparation for war or the continuation of war by other means. Complicated diplomatic arrangements were made to isolate the Dutch, but in the end the war needed to be won through swift action by the French armies. Failing to overrun Holland and Zeeland, in the end the French generals had to fight against a coalition which their delays enabled the Dutch to construct.

The French monarch apparently had a sound base on which to found his expansionist ambitions. During the twelve years between 1659 and 1672 (since the war of the Queen's Rights was little more than a parade of strength) Colbert enjoyed a period of peace during which to promote the national economy and regulate the royal finances at least by cutting out waste. The peace of Westphalia, to which Richelieu contributed so much, and the peace of the Pyrenees, negotiated by Mazarin, had already fortified the French frontiers. Nearly a million *livres* a year were then spent on commerce and industry and about three million *livres* on the navy. In 1667 an ultra-protective customs tariff was introduced with a view to stimulating French industry and damaging the Dutch. Yet when Colbert discovered that the Dutch were not intimidated, he became almost psychopathic about them. He spoke of 'the insolence and arrogance of that nation' and advocated war not for reasons of prestige but for economic reasons. 'If the King were to subject the provinces of the United Netherlands, their commerce becoming the commerce of His Majesty's subjects, there would be nothing more to be desired.' But though Charles II of England, the enthusiastic ally of France in the opening stages of the Dutch war, also dreamed the same dream for his own subjects, it was all a mirage. In 1674 Charles had to abandon the war, while the French fought on for another five years before agreeing to the treaty of Nymegen which actually benefited the Dutch since Colbert's tariff had to be reduced and commercial advantages conceded. And, while it is true that France also gained from the treaty, the King had made enemies who in time exacted their revenge.

Professor Goubert writes of the French in 1678 that they had suffered a severe check which had fearful consequences: 'Neither objective of the war had been achieved, neither that of the King nor of Colbert: the cheese merchants were not chastised in spite of their miserable army: Dutch shipping and the Dutch Indies had not been subdued.' Already the financial work of Colbert was undermined. Professor Robert Mandrou thinks that Louis ought to have been satisfied with the territorial gains won by his predecessors instead of claiming to be recognized as the greatest power in Europe, even including the Pope, from whom he demanded that he should treat the French ambassador at Rome as the leading representative of European sovereigns. The King's search for glory, sustained by war, Mandrou believes, was a ruinous dream aimed at putting the whole of Europe under the heel of France; war, he says, was a destructive whip permanently used upon France.

Is that a fair judgment? Professor Ragnhild Hatton, an eminent English historian of Europe, evidently does not think so; for she has written that in the Dutch war the French armies were successful enough and that afterwards as a result of it Louis XIV was clearly motivated by the need to close the gates of entry on his eastern frontier. She believes that the 'barrier of iron' planned and erected by Vauban saved France from being overrun in the eighteenth century and that the gains from the peace of Nymegen were sufficient to allow the French to call their King 'great'.

Certainly there are always two sides to every question and historians must not permit themselves to be influenced in any way by propaganda to make the French of the seventeenth century into ogres or criminals. They were, after all, the most cultured people in the Western world of their time; their drama, literature and painting were outstanding. It can be maintained that after 1678 all Louis XIV's wars were defensive, even the war that he began in 1688 in an effort to intimidate the Emperor. War does not necessarily ruin an economy if it is not fought on a nation's own soil. English historians have argued that in many respects war (which was the characteristic occupation of most governments in the seventeenth century) was a stimulant; for example, the output of the peasants fetched good prices from large armies that needed to be fed, provided that these armies did not forcibly plunder but rather bought what they needed. With the rise of national 'standing' armies after the Thirty Years' War, soldiers could no longer live off the countryside with impunity. War also stimulated industrial development. Ship-building, iron foundries and the cloth industry were given plenty of work. In fact France did not suffer economic ruin as the result of Louis XIV's wars.

In many ways then the France of Louis XIV was a land of contrasts: contrasts between the peasants who starved to death in years of bad harvests and the wealthy farmers who were able to provide for their posterity; contrasts between the economical procedures of Colbert and the lavish expenditure of his master on wars and building and gilding his palaces; contrasts between the gardens of Versailles with their fountains and lakes and the workmen who died of marsh fever in digging the canals that brought the water from the river to the palace. One may also contrast the teaching of Jacques Bénigne Bossuet, Bishop of Meaux, who preached on the divine right of kings with the writings of highly intelligent members of the same generation who enjoyed a freedom of mind not usually associated with countries where totalitarianism or tyranny prevail. François Fénelon, Archbishop of Cambrai, and Marshal Vauban had telling criticisms to make of the way France was governed and an 'opposition' to the King has even been discerned especially from the 1690s onwards. The French monarch craved, above all else, harmony and unity; yet as soon as he ceased to be a victorious conqueror and became a loser and a persecutor he no longer commanded adulation and died unmourned. The glories of Versailles had their seamy side. As Professor Albert Guérard wrote, 'The palaces of the time lacked elementary sanitation; the aristocrats bathed less frequently than in the Middle Ages; stench was fought with perfume.' 'Classical France', as it was called, was a way of life but had no philosophy. The Bourbons' failure to create political unity, to destroy the galling remains of feudalism or to accept religious toleration paved the way ultimately for revolution.

5 The Triumph of the Grand Alliance 1688-1715

Louis XIV's lightning attack on Germany in the autumn of 1688, which French historians usually call a 'preventive' war, was remarkable in two respects. First, it was a departure from the foreign policy practised by Richelieu and Mazarin. Their aim had been to rally the princes of Germany against the Habsburgs; in fact, to divide Germany against itself. Louis had no doubt hoped to strengthen his tactical position on the Rhine (for the territories of the Elector of Cologne included Bonn and Kaiserswerth on the Lower Rhine, while the Palatinate comprised fortresses along the Middle Rhine) as an insurance against a possible war of revenge organized by the Emperor because of the concessions forced from him by the truce of Ratisbon, an insurance to be taken out while the Emperor's back was turned on the west. But the dual threat to the Electorate of Cologne and to the Electorate of the Palatinate naturally aroused the fears and suspicions of every ruler in Germany. This was accentuated when for military reasons the deliberate and systematic devastation of the Palatinate was ordered for a second time, which made the French King's sister-in-law weep for her poor country. But Louis was not unduly worried about all this. He did not think that the minor German princes would act by themselves against him without the leadership of the Emperor; he believed that in the previous war of the Grand Alliance they had been subsidized by Dutch money to fight him. He distrusted their loyalty even if he bought their friendship. He was therefore less anxious than before to engage them on his side. In this he was unwise for the German Electors had substantial armies, notably that of Brandenburg, and soon the allies were to succeed in containing the French everywhere except in Spain.

The second feature of the war was that the English for the first time openly and definitely committed themselves to war against France. Some foreshadowing of this policy may be detected during the reign of Charles II, notably in 1668 and 1678. Louis XIV had

François de
Montmorency, Duke of
Luxembourg, who was
created Marshal in 1675
and was the principal
Grench general from 1688
to 1695.

never set great store by the friendship of Charles, whom he did not trust, but the English King was, after all, a French pensioner. When in 1685 James II concluded a treaty with the Dutch, Louis felt a sense of resentment and he did not hold out prospects of naval assistance to the English Roman Catholic monarch until he realized too late that William III of Orange was seriously intending to lead a Dutch armada across the North Sea in order to compel his father-in-law to join the anti-French camp or abandon his throne. When the French King welcomed James into exile in France and gave him the protection of his navy and the advice of his military experts to carry out a campaign against William in Ireland, Louis had again left it too late. It was in the first place unlikely that his fleets would be able to command the seas for long against the combined strengths of the English and Dutch navies, while his support of James, who had managed to make himself unpopular with most of his subjects, merely provoked the English governing classes into giving their assent to joining the Grand Alliance. Before the Nine Years' War (1689–97) ended English soldiers or German mercenaries in English pay totalled over ninety thousand men. No such comparable effort was made by an English government for many years.

Unlike the situation during the war of 1672–8, the French lacked allies, though admittedly they possessed the largest and best trained army in Europe, one which had been kept more or less on a war footing for ten years and had an outstandingly able commander in the sexagenarian Duke of Luxembourg, who did not allow his love of women and wine to detract from his military efficiency. The Swedes, to whom Louis XIV had been so loyal ten years earlier, preferred to remain neutral as they had no wish to attract the attentions either of the fleets of the maritime powers or of the French corsairs. The Danes were also neutral, although they were under obligations to the Dutch and hired out soldiers to William III. The Germans were alienated; the English had changed sides; even Carlos II of Spain and his ministers were sufficiently annoyed by the constant French infringements of their neutrality in the southern Netherlands to agree to frontier fortresses being occupied by Dutch troops. Since the death of Philip IV Louis, having grandiose ambitions in the Spanish empire, was not pleased with the Spanish decision and declared war with reluctance. The only result of the Spanish entry into the war was that in 1693 Catalonia was invaded and in 1694 Barcelona was besieged by the French. But in spite of this scarcity of allies the

French enjoyed one considerable advantage, unity of command and of policy. The King was supreme and his orders had to be obeyed. He determined, once the Grand Alliance had been formed, to act upon the defensive – hence the devastation of the Palatinate – expecting that a war of sieges inspired by the genius of Vauban would exhaust the allies and sooner or later compel them to seek peace. This policy was not precisely inspiring for the French generals; and it was victories won in the field, in northern and southern Europe, that enabled the French to hold their own.

The Grand Alliance suffered from contrasting disadvantages. They did not have initially a large united army. They had no generals comparable with Luxembourg and Vauban. William III's only claim to military greatness was that, like George Washington later, he never knew when he was beaten. The French King was right in thinking that as soon as difficulties arose the allies would fall out among themselves. Spain lacked the means to wage other than defensive war; the Duke of Savoy, who joined the alliance in the summer of 1690, found his territories invaded by a French army under Marshal Catinat, no mean general, was defeated in battle, and soon started trying to obtain an agreement with the French. The English Whigs were jealous of the Tory ministers on whom William III mainly relied, while many of the Tories soon tired of their saviour, and might have welcomed James II back to his throne if only he would change his religion, which he stubbornly refused to do. The merchants of Amsterdam disliked war on principle, and Dutchmen were uneasy as bedfellows of their former enemies. Nevertheless their Captain-General and Stadholder, though suffering constant ill health and feeling a hearty distrust of most English politicians, was the life and soul of the alliance. In spite of the federal character of the Dutch Republic, he was able by devious means to make his influence felt both in the States-General and in the provincial governments. He had a friend in Antonie Heinsius, now the Grand Pensionary of Holland. Moreover William stood for a principle; he thought that the health and well-being of Europe depended on a balance of power, a doctrine which had first been applied to the city states of Italy and was in the process of widening into a broader diplomatic concept. However innocent the French may themselves have felt about their watch on the Rhine, the aggressive policy of their king, backed by his formidable forces, had caused a fright and made men feel that his overweening ambition must be curbed.

William III, King of England and Stadholder of the Dutch Republic. He led the Grand Alliance of Europe against the armies of Louis XIV.

In 1692, James II, in exile in France, persuaded Louis to back him in a full-scale invasion of England. The French fleet assembled near Cherbourg and James joyfully set off from Paris to join it. However, all his hopes were wrecked by the battle fought at sea off Cape La Hogue. James fell into black despair and wrote to Louis asking for 'some small corner of the world' where he might live.

At first the war developed favourably for the French. Vauban captured Philippsburg by the end of October 1688 (though Louis XIV attributed the success to God); Heidelberg was set on fire and so was Coblenz to the north; in the spring of 1689 other Rhineland towns were destroyed, an action which provoked the Germans and allowed the French soldiers to get out of hand. In 1689–91 the refurbished French navy achieved some notable victories, particularly in defeating the English at the battle of Beachy Head, so that Louis was able to boast that the French now commanded the Channel as well as the Mediterranean. On 1 July the Duke of Luxembourg won a victory over the allies on land at Fleurus in Flanders. Far away the Turks staged a counter-offensive against the Austrians and retook Belgrade. In April 1691 the fortress of

84

Mons fell to the French; another French army occupied Nice, which then belonged to the Duke of Savoy; Barcelona was bombarded while later, in June 1693, the French navy destroyed or captured English and Dutch merchant vessels south of Portugal as they were returning loaded from Smyrna in Anatolia. The only bright spot for the allies during the first three years of the war was the defeat of James II in Ireland.

However, French resources were fully stretched and although it is perhaps an exaggeration to say that from then on the war became one of attrition, its fortunes swayed backwards and forwards. A decisive defeat of the French Channel fleet at the battle of La Hogue or Barfleur in May 1692, when the French admiral had positive orders to fight, and the bloody if inconclusive battle of Steenkirk in August were setbacks for the French. On the other hand, the Duke of Luxembourg had taken the town of Namur in June, the French defences along the Rhine were unimpaired, and an allied attempt, based on Savoy, to invade the south of France was frustrated. In 1693 Louis himself appeared on the war front for the last time; after that he retired to direct strategy from Versailles. The old order was changing; Louvois, the organizer of victories, died in 1691 while Luxembourg, the best French general, died in October 1695. Before his death Luxembourg won a victory at Neerwinden (July 1693) and Marshal Catinat was again victorious in Savoy. Victor Amadeus II of Savoy negotiated a separate peace with the French and after that had been arranged in the summer of 1696, the allies consented in the autumn to the neutralization of Italy. This was in fact the beginning of the end of the war. Both sides were economically and financially impoverished. Bad harvests in 1692 and 1693 had caused wide distress. Military actions cancelled each other out. In 1965 William III retook Mons and the French bombarded Brussels. Later in the year Namur was also recaptured from the French. In 1696 Louis XIV planned and then called off an attempt to invade England. But the capture of Barcelona by the French following the neutralization of Italy were setbacks to the allies. The French monarch, with his thoughts still largely concerned with what might happen when the childless King of Spain died, constituted himself the 'giver of peace', remarking in an expansive way that he deliberately sacrificed the advantages he had gained in the war to the needs of public tranquillity.

The Emperor agreed reluctantly to make peace. But he had been compelled, owing to the Turkish revival, to fight a war on two fronts, for it was not until 1697 that a rising Austrian general, Prince Eugene of Savoy, crushed the Turks at Zenta, some fifty miles to the east of the Danube. By the terms of the treaty of Ryswick Louis recognized William III as King of England (the main motive for which the English fought in the war) and the Dutch were granted a favourable commercial treaty. Neither of the two maritime powers sought or acquired new territory. The French, who surrendered most of their territorial gains obtained since the treaty of Nymegen and abandoned their effective occupation of Lorraine while agreeing to destroy all their fortifications along the Rhine, were permitted to retain Strasbourg. The Spaniards received back all the fortresses they had lost in the southern Netherlands; Luxembourg and Barcelona were also restored to them. As the historian Sir George Clark has noted, 'it soon began to be said that Louis, having shown the Spaniards how easily he could ruin them, now wanted them friends with an eye to the succession question'. 'Avoid anything', Louis ordered one of his ambassadors in the course of the negotiations, 'not to give any hope of my renunciation and that of my son to the succession in Spain.' It was clear that the peace of Ryswick was no more than a truce. Yet William III, a sick and lonely man, now a widower, sought to maintain the peace throughout western Europe.

When the Nine Years' War ended Carlos II of Spain was thirty-six. Although his death had been expected for a generation – a death which would surely upset the balance of power in the Western world – it now seemed clear that he was not going to live much longer, and, in any case, although he had been married twice, once to a French princess and once to a German, it was certain that he would never have any children. The question of who had the best claim to succeed him was incredibly complicated. There was no purely Spanish candidate and the two most powerful rulers in Europe, Louis XIV and the Emperor Leopold I, both of whom had had Spanish mothers and Spanish wives, emerged in the strongest position from the legal point of view. The Emperor Leopold felt little doubt that he would win in the end, for not only had his first wife, Margaret, the daughter of Philip IV of Spain, not renounced her succession rights, but the sister of his second wife was, opportunely, the second wife of Carlos II. In a secret clause of the treaty of the Grand Alliance the two maritime powers had in effect promised to support the right of the Austrian Habsburgs to succeed Carlos II if he died. So the Emperor waited phlegmatically for the event.

In 1697, the greatest Austrian general, Prince Eugene of Savoy, won a glorious victory over the Turks at Zenta, fifty miles east of the Danube. This led, two years later, to the treaty of Carlowitz and the cession of all Turkish-occupied Hungary to the Habsburg empire.

Louis XIV, for his part, had been fully aware that if Carlos II inconveniently passed away during the Nine Years' War, the chance of his profiting from the death of the Spanish monarch would be negligible. For he had actually been at war with Spain at the time and the maritime powers were the Austrian Habsburgs' allies. That, as has been seen, was one of the main reasons why Louis XIV agreed to peace in the autumn of 1697. However, he was not anxious to be immediately involved in another big war any more than were the other participants and he therefore reverted to the idea, first adumbrated in 1668, that the Spanish inheritance should be partitioned. An approach was made to his late enemy William III for whom he understandably had considerable respect, because he thought that a decision could be reached more rapidly with him than with either Madrid or Vienna, both notorious for

87

their delays in negotiation. William welcomed the approach first because he wanted neither England (which was now disarmed) nor the Dutch Republic (which was resuming its full commercial activities) to be dragged into another war and he was satisfied, as long as both countries enjoyed a reasonable share of trade with Spain, particularly across the Atlantic, to act as an honest broker and thus secure peace.

After much elaborate coming and going a partition treaty was signed in October 1698. By its terms the grandson of the Emperor, a child of eight, who was the son of the Elector of Bavaria, was to obtain the throne of Spain, Louis's only son and heir, the Dauphin, was to take Sicily, Sardinia, the Tuscan ports and the key Basque province of Guipuzcoa, while the second son of the Emperor Leopold would be awarded the duchy of Milan. The Elector of Bavaria had been appointed during the recent war to the post of governor of the Spanish Netherlands and after the peace of Ryswick the Dutch had been accorded the right to provide troops to man a barrier of frontier fortresses there under the command of the governor. Thus everybody would get something valuable out of the deal. Though it was true that the ultimate acquisition of ports in Italy by the French Crown was not to be looked upon with equanimity, at any rate neither the Dutch Republic nor the kingdom of England was to be menaced by the French acquiring such ports as Ostend and Antwerp.

The difficulty about this agreement was that neither the King of Spain nor the Emperor Leopold was asked for his opinion. Louis hoped that the maritime powers would bring pressure to bear in order to make them both acquiesce in the treaty. In this he was completely wrong. In any case the whole arrangement collapsed because within three months of its signature the child prince of Bavaria died, poisoned so the French alleged by his Austrian grandfather. However, negotiations were patiently renewed and in March 1700 another partition treaty was agreed to by the French and the maritime powers. The duchy of Lorraine was then added to the Dauphin's share, thus significantly extending the French eastern frontier, while Milan was awarded to the Duke of Lorraine in exchange. In return the second son of the Emperor Leopold, Archduke Charles, was to be awarded the whole of Spain, the southern Netherlands and the vast overseas possessions of the Spanish Crown. William in negotiating the second treaty was hardly being realistic and it caused an outcry against him in both London and Amsterdam.

The first partition treaty was, nominally at any rate, concluded in secret; but the second was an open treaty, since in order to make it workable it was necessary for the Spanish and Austrian Habsburg rulers to consent to its terms. The Emperor Leopold, who in 1699 at last concluded a treaty of peace with the Turks and thereby ensured his dominion over the whole of Hungary and Transylvania, was in no mood to accede to the treaty. Nor was the King of Spain. Spanish pride demanded that its empire (already shorn of the northern Netherlands and Portugal) should not be cut up. Carlos II therefore made a will. By a first will he had bequeathed all his possessions to the Bavarian princeling; by his second he bequeathed them not to Louis XIV's heir, the Dauphin, but to the Dauphin's second son, Philip of Anjou. If Philip refused this magnificent gift, it was to be offered to the Archduke Charles of Austria. Thus – in theory at least – whatever happened, the Spanish empire would remain intact and independent. Such was the belief that glowed in the cloudy mind of Carlos, who was at last really dying. He signed his second will in October 1700 and a month later 'the Sufferer', as he was called, expired.

Louis XIV had now to decide whether he should attempt to abide by the terms of the partition treaty or acquiesce in the will. The question was urgently debated in Versailles and who exactly said what is still disputed. It was plausibly reasoned that it was better that the Dauphin, Louis XIV's heir, should acquire Lorraine and southern Italy as French possessions in full sovereignty than that the Dauphin's second son should scoop the pool. For he would be required by the terms of the will to renounce his right of succession to the French throne and he might even (as in fact was to happen) become more Spanish than the Spaniards. The Dauphin, who was fat and usually apathetic, insisted that the will should be accepted: he was content to be the son of a great king and the father of a great king. Louis XIV himself was convinced that whatever else he did he would be obliged to fight against the Austrian Habsburgs again, for they were unlikely to accept meekly either a partition or the accession of a French Bourbon prince to the throne of Madrid. Moreover, however the new King of Spain behaved, a Bourbon alliance was surely likely in the future. Thus, as the Spanish ambassador to France remarked, the Pyrenees would 'no longer exist'.

For a few months it seemed as if the French decision to accept the testament of Carlos II was the right one. 'Some very wise men believe', wrote Madame de Maintenon, Louis XIV's morganatic wife, 'that there will not have to be a war and that we should have had a long and difficult one, ruinous to France, if Louis had insisted on the execution of the treaty.' French historians have supported her view, maintaining that the war of the Spanish succession, which began in full force in 1702, was the result of unscrupulous propaganda by interested parties such as the exiled French Huguenots. The only government which immediately thought of war was that at Vienna, where the Emperor Leopold had refused to agree to the two partition treaties on the ground that his family were the legitimate heirs to the whole of the Spanish inheritance. Nevertheless, there was the possibility that unless he could acquire allies the Emperor might have to agree to some compromise and that even if he would not, the war might be confined to northern Italy. Both the English and Dutch governments recognized Philip of Anjou, named Philip V of Spain, as heir. In business circles the hope was expressed that Philip would not prove himself to be a tool of France and that his succession might even be helpful to the expansion of trade.

William III, a sick and petulant man, had no such faith in the coming independence of Spain nor in the altruism of France. He had been disappointed in his opinion, formed after the peace of Ryswick, that Louis XIV had become a chastened and reasonable ruler ready to accept a balance of power in Europe. He told his friend, Heinsius, that they had been duped and regarded war as unavoidable. But he proceeded cautiously, anticipating correctly that public opinion in England and in the Dutch Republic might change when the significance of events dawned on them. Thus although he sent John Churchill, the Earl of Marlborough, an experienced diplomat and proved military commander, to The Hague to conclude another Grand Alliance with the Dutch and the Austrians, this was not, on the surface, a signal for war against France. It allowed for negotiations and it did not commit the maritime powers to obtaining the entire Spanish heritage for the Austrian Habsburgs. It was envisaged that the Emperor should acquire all the Spanish possessions in neighbouring Italy, that the Dutch should receive a barrier of fortresses in the southern Netherlands and that the maritime powers should gain commercial and colonial advantages. Louis himself seems to have been prepared to make concessions to avert another war. It is indeed ironical that after twelve years of fierce fighting a compromise, based on the idea of partition, was eventually to be reached.

Decisions taken in France and Spain in 1701 which, French

historians maintain, were misunderstood and distorted by un-scrupulous propagandists finally brought about the war. Shortly after the signature of the treaty of the Grand Alliance against him (7 September) Louis recognized James III, the son of James II who had just died, as the legitimate King of England, which natur-ally angered William and the Whigs. Permission was obtained from Spain for French soldiers to occupy the fortresses held by Dutch troops in the Spanish Netherlands. Swift action followed; the Dutch were surprised, disarmed and sent home. In Italy a French force was ordered to seize the duchy of Milan in the name of the new Spanish King. Furthermore, two diplomatic blunders of the first magnitude were committed. It was announced both in Madrid and in Versailles that Philip of Anjou had not re-nounced his right to succeed ultimately to the French throne: this was explained to be a mere statement of fact because con-stitutionally he could not do so. The other blunder was that the Spanish Regency, while awaiting the arrival of their new young King, invited Louis XIV to direct the government in his name. Fuel was added to the fire when the French were given exclusive trading privileges in Spanish overseas possessions.

All this meant – as William had expected – that effective public opinion in the two Protestant countries which he ruled, already largely antagonistic to France for historical reasons, became extremely hostile and militant. The English Whigs, who had asserted that William had acted unconstitutionally and foolishly in negotiating the partition treaties, were won over to the idea of war. In fact to a large extent the coming war was for these two countries one strongly influenced by economic considerations, for merchants did not relish the notion of the French winning a trading monopoly both in the Mediterranean and across the Atlantic. So an undeclared war began in 1701. In September Prince Eugene inflicted an important defeat on the French expeditionary force at Chiavi in the duchy of Milan. This put the allies in good heart. On 15 May 1702 they officially declared war on France.

The French appeared at first to enjoy several advantages in the coming war. Their army was well trained with some experienced generals who had emerged since the death of the Duke of Luxem-bourg. Initially it amounted to over two hundred thousand men and soon rose to a quarter of a million. Again, Louis XIV had unity of command and could operate defensively on inner lines. This time the French had the Spaniards for allies instead of enemies;

though they did not have much to offer in the way of troops or equipment, the loyalty of the bulk of the Spanish people to their new king was to prove a useful asset. The French also persuaded the Portuguese to become their allies. Thus the French had access to a large number of naval bases in the Mediterranean and the Atlantic and also, after their army had occupied the southern Netherlands, in the North Sea. Although the French navy was inferior to that of the English and Dutch combined, throughout the war much damage was inflicted on allied trade by French privateers. French diplomacy also enlisted the alliance of the Duke of Savoy, although in view of his behaviour in the previous war, they can scarcely have trusted him. However, his alliance facilitated their operations in Italy. Finally, the French obtained the alliances of the two Wittelsbach brothers (the Elector of Bavaria and the Elector of Cologne) who had always been envious of the Habsburgs. The Elector of Bavaria's accession to the French side constituted a threat to Vienna while his brother gave French troops manoeuvring power on the Lower Rhine. Furthermore the French encouraged and supported Francis Rakoczi, a proud Magyar magnate who had inherited a Hungarian nationalist tradition and enmity towards Austria. In 1703 he was to head a rebellion which was to distract the attention of Leopold I and his successors from the western theatre of war. Though the French were in no position to seek help in the Baltic, the fact that the Swedes were already engaged in fighting the Danes, the Poles and the Russians meant that the danger of the Grand Alliance finding active assistance from northern Europe was relatively small.

On the allied side an impressive accumulation of strategic resources was steadily built up. The Dutch and English rapidly raised large armies because they could afford to hire mercenaries from Denmark and the smaller German states. Brandenburg had a substantial army which was joined to the allied forces; for the Elector was anxious to please the Emperor who agreed to recognize him as King Frederick I in Prussia. In fact most of the German principalities consented to fight under the banner of the Holy Roman Emperor because they had been provoked by French aggression in two previous wars. But some of their soldiers proved pretty useless. Moreover the Emperor's attention was often distracted from the theatres of war in the Netherlands and in Spain because of the nearer problems he had to face in the Balkans and in Italy. However, he had a fine general in Eugene, just as the

British had in Marlborough, while Heinsius was the diplomatic heir of William III, who died in March 1702. Queen Anne, his sister-in-law, who succeeded as queen, boasted of her 'English heart' and proved more popular than Dutch William, whom the English political nation had never fully trusted. The wealth of the English kingdom and the Dutch Republic, deriving from commerce, industry and banking (the Bank of England, which lent money to the government, was founded in 1694) made them the paymasters of the Grand Alliance which was able finally to bring the Bourbons to heel.

The war of the Spanish succession ranged over much of Europe; it was fought in the southern Netherlands, in Germany, in Italy and in Spain. The French, although profiting from their inner lines of communication and their unity of command, were handicapped by their inferiority at sea, particularly in the Mediterranean. In the first two years of the war the allies pushed back the French defensive lines on the Meuse and the Lower Rhine. On the other hand, in 1703 the Marquis of Villars, a boastful and quarrelsome man, who proved himself to be easily the best of the French commanders, broke through the fortified lines of Stollhofen, which had been constructed by Prince Louis of Baden, one of the Emperor's generals, and which were intended to prevent the French from advancing north between the Black Forest and the Upper Rhine. Meanwhile in Italy the French had made progress in the duchy of Milan after a drawn battle fought at Luzzara in August 1702 between Marshal Vendôme, France's second best general, and Prince Eugene. In Spain, the allies had done well through the exertion of sea power. Cadiz was attacked and a Spanish silver fleet destroyed off north-west Spain at Vigo, the French escort squadron being destroyed. This episode made a profound impression on both Portugal and Savoy and induced them both to change sides. By the treaty with Portugal, signed in May 1703, the allies gained a valuable base at Lisbon. At the same time the Portuguese, who did not wish for a French prince as king in Madrid, insisted that no peace should be made without the Austrian candidate becoming the ruler of Spain. This commitment in fact prolonged the war, since it delayed the peace treaty being concluded on the basis of a division of the Spanish empire. The accession of Savoy to the alliance opened the opportunity for an attack on France from the south. But French troops immediately occupied both Savoy and Piedmont so the Austrians fighting in Italy became bogged down, to the disappointment of the Vienna

government which sought territorial gains in Italy rather than in Spain.

Villars's success in southern Germany (for which he was created marshal) and the seizure of the city of Ulm on the Danube by the French ally, the Elector Maximilian Emmanuel of Bavaria, opened up for the French a real offensive opportunity by allowing them to advance into Austria itself and by defeating the Emperor compel him to agree to peace. The scheme was that Villars

A bird's-eye view of the breaking of the boom by the English and Dutch fleets in Vigo Bay on 12 October 1702. The allied fleets were thus able to destroy the Spanish silver fleet with the French escort squadron.

should march through the Tyrol and link up with Maximilian Emmanuel, while Vendôme, leaving some forces to contain the Austrians in Italy, should join up with them through the Brenner pass. Meanwhile the rebel Hungarians, subsidized from Paris, would threaten Vienna from the east. Another French army under Marshal Tallard was sent to replace that of Villars in Alsace. However the scheme fell to pieces: Maximilian Emmanuel had ambitions of his own in the Tyrol; Vendôme was afraid to leave Italy; Villars quarrelled with Maximilian Emmanuel, who, as a prince, was his superior in rank. Nevertheless the French were not unsuccessful in 1703. The veteran Marshal Vauban captured the town of Breisach in Alsace, thus opening the long lines of communication between France and Bavaria. Prince Louis of Baden was defeated by the French at the battle of Höchstadt and the town of Augsburg on the river Lech, a tributary of the Danube, was occupied. Augsburg was on the route to Vienna so that the threat became obvious. But Louis made one fatal mistake. He recalled Villars and replaced him by an inferior marshal, Marsin.

The danger to the Grand Alliance was grave enough for the allies, led by Marlborough (who had been given a dukedom on account of his successes in 1702) and Prince Eugene, who had been recalled from Italy to the the Bavarian front, to concert a campaign to relieve the pressure on Austria. Marlborough skilfully led an army of twenty thousand (later to be swollen by German contingents to fifty thousand) from the Meuse to the Danube, a distance of two hundred and fifty miles, deceiving the French about his ultimate destination. Prince Eugene, who joined Marlborough fifty miles west of Ulm early in June, soon established a good relationship with him. It was agreed that Eugene should go west to prevent the French under Tallard from coming to the Danube, but in this he was unsuccessful, and Tallard met Marsin and the Elector of Bavaria at Augsburg on 5 August. On 13 August 1704 the two groups of armies confronted each other at Höchstadt, where Villars had won a victory for the French the year before. To distinguish the two battles the second one is known as the battle of Blenheim (Blindheim was a village not far from Höchstadt). Although the French and the Bavarians outnumbered the allies, a great victory was won by Marlborough and Eugene. Thus Bavaria, which had been systematically devastated before the battle, was knocked out of the war. The Elector Maximilian Emmanuel went back to his profitable post as governor of the Spanish Netherlands. The French lost over twenty thousand men in the battle and Marshal Tallard was taken prisoner. The blow to French military prestige was incalculable. Marlborough returned to the Moselle from whence he planned to invade France in the following year. Shortly before the victory at Blenheim an English admiral, Sir George Rooke, captured the Rock of Gibraltar and had the better of the French and Spanish fleets, which aimed to retake Gibraltar, in an engagement off Malaga. Never again did the French fleet seek battle with the allies nor were attempts to recapture Gibraltar effective.

1705 was another crucial year in the war. Marlborough's plan to advance into Lorraine from the Moselle was frustrated by the vigilance of Marshal Villars, who had been restored to command. In Italy, to which Prince Eugene had returned, his attempt to link up with the turncoat Duke of Savoy was withstood by Vendôme at the battle of Cassano in August. The only allied success was the capture of Barcelona, where the Catalans had rallied to the cause of the Archduke Charles. Next year, however, was a disaster for the French. On 23 May Marlborough won a big victory at Ramillies, north of Namur, which was more pregnant in its consequences even than Blenheim. For the whole of the Spanish Netherlands fell almost without resistance into the allied hands. In August the allies laid siege to Menin, a frontier fortress in France itself. A month later the Archduke Charles, who had landed at Lisbon in March 1704, marched into Spain and was crowned as Carlos III in Madrid. In September Prince Eugene, assisted by the Duke of Savoy, won another big victory over the French at Turin; Marshal Marsin was killed and the French field army was forced to retreat across the Alps.

It looked as if the war was at an end. Louis XIV put out peace feelers in the Netherlands, expressing himself as willing to concede the same kind of terms as those he had agreed with William III in the second partition treaty. The Dutch, who might have been willing to treat if promised a barrier of fortresses in the southern Netherlands, however, remained loyal to their allies. The new Habsburg Emperor, Joseph I, who had succeeded his father in 1705, wanted the entire Spanish inheritance for his younger brother (except for Milan which he intended to keep for himself). The English, committed by the treaty of 1703 with Portugal and fearful of a French predominance in southern Italy which might harm their Mediterranean trade, were adamantly opposed to any concession whatever. Thus the opportunity passed. Next year Archduke Charles was driven out of Spain after an allied army had

The War of the
Spanish Succession
1701-14

▨ Main areas of war

✕ Anglo-Dutch-Austrian victor

✕ French-Bavarian victory

--- Marlborough's march 1704

Vigo
1702 ✕

Valla

Salan
1706 ✕

Ciudad Rodrigo
✕ 1706

Alcantara
1706 ✕   Tagus   Mad

Lisbon

PORTUGAL

SPA

Cadiz   Malag
Gibraltar ✕ 170
captured by Br. 1704

96

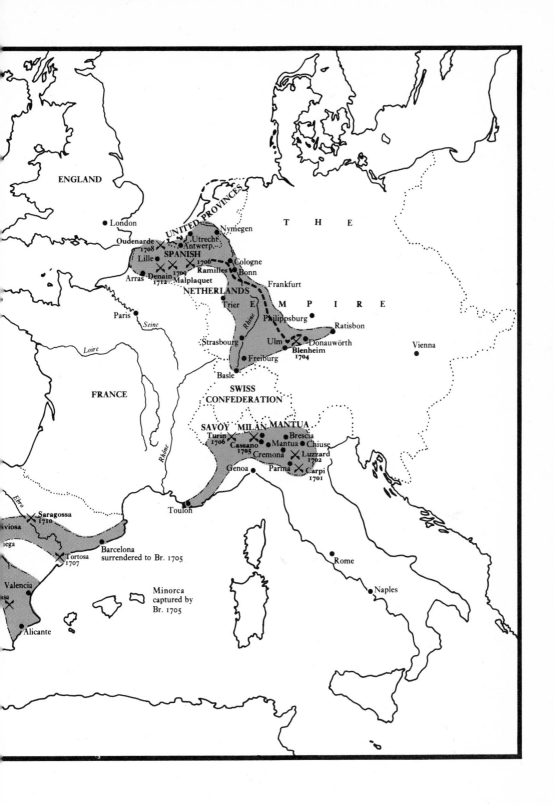

ENGLAND

London

United Provinces

Oudenarde
1708
Spanish
Lille
1706
Arras   Denain
         1712   Malplaquet
Netherlands

THE

Nymegen
Utrecht
Antwerp
Ramilles
1709
Cologne
Bonn

EMPIRE

Frankfurt

Paris
Seine

Trier

Rhine

Philippsburg
Ratisbon

Loire

Strasbourg

Basle

Freiburg

Ulm
Blenheim
1704

Donauwörth

Vienna

FRANCE

Swiss
Confederation

Savoy Milan Mantua
Turin
1706
Cassano
1705
Cremona
Brescia
Mantua   Chiuse
Parma   Luzzard
                 1702
Genoa   Carpi
         1701

Rhine

Toulon

Saragossa
1710

Barcelona
surrendered to Br. 1705

Tortosa
1707

Valencia

Alicante

Rome

Naples

Minorca
captured by
Br. 1705

been defeated by the French at the battle of Almanza. In 1708 the French began a counter-offensive in the southern Netherlands, but Vendôme was defeated at the battle of Oudenarde. However, stalemate developed. In the previous year a big allied operation against Toulon was a failure, while the Emperor, greedy for territorial gains in Italy, agreed to the convention of Milan with the French, enabling them to evacuate northern Italy and use the troops thus released to reinforce the other fronts. In 1709 the battle of Malplaquet, fought by Villars to stave off the threat of invasion of France from the north-east, was a murderous battle in which the Duke of Marlborough, though nominally victorious, had to sustain heavy casualties which deeply distressed him. Though he remained in command for two more years he did not fight another battle. In fact from 1709 onwards it was simply a question of negotiating a peace. As at Ryswick over twelve years earlier, the bargaining was long and complicated. But at last in April 1713 the maritime powers concluded a treaty at Utrecht in Holland with France, while the Emperor somewhat reluctantly came to terms with the French at Rastatt a year later.

The peace of Utrecht brought to an end the period which is usually called that of the ascendancy of France or the age of Louis XIV. The French King was now seventy-five years old and had seen his heirs dying off one after another until his great-grandson (the youngest son of the Duke of Burgundy), who was only two years old, was left as the direct heir. Louis believed that the loss of his grandchildren and his defeat in the war were punishments imposed upon him by God. Yet Jean-Baptiste Colbert Torcy, the son of Colbert and the grandson of a cloth merchant in Rheims, who was mainly responsible for the negotiation of the treaty, could write: 'God has crowned the Christian courage of the King in maintaining Philip v, his grandson, on the Spanish throne in spite of the efforts of a formidable league. . . .' Philip had to swear that he renounced his claims to the French succession before the *Cortes* in Madrid – for what that was worth. He retained not only the throne of Spain but all Spain's overseas possessions in the Americas and the West Indies. Furthermore he was given a free hand to deal with the rebellious Catalans as he liked, a gross betrayal by the allies. France itself was by no means shattered territorially by the conclusion of the prolonged wars. It kept Strasbourg, Franche-Comté and Alsace, though it was obliged to give up its conquests on the right bank of the Rhine such as Breisach, Kehl and Frieburg, and it did not lose all its colonies overseas.

Opposite: An English cartoon imagining the effect of the news of Marlborough's victory at Ramillies upon the French Court. A weeping Madame de Maintenon kneels before Louis, while the Duke of Anjou – Philip v of Spain – presents the requests for aid in the bottom left hand of the picture. Above them, the sun, the symbol of Louis, is shown in eclipse.

What did the allies gain? The Duke of Savoy, who had changed sides at a fortunate time, was among the best-off. He was given Sicily to add to his dominions of Savoy and Piedmont, while Nice was restored to him. He was also allowed to adopt the title of king, as, on the other side of Europe, was Frederick I, confirmed as King in Prussia. The Portuguese position in Brazil was strengthened at the expense of both the Spaniards and the French. The Emperor, who was now that very Archduke Charles who had aspired to the Spanish throne and who was known as the Emperor Charles VI, though he regretted not having achieved his full ambitions, did not do badly out of the peace, for as a result of it the southern Netherlands were added to his empire as was also much of Italy including the duchy of Milan and the island of Sardinia. Upper or Spanish Gelderland, however, was detached from the southern Netherlands and awarded to Prussia. The Wittelsbachs were restored to their Electorates in Germany. Henceforward the authority of the Habsburgs as the suzerains of Germany began to be steadily eroded.

What of the maritime powers? The Dutch gained remarkably little from a war in which they had expended so much money and so many lives. They had, it is true, realized William III's ambition of preventing the Spanish Netherlands from falling into the hands of the French and they had obtained a barrier of fortresses – though it excluded Lille – in that area to obstruct further French aggression. The barrier was not as comprehensive as they wished because the English who after a Tory victory in the general election of 1710 had reached a separate peace with France were not prepared to allow the Dutch all that the Whigs had promised them in a treaty of 1709, while the commercial advantages they won were small. They had to negotiate the details of their fortresses with the Emperor Charles VI. But in any case the whole idea of a barrier was a delusion. Never in the history of the Western world were the Dutch able by the mere possession of fortifications to stop invasion by more powerful enemies. Utrecht, wrote the distinguished Dutch historian, Pieter Geyl, ended the period of Dutch greatness, although, as has been noticed already, other historians do not agree with him.

England, or rather Great Britain, for the union with Scotland had at last been agreed to in 1707, benefited most from the war. It was given, much to the annoyance of the Dutch, a virtual monopoly of the slave trade with Spain, being permitted by what was known as the 'asiento' to carry some five thousand slaves a year to the

The peace of Utrecht, which was signed in April 1713. Of all the powers which signed the treaty, it was the English who were thought to have benefited the most, and this is reflected in the broadsheet, which shows the cornucopia of prosperity spilling out towards Queen Anne.

Spanish Indies. A ship was also allowed to carry goods to South America once a year and under the cover of that concession a busy smuggling trade grew up. England gained Gibraltar and Minorca, thus strengthening its naval superiority in the Mediterranean. Queen Anne (who died in 1714) was recognized as the legitimate Protestant Queen; this was necessary because the French and Spaniards had naturally backed the exiled Roman Catholic Stuarts during the war. Finally England made substantial gains overseas. Hudson Bay, Newfoundland and Acadia (Nova Scotia) were all recognized as British; St Kitts was added to the British West Indies; certain fishing rights in the neighbourhood of Newfoundland were all that were retained by the French. The French still ruled Canada and Louisiana in the north and south of the North American continent, but the colonies there were sparsely populated and had been neglected by Louis XIV. Thus the settlement at Utrecht not only presaged the building of the first British empire, but also the continuing expansion of the Western world across the Atlantic.

6 A Federal Nation in Embryo: the American Colonies to 1732

The outstanding accomplishment of the seventeenth century in American history [writes Professor Thomas Wertenbaker] was the planting of the colonies. In the year 1600 America north of the Floridas was inhabited by savage beasts and hardly less savage Indians; in 1690 the Atlantic Coast from Charleston to Nova Scotia was dotted with flourishing villages and towns, while many of the river valleys were covered with farms where comfortable homesteads nestled among fields of tobacco and wheat and corn.

Along the coastal plain, but shut in by the Allegheny mountains, a new Europe was in the process of coming into being. It has been estimated that by the end of the century the population was at least a quarter of a million white men and some twenty-five thousand black slaves; it was to multiply tenfold by the time of the American war of independence. Out of this population about a hundred thousand in roughly equal proportions were concentrated in the two oldest colonies, Massachusetts in the north and Virginia in the south, and nearly all the inhabitants of these colonies came from the British isles. They had arrived in search of an Eldorado or at any rate a cornucopia which would make them rich and free. Though the trading companies or proprietors had obtained royal charters defining their colonies geographically, it was obviously impossible for the government in London to exercise full political or economic control over this vast new area of the Western world. It is true that the voyage from England could at best take only a few weeks, but merchant ships and royal naval vessels might make the three-thousand-mile trip forwards and backwards across the Atlantic but once a year. Thus correspondence and news travelled slowly and orders sent to colonial governors from Whitehall would often be out of date before they arrived. From the very beginning the relative independence of the European colonists became an established fact.

Moreover two factors need to be taken into account. By the

last decade of the seventeenth century England had ceased to be the main source of emigration to the colonies. (The English are estimated to have formed only about sixty per cent of the total population when the war of independence began.) The religious persecution, which had been one of the principal causes of emigration before 1648, had ceased to be important by 1688, for with the triumph of William III dissenters had won toleration in England. Secondly, it came to be believed that North America was not a source of precious metals such as the Spaniards and Portuguese had discovered in South America. (One of the few requirements of the Stuart kings was that in return for the granting of charters five per cent of the gold found in the colonies should go to the Crown.) Thus the attraction for get-rich-quickly adventurers diminished. It was reckoned that the West Indian colonies were more valuable in supplying sugar and spice than the mainland colonies and were also useful bases from which to stage attacks on Spanish treasure ships. But emigration from outside the British isles swelled. The new emigrants included downtrodden German peasants, French Huguenots, Scots-Irish from indigent Ulster and poverty-stricken Swiss. These Europeans flowed mainly into the middle colonies. Though they became subjects of the British Crown and in time English-speaking people, they were antagonistic towards both English merchants and industrialists who tried to maintain monopolies and towards the Anglican Church. Furthermore those indentured servants who braved the horrific journey across the Atlantic and in time gained their freedom were not going to accept restrictions upon their new way of life. So North America became a melting pot of the Western world.

And not North America only. For it must be remembered that the West Indies too were the home of a mixed European community. 'The Caribbean', it has been said, was 'an area where Europe's frontiers met'. Here there were Spanish, French, Dutch and English colonies. Though the Spanish grip remained strong in the Greater Antilles, the Lesser Antilles was a no-man's-land.

Barbados and Jamaica were blessed with bold and unscrupulous governors who insisted that there was no peace beyond the line. The colonists who went there were seeking not so much religious freedom as economic gain. The English governor of Jamaica observed in 1673 that the Dutch had a motto: 'Jesus Christ is good, but trade is better.' More Negro slaves were brought there than to the North American mainland. Jews were welcomed and Negroes encouraged. The West Indian policy of the British government was to make profits out of the Caribbean islands and invest them in Jamaica. Both licensed and unlicensed commercial intercourse prevailed between the Spanish and English islands. Privateers raided Cuba and plundered Panama. In time of war the English government thought it worthwhile to dispatch frigates across the Atlantic to defend these valuable islands against the Dutch and the French. In defiance of acts of trade proclaimed in London a busy traffic grew up between the expanding American colonies, particularly Massachusetts, and the West Indies, which was to become a source of incalculable wealth in the eighteenth century.

Although Massachusetts was originally populated by the same kind of Puritans as those who fought against Charles I for religious freedom, the colony long remained an exclusive theocracy under intolerant Calvinists, led, for example, by the famous Mather family, which accepted the burning of witches; in other parts of America tolerance was real enough for dissenters. The Church of England, which came under the authority of the Bishop of London, took a hold only in the south. The Quakers, who suffered

The island of Barbados in 1657.

PENNS TREATY with the INDIANS, made 1681 with out an Oath, and never broken. The foundation of Religious and Civil LIBERTY, in the U.S. of AMERICA

William Penn making a treaty with the Indians in 1682. This marked the foundation of the state of Pennsylvania and was commemorated in the early nineteenth century in a painting by Edward Hicks.

persecution in England during the reign of Charles II, flocked to America. Their founder, George Fox, paid a visit there in 1672, while William Penn, who though a Quaker was a wealthy *persona grata* at the English royal Court, obtained a charter in 1681 to establish the colony later to be named after him which welcomed all dissenters. So did Maryland, for although it was founded by a Roman Catholic, Lord Baltimore, it admitted all Christians except Quakers, whose refusal to bear arms caused them to be oppressed there as well as in Virginia. But they became for a time a dominant force in Rhode Island, which as early as 1636 had split away from Massachusetts because of the harsh intolerance of its rulers. The Quaker diaspora helps to explain the long-enduring Puritan outlook of much of the United States of America.

By the end of the seventeenth century the English colonies in

America were twelve in number. (Georgia, the thirteenth, which received a charter in 1732, was named after King George II and though set up by philanthropists, later became a royal province.) Virginia received its charter in 1606 and New England was formed in 1620. New England became divided into Massachusetts (which included Maine), Rhode Island, Connecticut and New Hampshire. Maryland, named after Queen Henrietta Maria, the wife of Charles I, was founded in 1632, Carolina, named after Charles II, in 1663. This colony was first governed by a board, headed by the Earl of Shaftesbury, the celebrated Whig leader. New Jersey, so named after its first governor, Sir George Carteret, who came from Jersey in the Channel Islands, and New York, named after James, Duke of York, were finally wrested from the Dutch after the third Anglo-Dutch war. Pennsylvania was founded in 1681, in 1712 the Carolinas were divided into North and South Carolina, while Delaware, which had originally been New Sweden and then formed part of Pennsylvania, obtained a separate legislature from 1702.

The economic development of the American colonies went forward pretty rapidly, though it hardly realized the dreams of English capitalists and merchants. The idea that the colonies would supply essential goods previously imported from elsewhere – such as the naval stores normally purchased in the Baltic kingdoms – or would give England a monopoly in valuable imports which could be re-exported elsewhere in Europe met with early disappointment. Although the 'enumeration clauses' of the navigation code built up by Parliament during the reign of Charles II (notably in the Navigation Act of 1660 and the Staples Act of 1663) which laid down that specified goods, such as tobacco, sugar, cotton wool and indigo could be dispatched only in English ships directly to Great Britain and Ireland, were to some extent obeyed, in fact there was a good deal of illegal traffic which could not be prevented, and a regular exchange of commodities – for example, sugar for other foodstuffs – took place between North America and the French West Indies.

New England, because of its heavy clay soil and in the southeast its sandy soil, was not well suited to agriculture, especially as the summers were comparatively short and the winters long. But New England – like the United Netherlands – provided an example of challenge and response. The Puritan settlers worked hard and, overcoming the natural handicaps, grew food by means of intensive cultivation. But the numerous harbours and sheltered bays opening

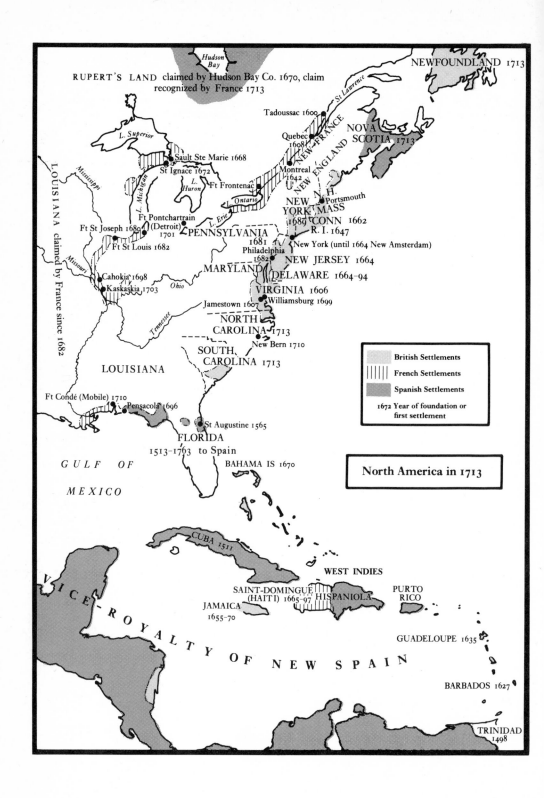

RUPERT'S LAND claimed by Hudson Bay Co. 1670, claim recognized by France 1713

Hudson Bay

NEWFOUNDLAND 1713

St Lawrence

Tadoussac 1600

Quebec 1608

NEW FRANCE

NOVA SCOTIA 1713

L. Superior

Sault Ste Marie 1668

St Ignace 1672

Ft Frontenac

L. Huron

L. Michigan

Montreal 1642

NEW ENGLAND

N.H.

Portsmouth

LOUISIANA claimed by France since 1682

Ft Pontchartrain (Detroit) 1701

Ft St Joseph 1680

L. Erie

Ontario

NEW YORK 1680

MASS

CONN 1662

R.I. 1647

Mississippi

PENNSYLVANIA 1681

New York (until 1664 New Amsterdam)

Ft St Louis 1682

Philadelphia 1682

NEW JERSEY 1664

Missouri

Cahokia 1698

Kaskaskia 1703

Ohio

MARYLAND

DELAWARE 1664-94

VIRGINIA 1606

Williamsburg 1699

Jamestown 1607

Tennessee

NORTH CAROLINA 1713

New Bern 1710

LOUISIANA

SOUTH CAROLINA 1713

Ft Condé (Mobile) 1710

Pensacola 1696

St Augustine 1565

FLORIDA
1513-1763 to Spain

GULF OF

MEXICO

BAHAMA IS 1670

	British Settlements
	French Settlements
	Spanish Settlements
1672	Year of foundation or first settlement

North America in 1713

CUBA 1511

WEST INDIES

V I C E - R O Y A L T Y

SAINT-DOMINGUE (HAITI) 1665-97

HISPANIOLA

PURTO RICO

JAMAICA 1655-70

GUADELOUPE 1635

O F   N E W   S P A I N

BARBADOS 1627

TRINIDAD 1498

on to the Atlantic were most helpful to fisheries – dried cod was a valuable export – and facilitated commercial progress. The forests yielded cheap timber and soon a prosperous ship-building industry developed. Other industries such as sugar refining, rum distilling, and cotton weaving followed. Such manufactures were based not on slaves or indentured servants but on free labour. Skilled workmen were better rewarded than they were in England; the evidence suggests that a higher standard of living was attained than almost anywhere else in the Western world. This agricultural and industrial progress was accompanied by the growth of banking and finance, while a New England merchant class expanded rapidly. Edward Randolph, who visited Massachusetts in 1676, reported home that thirty merchants there with capital varying between £10,000 to £20,000 had large estates and did a great deal of business. Outside Massachusetts the New England colonies benefited from a policy of religious toleration; for example, Dutch Jews settled in Rhode Island where they taught their acquired skills.

The middle colonies also flourished, but there the economy was at first largely based on agriculture. The soil was more fertile than in the north and the extent of arable land greater. Thus they produced all kinds of grain and fruit; cattle were kept and furs were bought from the Indians. The south was more or less a one-crop economy. That crop was tobacco. In both Virginia and Maryland tobacco was a unit of currency, which caused complications when the price of tobacco fell. Here were no compact settlements as in the north but moderately large estates owned by wealthy planters who dispatched their tobacco to England and received manufactured foods and luxuries in return. The mild climate was conducive to the output of ample food. Not only could cattle be pastured, but wild hogs were plentiful, wild ducks and turkeys were there to be found and every kind of fruit was abundant. The tobacco fields required no skilled labour so that at first indentured servants and then Negro slaves were employed by the planters. It has been estimated that in Virginia at the end of the seventeenth century about a fifth of the population consisted of indentured servants and slaves.

One must not, however, exaggerate the number of slaves that were employed in the English colonies at this time. Until the middle of the century the slave trade had been mainly in the hands of the Dutch and Portuguese and it was found most profitable to sell Negroes in the West Indies to work the sugar plantations.

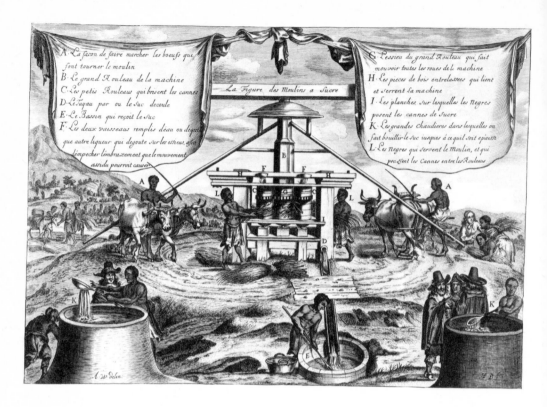

The manufacture of sugar on one of the Caribbean islands in the late seventeenth century.

However, when the Royal Africa Company was established in 1663 with the backing of the Crown, its aim was to provide three thousand slaves a year for the English colonies. After the Anglo-Dutch peace settlement at Breda in 1667 the Dutch renounced their exclusive rights in buying West African slaves. Nevertheless the price of slaves rose. Six thousand a year were sold to the West Indies and another twelve hundred to Spanish colonies. Evidently competition for slaves sent their price up. A fair price was thought to be £17 or £18 a head, but at one time they were bought in Jamaica at £24 a head and as much as £30 is known to have been paid elsewhere in the West Indies. Thus only a relatively small number of slaves were carried to North America. They were not concentrated in the South, but scattered along the Atlantic coast; for example, four thousand were to be found in New York, some of them working as household servants.

Because the colonists were absorbed in building up their economies and establishing a high standard of living, intellectual and cultural progress tended to be neglected. Harvard was founded in 1632 but it was chiefly devoted to training clergymen.

110

A Dutchman who visited the college in 1680 noted that: 'We found eight or ten fellows, sitting around smoking tobacco. We inquired how many professors there were, and they replied not one, there was not enough money to support one.' This report, however, has been condemned as unreliable. In fact the standard of education is believed to have been higher in New England than elsewhere in America. Secondary education was principally in the hands of the clergy who insisted on the reading of the bible, but schools were not numerous. Primary teaching had to be done at home, and it is thought that the wives of pioneers were so occupied with domestic and other duties that they could not have had much time for instructing their offspring.

Massachusetts and Connecticut were best provided with schools while New York and Maryland appear to have had none. Governor Berkeley of Virginia said in 1671: 'I thank God there are no free schools nor printing and I hope we shall not have [them] these hundred years, for learning has brought disobedience and heresy into the world . . . .'

Not only were schools relatively small in number but few public or subscription libraries were set up. Of course settlers from Europe brought books with them, but these were usually either religious in character or strictly utilitarian. The books written in America were, naturally enough, descriptive, throwing light on the early history of the continent and giving accounts of the Indians. Other books produced there were, again, religious. Cotton Mather was such a prolific writer that he had relatively little time for his pastoral duties. The first theatre was opened in Williamsburg in Virginia about 1716. But the Puritans did not approve of plays. Some of the southern planters must have been cultured men, but no leisured class existed to confer patronage on the arts. However, German immigrants promoted music. Possibly the outstanding cultural achievement of the early Americans was in their architecture; for houses and shacks built from logwood and mahogany as well as colonial churches could be extremely attractive.

It was only gradually that the English government formulated a colonial policy. Originally the Stuart kings had granted fairly liberal charters to either trading companies like those that founded Virginia and Massachusetts or proprietors such as the first Lord Baltimore and the second William Penn, who founded Maryland and Pennsylvania respectively. But to these were added royal provinces. In 1635 the company that founded Virginia surrendered

A page from a New England primer, printed in Boston in 1727.

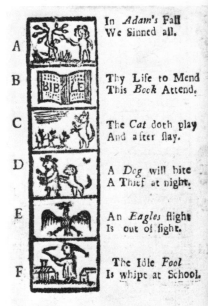

In *Adam's* Fall
We Sinned all.

Thy Life to Mend
This *Book* Attend.

The *Cat* doth play
And after slay.

A *Dog* will bite
A Thief at night.

An *Eagles* flight
Is out of sight.

The Idle *Fool*
Is whipt at School.

its charter to the King. When James, Duke of York acquired New York and New Jersey in the later half of the seventeenth century the former was destined to become a royal province, though James granted East and West Jersey to two of his friends. Yet the constitutions of the different American colonies were not widely different. They were ruled by governors, courts of assistants and elected assemblies. The principal difference between them rested on the right to appoint governors, who were the chief executives.

It was not until the 1650s that the government in London became plantation-conscious. The attempt by Virginia and Barbados to stand up for the Stuarts against the Parliamentarians, as well as the opportunity seized by Massachusetts to become a more or less independent state which attempted to establish in 1649 a union of New England, led the English Republic to take action. In 1650 and 1651 navigation acts were passed by the Rump Parliament restricting the right of the colonies to export their produce to Europe except to England in English ships. In 1655 during the Cromwellian Protectorate a Board of Trade was established in Whitehall to consider 'all ways and means for advancing the trade and navigation of the Commonwealth'. The main object of the policy was to draw valuable raw materials to England and to exploit the colonies as purchasers of English manufactures.

The same policy was continued after the restoration of Charles II in 1660. A new Navigation Act, more stringent than that of 1651, introduced the first regulations about 'enumerated commodities'. But the administration of the colonies was somewhat amorphous. A standing committee of the King's Privy Council set up after the Restoration was too large and its members were too deeply concerned with other affairs to do much useful work. In July 1670, however, a Council of Foreign Plantations was established containing a number of paid members, which was essentially a fact-finding body. In 1672 this council was combined with the Council of Trade which had dealt with commercial subjects since 1660; the Earl of Shaftesbury, who had been the principal founder of Carolina and was therefore reckoned knowledgeable about America, was appointed president and John Locke, the celebrated philosopher, became its secretary. But in the same year the third Anglo-Dutch war began, and the attention of Shaftesbury and his colleagues on the Council was somewhat diverted. Thus the new Council did not in fact accomplish very much, although the suggestion has been made that it had a 'more open-minded outlook on commercial affairs'. In 1674 it was superseded by a standing committee of the Privy Council, generally known as 'the Lords of Trade', and after New York was regained from the Dutch a more positive policy was pursued. A study of its minutes has indicated that while the West Indies were well known to its members, as were also the southern colonies of Virginia and Maryland, they were not at all familiar with New England nor with the Middle Colonies. However, the royal government was soon to learn about them.

An Act for the Encouragement of Trade (1673) had introduced a plantation duty which had to be paid by sea captains taking on board 'enumerated commodities' at the ports of clearance; in the case of tobacco the duty was a penny a pound. Collectors of customs were dispatched from England to America to ensure that these duties were paid. Edward Randolph, who was sent as collector to Massachusetts, reported home that the colonists were defiant and frequently failed to comply with the navigation acts. Even before this a royal commission sent to the colonies from England had experienced 'sullen resistance' and 'bitter protests' against the exercise of the authority given to its members, so that the King was pretty well informed about the independent-mindedness of the people of Massachusetts. The decision was therefore taken to revoke the Massachusetts charter and to convert the province into a royal colony. Writs were also issued calling in the charters of other proprietary colonies.

When James, Duke of York succeeded his brother in 1685 New York automatically became a royal colony as since 1664 James had been proprietor of the colony. The decision was thereupon taken to weld the whole of the New England colonies into a royal dominion and to abolish the representative assemblies. Sir Edmund Andros, a capable soldier who had previously been the governor of New York, was therefore sent to Boston to become Governor-General of the Dominion of New England, which was to include besides Massachusetts, New Hampshire and Maine, New York and the Jerseys and Delaware. Andros by no means behaved as a tyrant, but the New Englanders had grown accustomed to self-government, which was now denied them. They also strongly objected to paying the new taxes which Andros attempted to introduce. Nor were these enthusiastic Calvinists and witch-burners at all pleased to observe Andros's efforts to establish liberty of conscience, embracing Roman Catholics, Anglicans and Quakers (as James II was trying to do in England at the same time).

But Andros persevered and by 1688 Connecticut and Rhode Island were added to his dominion.

At the end of 1689 William III of Orange replaced his Roman Catholic father-in-law as King of England. The news of the 'glorious' and bloodless 'revolution' set the colonies aflame when it reached North America. The New York captain Jacob Leisler, a militia officer who came from Frankfurt and was a merchant of standing, led a revolt against the English Roman Catholic governor, while in Maryland a certain John Coode headed a rebellion against the proprietor, the second Lord Baltimore, vowing that he would deprive the Roman Catholics there of all their property. These two rebel leaders were improbably compared by their opponents with Masaniello (Tommaso Aniello) a fisherman who had directed mob warfare against Spain in Naples forty years earlier. In Massachusetts there was no Masaniello; the whole people resisted the unfortunate Andros. In 1691 the theocracy ceased to exist and Massachusetts became a royal province.

Once the news of William III's coronation at Westminster was known North America quietened. But the new King, though he accepted the restoration of the representative assemblies in New England, had no intention of abandoning the supremacy of the Crown in the colonies. Indeed if his attention had not been distracted by the war against France, he might easily have tried to consolidate the colonies and even have continued a dominion in New England. As it was, the navigation laws were maintained and Edward Randolph, once the agent of Charles II in Massachusetts, was appointed Surveyor-General of the customs in America.

The hostilities in Europe which involved England and France after 1688 had their repercussions on the English and French colonies. The French, whose fur trade and fishing industry in North America were valuable, had the strategic advantage of being able to attack New England from the rear along the St Lawrence and Hudson rivers. On the other hand, the English colonists greatly outnumbered the French. During the Nine Years' War (known in America as King William's war) Count Frontenac, the French Governor of Canada, threatened to attack the province of New York, but after destroying the town of Schenectady, withdrew. In 1690 a congress of four English provinces met at New York under the leadership of Leisler and made plans to conquer Canada. In that same year a force of New

Englanders occupied Port Royal in Acadia but then the war ended in small expeditions and Indian atrocities. In the war of the Spanish succession (known in America as Queen Anne's war) Port Royal was again captured and this time Acadia (renamed Nova Scotia) was ceded to the English by treaty. The main interest in these wars was the co-operation shown between the different New England provinces.

Three things emerge from a survey of English colonies in the late seventeenth and early eighteenth centuries. First, with the acquisition of Newfoundland, Nova Scotia and St Kitts from France, of Gibraltar and Minorca from Spain, and of trading privileges in the Spanish overseas empire, the ruling class in London, and particularly the Tory ministers who negotiated the peace of Utrecht, became conscious that Great Britain was a commercial, maritime and colonial power of future rich promise. Secondly, the American colonies, peopled not only with British emigrants but with other newcomers from all over Europe, who discovered a prospering economy and a rising standard of living, were not likely, if their liberties were interfered with, to stomach government by a small island kingdom three thousand miles away. Lastly, the abortive rebellions in both the 1640s and 1680s were a clear presage of what might happen one day as the American population grew. Furthermore, the New England confederation of 1649 and the dominion of 1686 as well as the New York congress of 1690, though not based on deliberate or spontaneous constitutional agreements, signalled that a federation of the colonies might be in the making. Only the policy of *quieta non movere* ('let sleeping dogs lie') pursued by the Whig government in England postponed the day of reckoning. Looking back, we can now see that the fashioning of the American colonies in the seventeenth century was one of the most striking events in the history of the Western world.

7 Western Society and Economic Growth in the Seventeenth Century

The price revolution – that is to say the six-fold rise in prices – which began early in the sixteenth century and was due in part to a population explosion and in part to the influx of precious metals from South America, continued, though at a decreasing pace, well into the first half of the seventeenth century. Whereas in Germany and Austria prices began to fall in the 1620s elsewhere in Europe they did not do so until the middle of the century. In the second half of the century, until the 1690s, prices were stagnant or actually fell. Since monetary wages altered comparatively little, it may be presumed that in this era of lower prices real wages may have improved or at least did not fall as they undoubtedly did in the sixteenth century. The testimony of travellers to the England of Charles II and to the Holland of the Stadholderless period suggests that ordinary people did not manage too badly – even in France they were not too miserable – while by the first decade of the eighteenth century, they lived comfortably enough. Daniel Defoe observed how the lower classes often ate meat and drank large quantities of beer. Cheap food was a boon to those who had regular work. But it has to be remembered that even in England there were about a million people who were either unemployed or only partly employed and that a million pounds a year was spent on the poor. Low prices, it has been conjectured, stimulated minor labour-saving devices, though no striking technological advances in industry were made until the eighteenth century.

Prices usually went up in times of war because of large demands for the supply and equipment of armies and navies. It has been calculated from price indices, based on such information as is available, that prices rose during the Anglo-Dutch wars and during the Nine Years' War, but it is remarkable that in France, according to the contemporary economist Pierre de Boisguilbert, food prices were low from 1660 to 1690 and so they were in England from 1702 to 1709. The evidence that we have, however, is subject to a good deal of guesswork for statistics were only in their infancy in the seventeenth century and mercantilist governments had only just started to use them. Even so, it is generally agreed that a minimum level of food prices was reached at the time when the Nine Years' War began, but bad harvests in the period from 1689 to 1691 and the very bad harvests of 1692–3 caused prices to shoot up and they remained high until the end of the seventeenth century. During the war of the Spanish succession prices were pretty steady everywhere but more bad harvests in 1708–9 brought a scarcity of food causing riots and unrest in France described by François de Salignac de la Mothe de Fénelon, Archbishop of Cambrai, as 'one great hospital' where men were dying of hunger. Facts like these contributed notably to ending the long and far-ranging wars in central and southern Europe. Although this scarcity of food did not reach famine proportions in either England or the Dutch Republic, the price of grain rose steeply and crop failures everywhere led to a high rate of mortality among the poorer classes. In fact the period from 1691 to 1697 was known as 'the seven ill years' and the population of Europe (as has been pointed out by Professor Karl Helleiner) 'declined here and there, as death and starvation stalked through the lands from Castile to Finland, and from Scotland to Austria'. The death rate is known to have been particularly high in the Baltic countries.

Other factors beyond crop failures help to explain the rise in prices during those years. One was a shortage of sound money. It is known, for example, that in England after the recoinage of silver in 1695 prices fell rapidly. Moreover the Bank of England, which had been founded in 1694, soon began to issue paper money based on the amount of its loans to the government. The repercussions of these two events were felt elsewhere in the Western world. Wealthy Dutchmen, for instance, bought stock in the Bank of England and in general the credit of the two maritime powers was improved. It was widely held that the currency was in some way or another the cause of economic depressions, though whether because there was too much bad money or too little good money is not altogether clear. Gerard Malynes, a Fleming, who regarded himself as a currency expert, believed that 'the want of money ... is the first cause of the decay of trade', a somewhat obscure observation.

One has to remember that money was not of the first importance in agricultural communities where men and women lived on a subsistence level, often engaged in barter, grew much of their own food, caught it in rivers or poached it, and even made their own clothes. Money was of significance as a standard of value (for example, for the fixing of wage rates) and as a means to foster international trade – yet, as we have seen, in Virginia tobacco was used for those purposes. The Western world was still a world based essentially upon agriculture, whether life was sustained by the growing of grain, the fattening of sheep or the planting of sugar. Even in England it has been calculated that not more than half a million people at the outside, that is to say only about one-eleventh of the total population, earned their incomes in other ways than from agriculture. As has already been noted in Chapter 2, five of the seven provinces in the Dutch Republic were more concerned with agriculture than with trade or industry and if the Dutch had to import wheat from Poland and elsewhere they exported butter, cheese and fish. If the two most industrially advanced countries, England and the United Netherlands, were still largely engaged in agriculture, it is clear that elsewhere in the Western world other countries were essentially dependent on the successful cultivation of arable land.

On 27 July 1694, the bank of England was founded. This is one of the earliest banknotes issued by the Bank of England in 1699.

The standard of living of landowners and of their tenants was influenced by two factors: first, the weather and secondly, the amount of their produce that had to be allocated for the support of the state and the Church. But everywhere these burdens of life

fell most directly on the peasants. When the crops were poor they starved or half-starved. Hardly a single modern historian when he is writing about his own country fails to stress the heavy taxation imposed upon the common people particularly in times of war. The prosperous Hollanders were said to have paid higher taxes than anyone else in Europe. During the Nine Years' War a Dutch pamphleteer wrote: 'of taxes there are in this republic so many and of such variety as has hardly been the case in all the world'. The large Dutch contribution to the costs of the Grand Alliance was paid for out of excises, property taxes, by borrowing and providing services such as banking and insurance. In England the landowning classes managed to escape from paying land taxes during much of the second half of the seventeenth century because the royal revenues were derived chiefly from indirect taxation, especially excise and customs duties, which made taxation regressive and which fell upon practically all articles of consumption including ale, the chief solace of the poor. Nevertheless the House of Commons did agree to a land tax to pay for the war against France, a unique example of landowners taxing themselves.

In France the privileged classes, the nobility and clergy, were exempt from land tax or *taille*. After the death of Colbert, however, the upper classes did become the subject of two other taxes, a *capitation* or poll tax and a *dixième* or tenth levied upon declared incomes. But the poll tax was suppressed during the interval of peace (1697–1701) while the tenth was not introduced until 1710. Neither of these taxes proved very satisfactory and they were often evaded; nor did the French government find it so easy to borrow money on the security of future taxation yields as did the Dutch and the English. Enlightened writers such as Marshal Vauban were conscious of the hardships suffered by the French peasantry through the various taxes they had to pay on top of their rents and feudal dues; it was for this reason that Vauban advocated the introduction of the tenth. But he wanted it as a substitute for other taxes, such as the *taille* and the *gabelle* or state salt monopoly, and not, as in fact happened, as an addition to them. Defoe thought that it was 'our own great felicity in England that we are not yet come to the *gabelle* or tax upon corn [grain] as in Italy and many other countries'.

One must not, however, exaggerate the plight of the peasantry in western Europe. In the first place many were legally free men and their status could hardly be debased. But the word 'peasantry' covers a wide category. Those who lived by agriculture might have a variety of tenures: there were sharecroppers, leaseholders, copyholders, cottagers and even, for instance in Wales and Scotland, landholders who shared ancient clanlands. Secondly, only the wealthiest peasant proprietors were exclusively engaged in tilling the soil. To increase their earnings they either spent part of their time working in rural industries or they found convenient supplementary employment. Professor Goubert has pointed out that it would have been an impossibility for a French peasant to pay his taxes, his tithes and his feudal dues and, if he was ambitious, to improve the welfare of his family, unless he multiplied his activities. That he succeeded in managing is suggested by the fact that no serious fall in the size of the population took place in the reign of Louis XIV. Indeed in spite of local and regional famines, wars, periods of anarchy and administrative incompetence, the French population actually increased over a period of twenty-five years from 1661 onwards. The French peasant was generally not only a gardener, a harvester, a horticulturalist, a wine grower and a stock-breeder, but also a spinner or weaver, a blacksmith or nailsmith, and sometimes an innkeeper, a poacher and a smuggler. '*Il faisait flèche de tout bois*,' writes Goubert ('He used every means to attain his ends'). In the Dutch Republic provincial and urban authorities encouraged the introduction of new ancillary industries outside Holland, for example in Utrecht. French refugees established a silk industry and the distilling of brandy. Such work commanded good wages and if agricultural workers did not themselves seek such employment, their wives and children might do so.

In England the situation of the peasant varied according to the area in which he lived. Peasants were generally better off in forest districts than where open fields predominated. For example, they could make good use of forest waste for feeding pigs. Where extensive common rights still existed they might keep large stocks of herds or augment their income by spinning and weaving, as game-keepers or foresters and by charcoal burning. Glove-making and lace-making also provided employment in some counties. Other employments were potting, tiling, nailing, carpentry and iron-smelting. 'Wherever peasant industries were combined with agriculture,' writes Professor Everitt, 'farmworkers tended to be relatively wealthy.' Some counties such as Hertfordshire or the Wealds of Sussex and Kent provided varied employment, whereas in Herefordshire, which had no rural industry at all, farm workers were very poor and were tempted to leave the countryside al-

together. Inventories examined both in England and in France indicate that quite a substantial number of wealthy peasants existed.

The interior of the cottage of a Dutch peasant family, a watercolour by Adrian van Ostade, executed in 1673.

Thirdly, it cannot be assumed that peasants always paid all their dues as well as all their taxes. In France peasants often paid their rents to the landlord or his bailiff who were on the spot while resisting the demands of tax collectors, trusting to the tacit or open support of the local nobility. The English peasants rioted against excisemen, and those who lived near the coast might frustrate customs officers by smuggling, especially in Cornwall and Devon and over the Kent and Essex marshes.

It can scarcely be doubted that the peasants elsewhere in Europe were infinitely worse off than those in England, France and the Netherlands, though in central Europe they had greater rights and led a less miserable existence than did those in Russia, Poland or Hungary. Most of Hungary was ruled until the end of the seventeenth century by the Turks who, though indifferent to the religion of their Christian subjects, were hard taskmasters. As a result of the taxes they exacted to pay for their perpetual wars the Hungarian countryside suffered depopulation and free peasants were reduced to the status of serfs. In Russia the combined pressures of rents, indirect taxes, fines and debts to money-lenders lowered the status of the peasants. A new code of laws *(Olozhenie)* introduced in 1649 aimed to stop the movement of peasants who frequently fled from the service of harsh landlords to avoid paying their taxes in order to seek better treatment elsewhere or work in towns. Landowners were required to register their peasants, and they gradually drifted for the most part into a position of legal hereditary serfdom. The families of such free peasants as there were lived continually on the verge of bankruptcy or famine. A bad crop or an epidemic was enough to ruin them. By the new regulations, which forbade the peasants to flee from their employment and imposed big fines if they were caught, the mass of the Russian people were reduced to complete serfdom by the 1670s. They could be whipped on their master's orders for neglect of duty. In Brandenburg-Prussia too the peasant's status was reduced. Owing to depopulation caused by wars and epidemics their landlords, the Junkers, took up deserted peasant lands, exacted heavy labour services and, because of the scarcity of labour, compelled even children to serve as menials on their estates. Peasants were, as in Russia, tied to the soil and virtually became serfs with few rights.

In other parts of Germany the peasants, although technically most of them were still serfs, were in practical terms much better off and were able to enhance their position because of the very shortage of labour. They were able to commute their feudal dues and serfdom began to disappear. Neither in Sweden nor in Finland was serfdom to be found although in both countries the peasants were severely taxed and were liable to starve when the crops failed. Bad weather in 1695-7 led to the death of thousands in Finland. There the peasants were described as 'the common people responsible for paying taxes to the crown' and in Sweden the nobleman, Per Brahe, proclaimed: 'We are all subjects of the Crown, the peasants directly and we indirectly.' Though peasant rights were defined by custom, the feudal privileges of the nobility remained. Thus in years of bad harvests much unrest prevailed. In Denmark also, though serfdom did not exist, the landowners' feudal rights could be oppressive and even when in 1660 Frederick III became absolute, he paid no attention to peasants' grievances. In Spain and Portugal too serfdom was disappearing. But taxes, seignorial oppression, a succession of bad harvests and much poor and uncultivatable land meant that most peasants lived on a minimum level of subsistence, though prosperous peasants were to be found, for instance in Catalonia. In Italy, where the soil was richer than in Iberia, peasants were also free but landlords were lazy and disliked spending capital on agricultural improvements. Broadly it may be concluded that nearly everywhere in Europe agriculture was handicapped by epidemics, bad weather, poor harvests and lack of enterprise especially on the part of the landlords. It was a different story in regard to commerce.

Although precise statistics do not exist, a commercial revolution was probably taking place in the Western world from the middle of the seventeenth century onwards. The explorers of earlier days had discovered the riches of the Americas and of Asia, but it took time for colonial settlements or trade posts (as in India and the East Indies) to become valuable exchange markets and thus expand international trade. But once half a million people had established themselves on the western side of the Atlantic this development was certain. The Dutch were the real pioneers. As we have seen in Chapter 2, although they had built up their economy by the expansion of fishing (often defiantly catching herrings off the mouth of the Thames) and of their mercantile marine, which actually carried goods for their enemies during the long contest with Spain, and had founded their bank at Amsterdam and their East and West India trading companies in the first half of the century, it was not until after their war with Spain that the Dutch could devote their full energies to increasing their foreign trade. The virtual monopoly which they established for themselves in the commerce of the Baltic and of the Far East became the envy of English merchants who had also founded their own East India Company at the beginning of the century and the French somewhat later. England, as an island which for the sustenance of its ordinary people and the welfare of its south-western mariners depended very largely upon fishing and which had to maintain a large navy to protect itself against possible invasion, became envious and anxious to emulate the commercial success of the Dutch.

Other wider factors no doubt contributed to the growth of commerce. The population explosion of the sixteenth century, the rise in prices which persisted into the seventeenth century, and the feeling that parts of Europe were overpopulated, all stimulated enterprise to meet economic demand. A consciousness arose of the need for a division of labour, since new products such as sugar and tobacco could be bought only outside Europe and had to be paid for either by exporting manufactured goods or,

123

since woollen textiles, one of the primary exports from western
Europe, were not particularly welcome in hot countries, by
exporting bullion. And bullion could most easily be obtained
by selling goods to Spain or services to South America. Thus the
huge influx of silver into Europe, which was brought across the
Atlantic in treasure ships and did not dwindle away until about
1630, was another factor in the growth of international commerce.

The evidence for the recognition of the importance of commerce by the end of the seventeenth century is to be found in
diplomatic negotiations. Under the Cromwellian Protectorate
treaties of trade were concluded between England on the one side
and France, Portugal and the Baltic kingdoms on the other, while

The town of Surat, on the mainland of India. It was captured from the Portuguese in the early seventeenth century, and became the seat of the presidency of the English East India Company. It remained the chief English trading port in India until 1668, when Bombay was obtained and became the capital of the Company's possessions.

the Lord Protector himself had hankered after a direct commercial treaty with the Dutch. In the negotiations which concluded the wars of the second half of the century questions of tariffs played a more significant part than ever before. The enmity between England and the Dutch Republic had been founded on commercial rivalry. By the time that the treaty of Utrecht was signed in 1713 economic considerations had become paramount, especially for these two maritime powers. For example, they refused to allow the southern Netherlands to fall into the hands of France, which was reckoned to be a growing commercial power, and though they let the Emperor Charles VI include the former Spanish Netherlands in his dominions, they would not allow him to re-open the port of Antwerp or use the serviceable Scheldt estuary lest it should become a rival to Amsterdam and London.

Another factor which helped the growth of commerce was the gradual reduction in trading monopolies. The Dutch and English East India Companies had been given exclusive privileges by their governments on the justifiable ground that heavy capital expenditure in building ports and trading stations was necessary to promote trade with Asia. (The same was true of Africa companies.) Other countries followed in their footsteps. Denmark, Sweden and France all created East India Companies, though their careers were brief and not always bright. But before the end of the seventeenth century the realization grew, in the United Netherlands and in England, though not in France, that free trade was more likely to promote mercantile enterprise than state or state-controlled monopolies. Monopolies had been the subject of criticism in England since Tudor days. Cromwell withdrew for the time being the privileges of the East India Company and two rival East Indian Companies functioned at the end of the reign of King William III. The Levant trade, which largely consisted in importing silks and spices from Turkey and Persia, and the Eastland trade to the Baltic were also thrown open. Only the Royal Africa Company maintained its monopoly in England until the end of the century but in the profitable slave trade much smuggling was done by interlopers. Pamphleteers in England and the United Netherlands praised the virtues of a free or open trade – it was, for example, one of the planks in the platform of the radical Levellers – while the growth of England's foreign trade, which doubled between 1660 and 1700, and of its mercantile shipping involved the breaking of a virtual monopoly in the export business previously enjoyed by London at the expense of other British ports.

125

One of the most remarkable features of the commercial revolution was the bulkiness of many of the goods transported by sea, such as the timber carried from the Baltic countries and the coal and iron exported from England. Dutch *fluitschips* or 'fly-boats', which were of a length of from four to six times their beam, had simple rigging and carried no guns, have been described as 'floating holds' and proved particularly valuable in the Baltic trade. The English Eastland Company tried to break the grip of the Dutch on the Baltic trade and claimed to send over two hundred ships a year through the Sound. They pressed for the maintenance of the Navigation Act policy so as to prevent Dutch ships from being used in carrying timber, pitch, tar, hemp and metals from the Scandinavian kingdoms to England. But the English carriers – even though they came to buy fly-boats manufactured in Holland – could not meet the whole needs of the royal navy for such materials and little attempt was made rigorously to enforce the prohibition on Dutch ships fetching goods from the Baltic. Similarly the carrying of coal (now increasingly used instead of timber, especially in industrial processes) required larger vessels. The number of colliers grew and the size of colliers expanded both in order to bring coal from Newcastle to London and to carry English coal and iron abroad.

The Dutch were at an advantage in their dealings with the Scandinavian kingdoms, Poland and Germany in that they were able to meet their need to export grain (another bulky cargo). Grain was brought from the Baltic countries and Poland via Danzig and Königsberg, half of it being used by the Dutch themselves to meet their own needs in the form of food and drink, but nearly half of these cargoes were re-exported to Portugal, Spain and parts of Italy which did not grow sufficient grain for their populations. The English also exported grain in years of good harvests, a bounty being paid on exports when the price was reasonably low. France was paradoxically both an exporter and an importer of grain. The country being large and internal communications poor, one part of France might starve while another had a surplus of grain for export. Thus the Amsterdam grain market was huge. It fed France and Spain, Italy and Germany (sending boatloads up the Rhine) and it also sold imported feeding stuffs for its cattle, wheat for its bread and barley for its gin and beer. England after the bad harvests of the 1690s was also an important dealer in cereals, particularly rye, while Scotland exported malt and barley.

126

The principal English export was still cloth (in which it forged ahead of its rivals), as it had been for many years, but re-exports of goods brought in from North America, the West Indies and the Levant such as sugar, tobacco, indigo, silks and spices became more and more profitable. If one adds linens, dried cod *(bacalhau)*, clothes, including hats and stockings, as well as the bulky goods, it is clear that English exports were becoming more varied. In fact the export trade was growing, while that of the Dutch was beginning to contract, although it still remained predominant in the Western world.

Towards the end of the century luxury or semi-luxury goods formed a big part of international trade. Tea and coffee came from Asia. Wines were exported from France (claret not burgundy), from Portugal (but not yet vintage port), from the Moselle via Holland, and from Spain. Caviare already came from Russia. Silks were exported from many countries inside and outside Europe (they were woven in England during the French wars); so

An early eighteenth-century tobacco label, advertising one of the chief commodities of the North American export trade.

127

were linens; while porcelain was brought in from China and successfully imitated in France, Italy and Delft in Holland. Of course the upper classes in most countries had always bought imported luxury goods, such as jewelry and rich clothing, but by the beginning of the eighteenth century the importation of such luxuries had ceased to be officially frowned upon.

Much ink and paper has been expended by historians in analyzing the 'mercantile system' which is said to have prevailed in the organization of seventeenth-century commerce. Sometimes it is briefly stated that particular governments followed a 'mercantilist policy'. But like many historical theories – above all in regard to 'systems' like the feudal system, the manorial system and so on – the mercantile system is increasingly seen to be a nebulous and even meaningless term, a mere jumble of nationalist prejudices. Governments naturally sought to obtain the best terms for their countries in the pursuit of international trade, and economic pamphleteers and interested industrialists or shipping magnates advocated economic policies in patriotic language. It is said that governments sought to achieve a favourable balance of trade with exports exceeding imports either in order to get hold of precious metals or to maximize national welfare or to make themselves more powerful. Colbert once said: 'Manufactures will result in obtaining silver: that is the only aim of commerce and the only means of increasing the grandeur and power of the State.' But practising merchants did not believe that, and both Dutchmen and Englishmen were well aware that to procure necessary goods from the Baltic, muslins from India or pepper from the East Indies they would have to be paid for with bullion. Goods thus bought could be re-exported and sold at a handsome profit. Some governments introduced prohibitions on imports, subsidies for manufacturing industries and for shipping and bounties on exports. There was nothing new about such policies and they would not be thought novel today. What remains true is the belief at the time that the export of manufactured goods exchanged for raw materials could raise a nation's standard of living. That is what happened in seventeenth-century England when it was ceasing to rely, as it had done in earlier times, on the export of raw wool, unfinished cloth, tin and lead, and was being transformed from an 'under-developed' country into a developed one by increasing its production of these traditional commodities. How far this commercial revolution in the Western world exemplified the beginnings of modern capitalism is debatable. The historian, Henri Sée, thought that Colbertism actually retarded the growth of capitalism in France. But the truth is that the 'capitalist system' is extremely hard to define. All that can safely be said is that some kind of commercial revolution took place during the seventeenth century, stimulated by the extension of the Western world across the Atlantic, and by its accumulation of wealth paved the way towards considerable industrial advance. How far warfare interrupted such economic progress is again difficult to decide. War was commoner than peace in those days; but in the twentieth century we have learned that output can be increased rapidly by the demands of total war. Most practising merchants may not have liked disruptive wars, but they almost certainly increased national incomes in the seventeenth and eighteenth centuries both directly and indirectly. Though it is often claimed that nations such as France and Spain were 'ruined' by wars, they recovered from them just as easily as Germany and Japan have done from total wars in the twentieth century.

8 Western Science and Philosophy in the Seventeenth Century

The seventeenth century has been called 'the century of genius'. 'Almost everything that distinguished the modern world from earlier centuries', wrote Bertrand Russell, 'is attributable to science, which achieved its most spectacular triumphs in the seventeenth century.' (What we mean today by science was then described as 'natural science'.) It is impossible to state a precise date when thinking men abandoned medieval outlooks and their customary dependence on the polymathy of Aristotle, but it can be argued that the changeover was becoming clear about the middle of the century. Before then physics and astronomy had already made large strides. Galileo Galilei, who had been persecuted by the Roman Catholic Church for claiming that the earth revolved round the sun, died in 1642 and in that same year Isaac Newton, who accepted without question the mechanical explanation of the universe, was born. In the late 1640s men who were to form the nucleus of the Royal Society gathered in London to discuss experimental problems, while French *savants*, who were meeting at the same time in Paris under the presidency of Pierre Gassendi, the atomic scientist, later became members of the Académie Royale des Sciences. In 1650 René Descartes died in Sweden, having published his book *Principia Philosophae* six years earlier, while in 1651 a completely different kind of book, *The Leviathan*, appeared from the pen of the English philosopher, Thomas Hobbes. Both these books were anathema to traditional Christians.

The teaching of Descartes, though not universally accepted, dominated the Western world – at any rate outside England, where empiricism ruled – for almost a century. Descartes's philosophy was dualism. The orthodox belief had long been that the mind ruled the body, but Descartes held that the mind does not move the body nor does the body move the mind. The body – or 'matter', 'extension' or 'movement' – was governed by unchanging laws

of physics and the material world was therefore rigidly deter-
ministic. On the other hand, the mind – or the soul – was distinct
from the body and easier to know than the body. The mind would
be what it was even if there were no body. Moreover the existence
of the mind was simpler to prove than the existence of the body.
The first task of philosophy, Descartes thought, was analytic,
the second synthetic. Analysis proved the certainty of being because we know intuitively that thoughts exist. This is beyond
doubt. Man is a thinking thing and in that he differs from the
animals who have only senses, not thoughts. Therefore Descartes
did not, like the English empiricists, really base his philosophy on
scientific analysis; he founded it on intuitive certainty. From this
primary belief in self-consciousness Descartes went on to maintain that everything was true that was clear and distinct as in one's
own self-consciousness. These were in fact 'innate ideas' which led

Réné Descartes,
mathematician and
philosopher. Portrait by
Frans Hals.

on to a series of further propositions. For example, we are conscious that we are finite and imperfect beings; from that it can be deduced by contrast that there must be an infinite and perfect being, in other words, God.

Thus Descartes deduced from his original premise 'I think therefore I am' the existence of God. But that was not his only argument in favour of divinity. For he also maintained that the mere possibility of our thinking about a perfect being proved that a perfect being must necessarily exist. This is known as 'the ontological argument', which was earlier put forward by St Anselm. It is extraordinary, in view of the way in which Descartes laboured to prove by different kinds of reasoning the existence of God, that he should have been condemned by many churchmen of his time as an atheist and a materialist. They derived this opinion not from Descartes's views about the mind, but from his insistence that matter was moved mechanically, like a wound-up clock. Christians, or at any rate Christians such as the Jesuits who believed in free will and taught that God could forgive sins and wipe men clean of them, refused to regard God as a mere clockmaker who, having started the clock, then ceased to interfere with it. Moreover they were reluctant to accept that the mind or the soul had no control over the body. Descartes himself never satisfactorily explained the relationship between the mind and the body, the dualism which lay at the root of his philosophy. But his later followers or Occasionalists contended that the mind and the body harmonized like two clocks that always struck simultaneously. Thus when the body felt pain the mind experienced sorrow.

Blaise Pascal, who died in 1662 at the age of thirty-nine, like Descartes a mathematician, refused to accept Descartes's deductive evidence for epistemology, that is to say his theory of knowledge. Pascal held that other sciences were not dependent for their proofs on mathematics. Indeed few rational deductions were productive of certainties; they did not, for example, solve the problem of dualism. Therefore why not revert to one's original intuition – one's feeling that one exists and that God exists? As he wrote, 'the heart has its reasons of which reason is ignorant'. Other thinkers – Newton, for instance – while accepting that the laws of physics were mechanical, did not agree that this meant that God removed himself from the world once he had started it – that Nature was 'despiritualized'. The clock might go wrong and God might decide to intervene and mend it.

Descartes did not altogether divorce himself from scholastic

A View of Bethlehem one of the Brethren's Principal Settlements in Pensylvania, North America.

Vue de Bethlehem, l'un des principaux établissement des Frères Moraves en Pensylvanie, Amerique Septentrionale.

methods of thinking. His arguments for the existence of God had been anticipated in the Middle Ages, while his belief that there were three distinct 'substances' – God, mind and matter – was a scholastic way of putting things. Western philosophers did not entirely shake themselves free from thinking in terms of 'substances' until the next century.

Thomas Hobbes, the English philosopher, also followed purely deductive methods to reach his conclusions. But whereas Descartes considered it easier to prove the existence of the mind than that of the body, Hobbes insisted that philosophy could treat only of bodies and left the existence of the mind or the soul to faith. To think is to reckon things by means of verbal signs. One must define one's terms carefully and in doing so, one can see that everything is determined by the pressure of external objects on the senses. Thus a train of thought is regulated by desires or fears and is governed by laws of association. Though some modern writers have tried to prove that Hobbes preached a pure sense of duty and even held Protestant religious beliefs, the view of contemporaries and of his immediate critics that Hobbes was a determinist, a materialist and a rationalist is hard to disprove. No convincing evidence has really been found to the contrary. But Hobbes, like Gottfried Leibniz later, was a timid philosopher and though he wrote with extraordinary clarity, he took care not to lay himself open to punishment or persecution for what he wrote. Hobbes in fact was the most modern of seventeenth-century philosophers and that is why his works exert a permanent fascination for historians and political scientists.

Spinoza, who died in 1677, like Descartes and Hobbes a bold and original thinker, did not publish his main work during his own lifetime. He solved Descartes's problem of dualism by maintaining that only one 'substance' existed and that was God. God was the universal essence and both mind and matter were simply aspects of the divine being. This line of thought has been called 'logical monism' or pantheism. But the existence of God is simply assumed and not proved. He is neither mind nor body; all that can be said of him is that he is all-embracing Nature. Thus what men are required to do is to seek to know God and to love him intellectually. By doing so passions can be eliminated. Both hope and fear – the passions that played such a large part in Hobbes's philosophy – are to be condemned. In fact Spinoza can be described as a kind of Stoic. Every evil, he believed, could be overcome by understanding and by love.

Above: Benedict Spinoza, the Dutch philosopher. Most of his important writings were published after his death in 1677.

Opposite above: Tyrolean Lutherans, persecuted in Catholic Salzburg, set off on their long journey to Georgia in North America, 1732.

Opposite below: Farmlands in Bethlehem, Pennsylvania, transformed from a wilderness into fertile arable lands by Moravian settlers within twenty years. Painting of 1757 by J. Naval.

Leibniz, a German born in Leipzig, the son of a philosopher who served the House of Hanover, was, like Descartes, an outstanding mathematician as well as a moral philosopher. He was born in 1646 and died at the age of seventy, but, like Spinoza, he put forward his views cautiously and concealed some of them. Leibniz denied the reality of matter and substituted an infinite family of 'souls', 'substances' or 'monads', some small and some great, which progressed from mere constituents of what was called matter to the central monad or God. In his published writings he admitted the existence of free will since 'every soul was a world apart, independent of everything else except God' who had made men free. Nothing happened without a reason. God had deliberately made men liable to sin so that they were given a free choice between good and evil. Because the choice was offered it was the best of all possible worlds that God had designed. Leibniz was a great logician and thought that logic was the key to metaphysics. But Bertrand Russell has argued that at root Leibniz's logic led him to believe not in free will (as he claimed in his published writings), but in determinism. Thus at heart he did not accept the reality either of sin or of free will. According to Russell, Leibniz believed that everything that did not exist struggled to exist. God was therefore not the creator. Finally, Leibniz distinguished between universal truths and the facts of experience – between necessary and contingent truths – just as Descartes distinguished between empirical truths and logical truths. Such distinctions enabled Leibniz to argue that a reconciliation could be effected between the different European religions, but his efforts to achieve this failed. Perhaps he believed that to wise men all religions are the same.

With John Locke, who was born in Somerset in 1632, one moves away from the French and German abstract philosophers to the British empirical school of philosophy which has continued until our own time. In his *Essay Concerning Human Understanding* Locke wrote modestly that it was 'ambition enough to be employed as an under-labourer in clearing the ground a little and removing some of the rubbish that lies in the way of knowledge'. Locke rejected Descartes's belief that knowledge is derived from innate ideas and maintained that the mind was a clean sheet on which experience inscribes ideas either simply or through complex reasoning: therefore both primary and secondary ideas exist, but men are limited in what they are able to discover. We cannot expect to know the nature of the sun or the stars or penetrate the mysteries of the next world. What we can do is to procure for man happiness on earth. 'Man's proper business,' he wrote, is 'to seek happiness and avoid misery'. Locke was little concerned with metaphysics as the scholastics or his contemporary French and German philosophers had been. He concentrated on ethics which for him were utilitarian. Christian ethics were to him natural ethics which aimed at making men happy but not at giving them short-term pleasures (as with the hedonists). Ultimately Locke's philosophy ousted that of the Cartesians, and through his disciples and through the genius of Voltaire, it was to come to dominate almost the whole of the Western world, including North America, by 1775.

Three important facts may be noticed about the philosophers of the second half of the seventeenth century. The first is that they were all polymaths. No distinction was drawn between pure philosophers and 'natural philosophers', that is to say, scientists. Descartes and Leibniz were first-class mathematicians. Hobbes was a pioneer psychologist and a political scientist. Pierre Gassendi was a philosopher as well as an atomic scientist. Isaac Newton wrote on pure mathematics as well as physics and was a busy theologian. Both Newton and Locke were engaged on the reform of the currency. Locke too was a political scientist, an educationist and a theologian. Secondly, these thinkers were all gradually being weaned from medieval modes of thought, though, except for the British school, they were still preoccupied with metaphysics. It is not, however, true that they broke with the great classical philosophers. Many of the arguments they used are to be found in Plato or Aristotle. Lastly, these men were all aware that in contradicting some of the accepted beliefs of Christian teachers they ran the risk of suffering the fate of Giordano Bruno (who rejected Aristotelean astronomy and was burned at the stake) or Galileo. The Papacy was still powerful in Roman Catholic countries. Much of what was daringly written about the ultimate truths of life was published anonymously or not published, as in the cases of Spinoza and Leibniz, in the authors' lifetimes. And though men like Descartes, Leibniz and Newton maintained that they had proved the existence of God, it was not necessarily the Christian god of orthodox faith. Therefore, unwittingly perhaps, they undermined faith and by doing so ultimately contributed to political as well as philosophical revolutions.

Political science in the Western world may, like modern physics, be roughly dated from the second half of the seventeenth century.

John Locke, the English philosopher whose work was to influence the political ideas of the Western world throughout the eighteenth century.

It is true that Niccolo Machiavelli, following Aristotle, had separated politics from ethics and had laid down rules whereby a prince or a government might hope to strengthen and secure the state against foreign enemies, but he had looked at the problem more as a practical politician than as a political theorist. Jean Bodin, a French writer who was much read in England, had propounded at the end of the sixteenth century a doctrine of *puissance souveraine*, consisting of an absolute, unlimited and indivisible authority to make laws. But Bodin was still influenced by the medieval view that a ruler must obey natural and divine laws and that a subject was permitted to disobey a secular government if its commands were inconsistent with the laws of God. It was not until Hobbes that political theory ceased to centre upon the medieval controversy about the relationship between temporal and spiritual power.

Hobbes's teaching was based upon two premises: the first was that an effective sovereign must be absolute and supreme, indivisible, inalienable and unlimited. What the sovereign commanded was the law and whoever disobeyed the law was wrong. 'Such authority', he wrote, 'is to trump in card-playing, save that in the matter of government, when nothing else is turned up, clubs are trumps'. His second premise was that men had no right to disobey the sovereign except in the cause of self-defence. He justified his view of the state by arguing that the acceptance of an absolute sovereign was the only way to ensure peace. Men are naturally ambitious and jealous and to prevent anarchy it was essential for every man to give his assent to the absolute power of the government. No subject might rebel because that would mean the dissolution of the state and reversion to anarchy. Hobbes's overriding consideration in the 1640s and '50s, in an age when rebellion was erupting all over the Western world, was to ensure peace and order. Yet it has been argued that Hobbes also believed that 'political society can be established and sustained only if there are a certain number of men who are generally prepared to do their duty'.

Spinoza is known to have read and been impressed by the work of Hobbes. Like Hobbes, he thought that the sovereign could do no wrong, must be supreme in the state and also must, as English monarchs did, govern the Church. He too believed that law was what the sovereign ordered. But Spinoza's approach to political questions was more liberal and more optimistic than that of Hobbes. He thought that political consent and obedience could be justified as rational self-interest and, unlike Hobbes, who considered that monarchy was the best form of government, Spinoza preferred democracy as the most natural form. Furthermore he believed that a good government should aim to secure not only peace but intellectual freedom within a State and that if it failed to do so, resistance was permissible. Thus to some extent Spinoza's political theories were half-way between those of Hobbes and those of John Locke, who insisted upon the right of rebellion against any government that abuses its powers.

The German, Samuel Pufendorf, who died in 1694, also attempted to reconcile the authoritarian view of the state with the rights of the individual. He did not agree with Hobbes that men are naturally warlike and that to ensure peace they had to surrender all their rights to the sovereign power. But he accepted that a government must be strong enough to protect the institution of private property. Governments should therefore be bound by a contract with their subjects to secure specific ends. If governments failed to fulfil their contracts then other governments should replace them.

John Locke also thought that the rights of a government could be defined by a direct contract or covenant and that through such a contract individuals should be allowed to retain a number of natural rights which the government might not take away from them; these included the right to life, liberty and property. If this contract was broken by a government it could legitimately be overthrown. Thus men could both be ruled and be free. Locke's political theories were not published until 1688 and then anonymously. They were to have much direct and indirect influence upon the Western world in the eighteenth though not in the seventeenth century.

Other political theories which were expounded at this time related to 'mixed monarchy' as opposed to absolute government. This meant that the executive, legislative and judicial authority in a state should be separated or balanced. But the idea of mixed monarchy, though accepted by most English royalists, met with criticism during the civil wars. Henry Parker, for example, maintained in pamphlets published at the outset of the wars that Parliament was or must be sovereign. James Harrington, writing at the end of the English civil wars, contended, on the other hand, that security could best be attained by a balance of property and a rotation of government. Sir Robert Filmer, whose *Patriarcha* was published posthumously in 1680 and whose views were

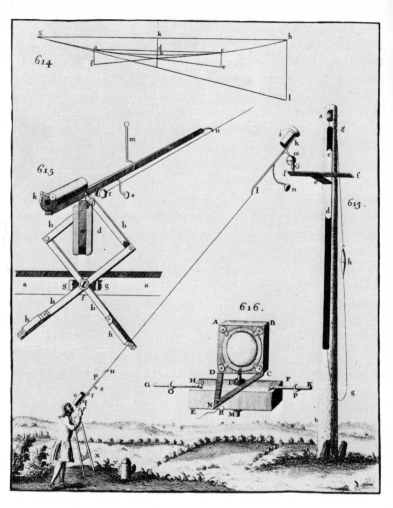

The aerial telescope of Christiaan Huygens, from an engraving in Smith's *Opticles*.

contested by Locke, thought that a 'pure absolute monarchy' was the best form of government because it was based upon the needs of a patriarchal society and therefore could not be a tyranny.

The fascinating point about these seventeenth-century political theories was that the majority of them were arguments for the absolute supremacy of governments. They rejected the medieval idea that sovereignty was divided between the state and the Church and that a secular ruler was obliged to obey traditional unwritten laws – the 'natural law' or the 'moral law'. A case was therefore made out in favour of monarchical absolutism, which had become the characteristic form of government in Europe by the outset of the eighteenth century. Only the North American colonies, the Dutch Republic, one or two Italian and German city states,

Switzerland and Sweden after 1718 were definite exceptions. Even in England Charles II and James II tried to strengthen the effective power of the monarchy. For the last four years of his reign Charles II ruled without a Parliament and James II soon got rid of his first Parliament, though he attempted to pack another one to do his will. English judges were picked and dismissed by monarchs. But two other considerations must be taken into account. The first is that the political theorists rarely invented anything new; what they did in fact was to justify existing forms of government. Secondly, though one speaks of untrammelled absolutism in France, Prussia and Russia, it must be remembered that in fact the aristocracy acted as a balancing force and monarchs were scarcely able to do what they wanted unless they persuaded the aristocracy to back them.

More interesting than political science was the advancement of scientific knowledge in the second half of the seventeenth century. Most of this, though vastly important, was highly theoretical. Progress was made in mathematics, including geometry, by the Dutchman, Christiaan Huygens, by Robert Hooke, Isaac Newton and Leibniz. Calculations were applied to the movement of the planets. Newton showed how they were drawn·towards the sun by a force which varied in inverse proportion to the square of their distance from the sun. Robert Boyle in his *Sceptical Chymist* (1661) refuted the Aristotelian idea that only four elements existed: earth, water, air and fire – and the view of the alchemists that matter could be resolved into sulphur, salt and mercury. But in general his work was destructive rather than constructive. As Professor A. R. Hall has noted, 'In the end Boyle failed not only to draw up his own list of chemical elements, but even to decide definitely whether such simple substances existed at all.' The Italian Gian Alfonso Borelli and the Dane Niels Stensen applied mechanical principles to anatomical questions, while there was a growth in the study of corpuscular theory associated with the names of Gassendi and Boyle, who wrote a book entitled *Of the Reconcilableness of Specific Medicines to the Corpuscular Philosophy*.

But none of these scientific theories or discoveries immediately contributed to technological advance. It may, however, be pointed out that the science of statistics originated in the second half of the seventeenth century when it was associated with the names of two Englishmen, William Petty and Gregory King, and of the Frenchman Sébastien Vauban. Commercial statistics began to be kept from the end of the century, but it was some time before population statistics, which needed to be based on a census, were also generally kept. It has been claimed that agriculture benefited from new methods of tillage and the introduction of fertilizing crops like clover. But if so it applied only to parts of England and the United Netherlands.

The scientists were, on the whole, more absorbed in justifying the ways of God to men than in helping along agriculture or medicine, which remained primitive. Not only Descartes and Leibniz but Newton and Boyle were anxious to show conclusively that God existed, while the two latter scientists maintained that God was necessary not merely to set things in motion but to co-operate with mankind.

How far did these philosophical theories and investigations by scientists, especially by physicists, in fact undermine belief in Christianity? Unquestionably the age of Spinoza, Newton, Locke and Leibniz was one of the greatest intellectual moments in the history of the Western world. The French historian of ideas Paul Hazard wrote that 'minds and consciences were deeply stirred by the startling influx of new ideas, and, by the time the [seventeenth] century was drawing to its close, the effect was clearly visible'. In his *Éloges* Bernard Fontenelle, who was, with another French-man, Pierre Bayle, one of the first authors to translate scientific and philosophical ideas into popular language, collected the funeral orations he had given as secretary of the French Academy after the deaths of French scientists. The *Éloges* show that many of these scientists had originally been educated for the Church, but because they found their teachers uninspiring turned voluntarily to the study of philosophy, mathematics or physics. Denis Diderot, the chief editor of the French *Encyclopédie*, published in the middle of the eighteenth century, was a supreme example of a middle-class man intended for the Church (he was educated by Jesuits) who later devoted himself to scientific expositions which undermined religion.

On the other hand, as has already been emphasized, the great scientists like Descartes and Leibniz believed that they had proved the existence of God and were not concerned with demolishing orthodox Christianity. Thus it may be said that it took a hundred years for their discoveries to percolate through to influential figures like, say, Benjamin Franklin or Jean Jacques Rousseau, who were both deists and both helped to effect revolutions in thought and deed. Meanwhile other factors contributed to what Hazard called the immense secularization of European thought.

One such factor was travel and travellers' tales. The merchant adventurers and Jesuit missionaries had not only penetrated into South America but also into India and China. Here they discovered moral ideas and practices very different from those traditionally held in the West. Sir William Temple devoted his retirement from active politics to the study of the moral and political history of China, Peru, Tartary and Arabia. Other students of the universe were puzzled by the fact that the aboriginal American Indian was not the son of Shem, Ham or Japhet. La Bruyère, writing about free-thinkers, observed: 'Some complete their demoralization by extensive travel, and lose whatever shreds of religion remain to them. Every day they see a new religion, new customs, new rites.'

Another and possibly more important factor in undermining religion was that so many different forms of Christianity were now being permitted to exist side by side. The peace of Westphalia had allowed German rulers to choose between Roman Catholicism, Lutheranism and Calvinism. In some cases, for instance in Brandenburg, a Calvinist prince might rule over a mainly Lutheran country. France had been split asunder between the followers of the Jesuits and the so-called Jansenists. The Jesuits were accused of being 'laxists' because in their ardour to effect conversions to Christianity in pagan countries they adapted their behaviour and teaching to the needs of their proselytes. For example, in India they made concessions to Hindu notions of caste, while in China they embodied the precepts of Confucius in their morality. The Jansenists, on the other hand, were convinced that conversion, based on the descent of special grace, was essential to a Christian and that those on whom such grace did not fall were destined for perdition. Many leading Frenchmen and women – Cardinal de Retz, Blaise Pascal, the dramatist Jean Racine, the theologian Antoine Arnauld, who was a friend of Leibniz, and Madame de Longueville, the celebrated Frondeur *intrigante*, were all at one time or another Jansenists. The Cistercian monastery of Port Royale in Paris was the headquarters of the movement. Jansenism also spread outside France, for instance to the university of Louvain in the Spanish Netherlands. Though Jansenism was condemned as heretical by Pope Clement XI in his Bull *Unigenitus* (1713), it persisted and intermingled with the train of thought which culminated in the French Revolution.

Louvois's harsh treatment of the French Calvinists or Huguenots also created an underground movement in France, while the dispersion of many Huguenots throughout Europe, including Roman Catholic countries like Spain, made for the diversification of religions. The Huguenots were welcomed abroad for economic reasons and so were the Jews. Cromwell allowed the Jews a synagogue to the east of London; the Dutch let them establish synagogues in Amsterdam and The Hague; the Great Elector of Brandenburg and Frederick William I of Prussia welcomed them as merchants who could increase foreign trade. This diversification applied not only in western but in eastern Europe. In Poland the Greek Orthodox Church, the Roman Catholic Church, Protestants and even Socinians (who did not believe in the doctrine of the Holy Trinity) were to be found. In Russia a remarkable and ambitious ecclesiastic, Nikon, who became Patriarch at Moscow in 1652, vainly tried to suppress other religions, which ranged from the Uniates (who were willing to reconcile Orthodox practices with papal authority) to Protestants who drifted into Russia from northern Europe. In England the ousting of the Roman Catholic James II, who had ruled over a Protestant realm and tried to achieve civic equality for all sorts of Christians, was followed by an act of toleration introduced soon after William III was crowned; and although neither in Great Britain nor in the United Netherlands was civic equality granted to all kinds of Christians, every form of Christian worship was henceforward permitted in practice. In England the nonconformists were allowed to build their chapels and set up their dissenting academies, which became educationally influential; in the Dutch Republic, though the official religion was Calvinism, a third of the population were Roman Catholics.

To sum up, during the fifty years or more between the time when Louis XIV assumed full authority over his country and his death in 1715 a change occurred in the whole intellectual atmosphere of the west. Louis had refused to allow the body of Descartes to be buried with religious ceremony in France; Spinoza and Leibniz did not dare to publish their true philosophies while they were still alive for fear of persecution; even Hobbes and Locke were extremely cautious and anxious to avoid accusations of unorthodoxy or materialism. But the wider knowledge of the non-Christian world and the spread of religious toleration alike in Russia and North America, the giants of the future, in effect destroyed the power of monolithic state religions by the middle of the eighteenth century.

9 Western Civilization and Culture in the Seventeenth Century

This period in the history of the West is often said to belong to 'the age of baroque'. But two important qualifications need to be made. The first is that no complete agreement has been reached among experts about the precise significance of baroque and, secondly, that the baroque style was by no means the only aesthetic style that prevailed during the second half of the seventeenth century. Baroque was first employed as a deprecatory term in the second part of the eighteenth century. It was said, for example, to represent 'in painting, a picture or figure ... in which the rules of proportion are not observed and everything is represented according to the artist's whim'. Or, again, it has been described as the art preferred by the Jesuits, or as the fulfilment by painters in Roman Catholic countries of the aims agreed upon at the Council of Trent which launched the Counter-Reformation. Unquestionably it originated in Rome where artists from all over the world were sitting at the feet of two individualist painters of genius, Michelangelo Caravaggio (1573-1610) and Annibale Carracci (1560-1609). Its appeal was to the emotions rather than to the intellect. The classical Renaissance style, it has been suggested, was intended by its geometrical designs and its knowledge of antiquity to attract the favour of a comparatively limited educated class of humanists. The Roman Church, on the contrary, gloried in the traditional beliefs, in its saints and in its martyrs. Through baroque art the saints were made insistently real in their ecstacies and their sufferings. Elaborately designed ceilings in churches were intended to overwhelm the feelings of the beholder. As Sir Kenneth Clark has observed, 'the Church gave imaginative expression to deep-seated human impulses'.

But by the middle of the century the days of some of the finest baroque geniuses (such as Peter Paul Rubens – 1577-1640) had ended. One genius, however, was to survive until 1680; this was Giovanni Lorenzo Bernini (1598-1680), who enjoyed the patron-

age of five popes and at the age of sixty-two was invited by Louis XIV to Paris. Though best known as an architect because he designed the piazza in front of St Peter's Cathedral in Rome and because he was invited to plan a new palace of the Louvre, he was in fact a magnificent sculptor. In his *The Ecstasy of St Teresa* in Santa Maria della Vittoria in Rome, completed in 1648, he combined sculpture, architecture and painting. Such blending of different arts and the powerful emotional appeal of the finished tableau was typical of the art of the high baroque. Another creation of Bernini was the tomb of Pope Alexander VII who died in 1667. The Pope kneels in prayer, while beneath him allegorical figures mourn him and death lies prostrate holding an hour-glass. By his invention, his illusionism, and the use of highly coloured marbles Bernini created a splendid tableau. Painting, architecture and sculpture, all pitched at a higher and more emotional key than that used by the Renaissance artists, together with the bold use of colour, characterized the achievements of the best baroque artists. Later in the century their art tended to be overpitched, as in some of the paintings of Salvator Rosa (1615-73) and Guido Reni (1575-1642). But two other architects, whose church façades exemplified baroque at its most characteristic and who did not overdo their effects, were Francesco Borromini (unlike Bernini, he was not a sculptor as well), who died in 1667, and Pietro da Cortona, who died in 1669. Both of them used contrasting curves and pillars to attract the eyes of spectators.

The development of baroque with the enrichment of public buildings after 1643 culminated in the interiors of Roman Catholic churches from Spain to Bohemia and in secular palaces and other buildings scattered throughout eastern Europe, in southern Germany, Austria and Russia. Michael Kitson has written that 'the Church's attitude towards art was still comparatively austere in the first half of the period though as much perhaps for reasons of economy as from principle; the rich baroque altars and decorations that fill Catholic churches today were only introduced in the second half of the 17th and the 18th centuries'. He thinks that artists, when restraints were no longer imposed upon them, let themselves go and that it was they and not the Jesuits who invented baroque. Among the decorations which they used were frescoes; and they experimented with illusionism of one kind or another. Yet whereas some baroque artists went to extremes of illusionism, others renounced such ingenuities in favour of more classical methods. Thus while Giovanni Battista Gaulli (1639-

Opposite: Bernini's sculpture of *The Ecstasy of St Teresa* in Santa Maria della Vittoria in Rome – to many the epitome of high baroque art.

147

The façade of the church of St Maria in the Via Lata in Rome, designed by Pietro da Cortona.

1709) blended fresco and painted stucco to obtain his effects and allowed parts of the painted ceiling to spill over to lower parts of the church, Carlo Maratti (1625–1713) eschewed illusionism and followed a style rather confusingly called 'baroque classicism' which he had learned from his master, Andrea Sacchi.

Some of the buildings in central Europe, where baroque spread from Italy later in the seventeenth century, nevertheless exemplified the most gorgeous kind of baroque. Though, apart from Andreas Schlüter (1664–1714), a north German sculptor most famous for his equestrian statue of the Great Elector of Brandenburg, the native painters and sculptors were not outstanding, several celebrated architects arose, notably Johann Fischer von Erlach (1656–1733) and Johann Lukas von Hildebrandt (1663–1745). They designed imposing palaces and extravagant churches,

The interior of the
Schloss Pommersfelden
in Bavaria, showing how
Johann Lukas von
Hildebrandt blended the
architecture with the
decorative sculpture and
painting.

based upon knowledge which they had derived from western
Europe; Hildebrandt planned the Upper Belvedere in Vienna for
Prince Eugene of Savoy and in the Schloss Pommersfelden in
Bavaria he blended painting, sculpture and architecture much as
Bernini had done in Italy. Von Erlach did the same for Prince
Eugene's Stadt-palas in Vienna. Both these artists obtained
wonderful results with the siting and embellishment of massive
internal staircases. The same kind of extreme elaboration was
employed in ecclesiastical architecture. Fischer von Erlach's
Kollegienkirche at Salzburg combined a curved portico, two
towers surmounted by sculpture, and a central dome, while at
Gabel in northern Bohemia Hildebrandt employed what were
called 'three-dimensional arches' (curved in plan as well as
elevation) beneath the dome. Another extraordinary baroque

ecclesiastical building was the Benedictine monastery of Melk
towering high above the Danube. John Summerson tells us that its
architect was Jakob Prandtauer, a sculptor-mason, neither
travelled nor deeply read. The monastery rose bastion-like from
the rock on which it was built; it showed that an ambitious abbot
could vie with princes in 'sheer lust for architectural performance'.

Such was the variety of late baroque with its challenging
adventurousness and deep emotional appeal, the culmination of
a style that intervened between the classical style of the Renaissance and the impressionist and post-impressionist achievements
of more modern times. But if this style dominated Italy, Spain
and Austria, two other styles, French neo-classicism and Dutch
realism, were contemporaneous with it in the second half of the
seventeenth century.

It is curious that the two painters who most influenced the
French classical style were Nicolas Poussin and Claude Lorrain
for both of them spent most of their working lives in Rome. There
in fact a classical reaction took place after the deaths of Carracci
and Caravaggio and painters began to look back with admiration

150

upon Michelangelo and Raphael. Poussin, who was invited to Paris by Louis XIV in order to take part in the decoration of the Louvre, was not happy there and returned to Rome as soon as he could. He died in 1665, but Claude, who was seven years younger, lived on until 1682. Poussin was an extremely studious painter fully aware of what he was trying to do. His ideals were order, clarity, harmony and balance. He even discarded brilliant colour because he believed it interfered with clarity and precision. If Poussin was absorbed in the exploration of antique sculpture, Claude was more deeply attracted by Latin than by Greek models. He painted the Virgilian countryside outside Rome and as with Poussin in his figure painting, took enormous care in his arrangements of hills and trees. Neither of these painters aimed at realism; on the contrary, both Poussin's religious paintings and Claude's landscapes were idealized.

French neo-classical art was essentially academic, moral and rather austere. It was academic because it conformed to definite rules. But Poussin's and Claude's paintings were bought in Paris where they exerted a profound influence even upon sculpture. Georges de la Tour (1593–1652), a painter in Lorraine, who had been a disciple of Caravaggio, nevertheless eschewed the emotional appeal characteristic of baroque artists. In the sculptures of François Girardon (1628–1715) and Charles Antoine Coysevox (1640–1720), for example, in Coysevox's tomb of Cardinal Mazarin, can be seen an almost purely classical arrangement. The classical movement spread to French architecture; even the palace of Versailles, which is sometimes wrongly described as baroque, contained only a few baroque elements. The gardens of Versailles were laid out geometrically along classical lines and were decorated with classical statues. The French believed in order and grandeur.

In the Netherlands the greatest artistic age had largely passed by the middle of the seveneenth century. Both Hals and Rembrandt died in comparative poverty because their genius was insufficiently recognized. Rembrandt survived until 1669, but his popularity in Amsterdam decreased as his art became more profound and uncompromising. He eked out a living by selling etchings. Among the best artists of the second generation were Jacob van Ruisdael (1628/9–82), who lived in Haarlem, and held up a mirror to nature, and Jacob Jordans (1573–1678), who dwelt in Antwerp and portrayed Flemish life. Another magnificent painter almost supreme as a colourist was Jan Vermeer of Delft, but he died in 1675 at a relatively early age and few of his wonderful

Opposite above: The baroque monastery of Melk, rising from above the Danube. This was the work of the sculptor-mason, Jakob Prandtauer.

Opposite below: The Upper Belvedere in Vienna, which was built for Prince Eugene of Savoy by the baroque architect, Johann Lukas von Hildebrandt.

153

paintings have survived. Other painters who did *genre* and conversation pieces included Gerard ter Borch (1617–81) and Pieter de Hooch (1629–*c*.83).

The Dutch never accepted the full baroque style, but painted the sea, the sky and landscapes as they saw them. It has been argued that one ought not to overstress Dutch realism, that in fact, as Huizinga remarked, 'every bloom in every flower is a symbol'. What seems to be unquestionable is that too many Dutch artists were trying to gain a living and that overproduction resulted. Portrait paintings were done to order and were not generously paid for. The other artists, the *genre* and the landscape painters, did so on speculation and often had attics filled with unsold works. Towards the end of the century Gerard Lairesse (1641–1711) a second-rate painter who lectured and wrote about the principles of art, condemned what Professor Rudolf Wittkower has called 'a hitherto unknown revelation of microscopic life in all its facets'. Lairesse thought that the Dutch school merely imitated life instead of idealizing it. For a time a reversion took place in favour of the French classical style. The Dutch produced no outstanding architects though the elegance of the tall houses that line the Amsterdam canals have survived for the enjoyment of posterity. The Dutch excelled, however, in the making of beautiful clocks and vases.

In England the finest artist after the the restoration of Charles II was Christopher Wren (1632–1723), who had been trained as a mathematician. Soon after the Great Fire of London in 1666 he was appointed Surveyor-General by the King and he planned fifty-five churches including the new St Paul's cathedral. Perhaps he may be called an eclectic artist for he drew upon classical and baroque models including the work of both Inigo Jones and Bernini. His style has been described as that hybrid, 'late baroque classicism'. His successors such as Sir John Vanbrugh (1664–1726) and Nicholas Hawksmoor (1661–1736) were more baroque and less classical. In painting England showed little distinction. The best portrait painter of the century, William Dobson, had died in 1646, five years after Van Dyck. Portrait painting thereafter was dominated by Peter Lely (1617–80), who learnt his art in Haarlem, though he came from Westphalia, but his solid Dutch style was not well adapted to depicting the languorous beauties of Charles II's Court, even though he did his best to imitate Van Dyck; he was better at painting admirals.

The art of the later seventeenth century was dependent on

Opposite: Sir Christopher Wren's designs for the rebuilding of St Paul's Cathedral after the Great Fire of London underwent many alterations and modifications before construction. This is one of his last drawings and closely resembles the building as it was completed.

154

39

patronage and therefore had to be linked to the structure of society. During the first half of the century the popes had been leading patrons and that was why many artists gravitated to Rome. But after the death of Alexander VII in 1667 this patronage was reduced. However, patrons were to be found in a number of Italian states, for example Florence, Genoa, Venice, Piedmont and Naples. Guarino Guarini, a theologian and mathematician, settled in Turin in 1666 and soon proved himself to be an architectural genius. His work exemplified baroque at its most daring. In the Chapel of the Holy Shroud he erected a dome with transverse ribs and a pagoda-like lantern with the drum pierced by windows, which Michael Kitson describes as 'the ultimate expression of the baroque conception of space in Italy'. In France, until Louis XIV's funds were chiefly diverted to his wars, the Court provided much patronage. Colbert set up an academy not only in Paris but also in Rome. Thus French artists became the servants of a centralized autocracy and were expected to follow the classical style practised by Poussin and inculcated by Colbert's agent, Charles Le Brun. Bernini criticized the slavish submissiveness of his French colleagues, understandably since his own designs for the Louvre were rejected by Colbert. After Colbert's death French architects and painters felt a fuller sense of freedom and were able to abandon the *style Louis XIV* but enjoyed less patronage.

In the United Netherlands, as has been noticed, the numerous Dutch painters were dependent on the patronage of the bourgeoisie, even shopkeepers buying their work. In England the Court was not the fountain of patronage that it was in the time of Charles I who had collected the Italian works of art which were later dispersed to pay the debts of the Commonwealth. Charles II was more interested in science and naval architecture than he was in painting. However, the English aristocracy was often, if not always, the source of enlightened patronage. Portrait painting was to the seventeenth century what fashionable photography is today. So heavy was the demand for the work of Sir Peter Lely that he was able to employ a dozen artists in his studios. One of them told Lely that he could copy his work better than Lely could do it himself. In fact it has been said that for every genuine Lely that comes into the art market, five copies can be found. Other painters came from the Netherlands, such as Jacob Huysmans from Antwerp and William Wissing from Amsterdam, to make an adequate livelihood in England.

In Spain it is not unfair to say that painting and architecture declined in quality at much the same time as the kingdom's political greatness came to an end. Philip IV, who was a considerable patron of the arts, died in 1665. His Court painter Velazquez predeceased him in 1660. Francisco Zurbaran, celebrated for his symbolic portraits, died in 1664. Alonso Cano, who was a sculptor as well as a painter and designed a startling façade for Granada cathedral, died in 1667. Zurbaran it has been said gave the impression long before his death of having worked himself out; he was jealous of the rapid success of Bartolome Esteban Murillo (1618–82) whose reputation has fluctuated throughout the centuries. Once described as the Raphael of Spain, his paintings came to be regarded as mawkish and his religious studies oversentimentalized. In regard to architecture Spanish baroque was richly ornate especially in relation to the interior of churches with elaborate altars and altar screens. But in general Spanish late-seventeenth-century art cannot be compared with the era of Velazquez, Rubens and Zurbaran.

During the baroque period it has been said that painting and sculpture declined as independent arts, but this is a doubtful generalization. It is, however, true that the leading patrons in Russia, in Austria and in Bohemia, as well as in Italy and France, were princes and dukes on the one hand and the Church on the other, and that they required the collaboration of a variety of artists to meet their grandiose needs. The Roman churches (and also those in Turin or Toledo) filled the imagination of the age and needed a blending of arts and crafts. Baroque seldom followed a set pattern and patrons drew on artists influenced or taught by different masters in Italy and elsewhere, whose work can still be seen for example in the Belvedere or in Austrian churches. After the death of Colbert there was a late flowering of French baroque. An important debate took place in the French academy in which 'the colourists', who were followers of Rubens, defeated the neo-classicists inspired by Poussin. Thus French baroque was to play its part in developing German and Russian ideas for palaces and churches in the eighteenth century.

Music, in common with painting and architecture, was an international language and the adjective baroque has been applied to late seventeenth-century musical composition. A parallel may be found with painting in that the somewhat austere techniques of Renaissance music were abandoned in favour of emotionally expressive melodies. Although opera was first written at the beginning of the century and an opera house was built in Venice during

157

The Flower Garden by
Pieter de Hooch, an
example of his 'classical'
phase when he was
strongly influenced by
artists such as Jan
Vermeer of Delft.

1637 the general popularity of opera grew up later and spread
from Italy into Austria and Germany. Both opera and the concerto
have been described as the products of the baroque spirit.

In considering the relationship between art and society one must
not only appreciate the nature of patronage but also the changing
fashions which artists followed. Professor Wittkower has exemplified the changes in fashion with reference to de Hooch. His
earliest phase, characterized by strong chiaroscuro, is linked with
Frans Hals and his circle; his second or 'classical' phase was

influenced by artists such as Vermeer; finally, came an 'academic' phase under French influences. Thus, writes Professor Wittkower, his 'development echoes three social phases: the heroic age following the war of Dutch liberation, the comparatively peaceful phase of the thriving Dutch bourgeoisie, and the aristocratization of society under the shadow of Louis XIV's supremacy'. In the second place, it may be said that in Western society where monarchs and nobilities exerted the greatest influence, artists were expected to pander to their wish for grandeur and display. In England the aristocracy often commissioned the building of vast country houses which they could not hope to live to see completed. Blenheim palace, built to commemorate the Duke of Marlborough's victory in 1704, is a case in point. In France the glory of Louis XIV at his prime had to be reflected by artists, while the German princes, who envied his achievements, imitated his buildings at Versailles and elsewhere. Few artists except Rubens were other than the paid servants of royalty or of the aristocracy; even in the United Netherlands painters were expected to enhance the prestige of the Regents. Similarly the wonderful baroque churches were intended to glorify not only God but also the ecclesiastical princes of the time. Compared with the rich furnishings of these churches calculated to dazzle the eyes the Gothic cathedrals with their flying buttresses and soaring spires were severe and other-worldly.

Sir Kenneth Clark has an illuminating comment on baroque. After praising the talent and versatility of Bernini and asserting that he produced one of the most deeply moving works in European art (*The Ecstacy of St Teresa*) he observes that such work can arouse misgivings. These misgivings, he says, may be summed up in the words 'illusion' and 'exploitation'. Baroque, he suggests, escaped from reality into the world of illusion. Although the Roman Catholic Church came down sharply upon the worship of graven images, the emotional appeal made to the masses through illusionism was in a sense exploitation. The exuberance of baroque, one may argue, was furthermore a kind of attempt to impress the masses and induce them to forget the drabness of their own secular lives. 'The sense of grandeur', says Sir Kenneth, 'is no doubt a human instinct, but if carried too far, it becomes inhuman'. The masterpieces of baroque (and later of rococo) were in fact the last proud fling of a dying society which was to be overwhelmed by the American and French Revolutions.

10 Russia Enters the West 1682-1772

A Russian boyar, a painting from the notebook of a seventeenth-century German traveller.

In the middle of the seventeenth century Muscovy or the state of Moscow was still an underpopulated and relatively isolated part of Europe. It was more or less untouched by the Renaissance or Reformation or by the philosophy and science of the West. Politically it had not yet become an autocracy. The first Romanov Tsar (Michael I) had been elected by a representative national assembly, the Zemsky Sobor, and had been advised by a duma of boyars or council of the nobility. Alexis Michailovich, who with the approval of a Zemsky Sobor, succeeded his father in 1645 and was known as the Gentle, had some of the attributes of a constitutional ruler and relied on the advice of an outstanding Foreign Minister, Ordyn-Nashchokin and of the Patriarch Nikon, a peasant by birth who rapidly climbed the ecclesiastical ladder. In some directions the Muscovite empire was expanding, in others contracting. During the reign of Alexis, Smolensk and Kiev near the Lithuanian border were yielded by the Polish-Lithuanian Commonwealth to Russia. The Cossacks – mounted frontier warriors of independent character, who lived on the left bank of the river Dnieper – acknowledged the suzerainty of the Tsar in much of the Ukraine. Thus Russia was expanding westwards. Southwards the authority of the Tsar stretched from the Dnieper in the west to the area watered by the Lower Volga, which emptied into the Caspian Sea at Astrakan, and had been conquered by the first Tsar, Ivan the Terrible.

But Russia had no satisfactory outlet for foreign trade which would have brought the country into closer contact with the Western world. The port of Archangel in the White Sea was rendered impassable by ice for much of the year. The Baltic, as has been noted, became largely a Swedish lake after the conquests of Gustavus Adolphus. The Black Sea was a Turkish lake, its northern shores being chiefly dominated by semi-independent Tartars who paid tribute to the Sultan. Hence to secure further expansion westward towards the Baltic and to obtain access to the Black Sea, wars with Sweden and Turkey were practically unavoidable, while an alliance with Poland-Lithuania was necessary to protect the

Russian peasants, seen through English eyes: an illustration from John Mottley's *The History of Peter I, Emperor of Russia*, published in 1693.

western frontier. To the east, however, the Muscovite empire was rapidly expanding not so much because of the efforts of the government as through the enterprise of pioneers, chiefly the Cossacks of the Dnieper and the Don. Indeed the advance has been compared with the astounding deeds of the Conquistadores in Central and South America. During the reign of Alexis the port of Okhotsk on the Pacific was founded and the first treaty between Russia and China was concluded in 1689. Beyond the Urals a valuable fur trade developed.

Not only did Alexis conclude peace with the Poles and win the allegiance of the unruly Cossacks, but he attempted administrative reform. In 1649 he issued a new code of laws *(Olozhenie)* in an effort to establish internal peace. The Russian landowners had constantly pressed the Tsars to prevent the flight of peasants from one part of the country to another. The peasants, who lived mostly on a meagre margin of subsistence, understandably sought out generous masters or joined the semi-independent Cossacks of the south. They also attempted to escape from their oppressive feudal obligations by becoming monks or priests, and to get away they often murdered their masters and set fire to their houses. Alexis's legislation made serfdom into a state institution. Henceforward all peasants had to be registered by their masters. Registered peasants who fled could be severely punished when caught; those who received them could be fined heavily. To ensure justice masters might flog their serfs, who were given no reciprocal rights.

It was no wonder that peasant revolts, like those of Stenka Razin in the 1670s, were endemic or that the Cossacks were frequently reinforced. In any case the bulk of the people were illiterate, superstitious and poverty-stricken. Quarrels inside the Orthodox Church brought it into contempt with the nobility. To maintain order the government became increasingly autocratic. No Zemsky Sobor was summoned for nearly thirty years. The duma of boyars continued to decay. With the aid of a bureaucracy at the centre and governors who acted as both military officers and judges in the provinces, the government aimed at centralization as well as autocracy.

Alexis (a Romanov) died in 1676, leaving two weak-minded sons and a strong-minded daughter, Sophia, by his first wife, and a son, Peter, the future Peter the Great, by his second wife. Peter was only four when his father died. For twenty years until in 1696 when Peter became sole Tsar constant squabbles took place over the question of who should rule the Muscovite empire in which the palace guard or streltsi played a leading part. Fortunately for the Russians their foreign enemies were quiescent during much of this period. The able King of Sweden, Charles XI, who attained autocratic powers, used them to keep his kingdom out of war. When he died in 1697, leaving a boy of fifteen as his successor with the title of Charles XII, it looked as if Sweden would become a victim rather than a predator. The Turks had their hands full resisting the offensive by the Austrians and the Poles in the Balkans, the humiliated Sultan, Mehmed IV, having been dethroned and put in a cage in 1687. Peter the Great's half-sister, Sophia, who acted as Regent of Russia for seven years and had a capable chief minister and cultured lover in Prince Vasily Vasilyevich Golitsyn, took advantage of the Turks' difficulties to declare war upon them in the hope of expanding Russian power to the Black Sea, but Golitsyn proved unable to overcome the Tartars of the Crimea and the Turkish war was still in progress when Peter I assumed full authority as Tsar.

Peter was a dynamic, violent and self-educated ruler who, it has been said, worked upon Russia 'like nitric acid on iron'. He proved himself to be a superb technician, a considerable general and a first-class administrator. He was liable to terrible rages, could drink anybody under the table, and soon got rid of the dull wife his mother had provided for him and took as his chief mistress a peasant girl from Livonia, Catherine, whom afterwards he married. She accompanied him to the wars and was to succeed

Peter the Great's fleet anchored in the harbour of Archangel, from an engraving made by Kort in 1700.

him as the Tsarina Catherine I. The story of how, soon after his accession to full authority, Peter insisted on visiting England and Holland incognito to learn the art of shipbuilding is familiar. From the first he realized that Russia needed modernization and that required technical advice from the West. He also appreciated that to expand Russian territory at the expense of his neighbours and to obtain access to the seas, he needed an army, a navy and a munitions industry. He learned quickly from experience, claiming to have mastered the art of shipbuilding in four months. The war with the Turks had dragged on. Instead of fighting in the Crimea as Golitsyn had done, Peter attacked the fortress of Azov to the north-east of the Black Sea and captured it at his second attempt. He then chose Taganrog, which lay west of Azov on the open sea, as a naval station. He also found allies against the Turks in the Venetians and Austrians, whose distinguished general, Prince Eugene, halted a Turkish counter-offensive at the battle of Zenta in Hungary. The battle, which took place in September 1697, resulted in the death of thirty thousand Turkish soldiers and the mutiny of others who assassinated the ill-advised Grand Vizir. Thus the Turks, though always resilient, were obliged to stop fighting for the time being. By the treaty of Carlowitz (January 1699) they gave up all claims upon Hungary and Transylvania and conceded the Morea and Aegina to Venice. They also agreed to a two-year truce with Russia and in 1700 by the treaty of Constantinople surrendered Azov and Taganrog.

At this time Charles XII of Sweden was only eighteen while Peter was twenty-eight. Charles was a very different character from Peter. He had enjoyed a happy childhood and was devoted to his mother and his sister. Stockholm was a much more cultured town than Moscow, having long been under German, Dutch and latterly also French influence. Charles knew French and German, read the works of the leading French dramatists, studied mathematics, and learned history from textbooks written by the eminent Swedish historiographer royal, Samuel Pufendorf, the German philosopher, lawyer and political scientist. After Charles became king he spent much time with a leading Swedish architect, Count Nicodemus Tessin, and planned the building of a palace if not as imposing as that of Versailles at least as grand as that in Copenhagen. On the whole, however, his tastes were austere. He never married and suffered from sexual frustration; he always preferred to drink water or small beer; and he studied the Bible and Lutheran religious books. His ancestors had left him a magnifi-

Charles XII of Sweden, who spent almost the whole of his reign conducting military campaigns against the Danes, Poles and the Russians.

cent empire not only in Sweden proper, but also Finland, Karelia (adjacent to Finland), Ingria, Estonia, Livonia and farther to the west, Swedish Pomerania, Stralsund, Bremen and Verden. Neighbouring Denmark was not only surrounded by Swedish possessions but by the ducal parts of Schleswig and Holstein, which had been alienated by the Danish Crown, and were ruled by the Duke of Holstein-Gottorp: Charles XII's grandmother was a member of the ducal family which was therefore pro-Swedish. All these territories none the less had a population of fewer than three million inhabitants and although Charles's father, who was exceptionally parsimonious, had left his son a full treasury and one of the finest armies in Europe, imbued with the traditions of

165

Gustavus Adolphus and Charles X, the young King at once became the potential prey of envious neighbours.

A coalition aiming at the dismemberment of the Swedish empire was soon formed in the hope of overthrowing the new King before his rule was firmly established. It was partly inspired by Charles XII's own cousin, the ambitious Elector Augustus II of Saxony, who was also the recently elected King of Poland succeeding John Sobieski; it was partly too the work of a Livonian nobleman named Johann Reinhold von Patkul who dreamed of Livonian freedom; and it was joined by Peter I of Russia who was hopeful of gaining or regaining territory on the Baltic seaboard, but refused to commit himself to attacking Sweden until his war with Turkey had ended. Charles XII, however, proved himself to be a military genius and in addition to possessing a useful navy of his own received naval assistance from the Dutch and the English. In July 1700 his troops landed on Danish Zealand and threatened Copenhagen with bombardment and blockade. Frederick IV of Denmark gave in and by the treaty of Travendal opted out of the war.

Meanwhile Tsar Peter had concluded peace with the Turks and declared war on Sweden. But the treaty of Travendal was a blow to his plans. He had begun the war by massing his troops against the port of Narva at the junction of Estonia and Ingria, while Augustus II was leisurely moving against Riga in Livonia. Charles XII now surprised the Russians just as he had surprised Frederick IV. Re-embarking his troops from Zealand, he landed them in Livonia and routed the ill-trained Russian army, which had been besieging Narva in Ingria, during a snowstorm. Though Charles XII was advised to finish off the Russians, he preferred to turn his army back against his third enemy, his cousin Augustus, and spent the next six years fighting in Poland and Saxony. This gave Peter, who had not himself been present at the battle of Narva, a breathing space. He built up and trained a new army, based on Western models; he purchased flintlock muskets abroad, but inculcated the lesson that battles are won by cold steel. While Charles XII was absorbed in Poland, Peter retook Narva and overran much of Ingria and Livonia. He also planned a new capital to be named St Petersburg near the Finnish frontier and a naval base on the island of Cronstadt to protect it.

At the end of 1706 Augustus made peace with the victorious Swedish King on humiliating terms. He resigned the crown of Poland, which was taken up by Stanislas Leszczynski, a native

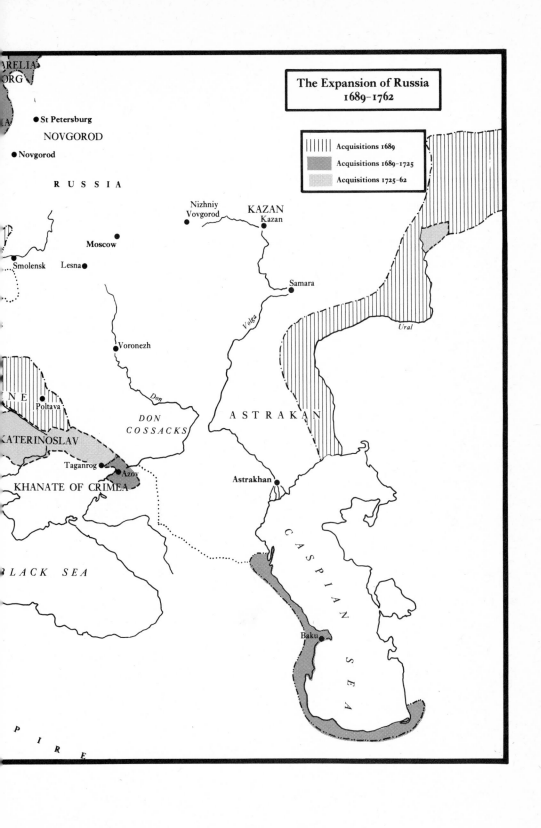

The Expansion of Russia
1689-1762

	Acquisitions 1689
	Acquisitions 1689-1725
	Acquisitions 1725-62

ARELIA
ORG

● St Petersburg

NOVGOROD

● Novgorod

R U S S I A

Nizhniy
Vovgorod

KAZAN

● Kazan

● Moscow

Smolensk   Lesna●

Samara

Volga

Ural

● Voronezh

Don

N E
● Poltava

DON
COSSACKS

A S T R A K A N

ATERINOSLAV

Taganrog ●   ●Azoy

KHANATE OF CRIMEA

Astrakhan ●

C
A
S
P
I
A
N

S
E
A

B L A C K   S E A

Baku ●

P

I   R

E

Polish nobleman, who was Charles's nominee, and he handed over Patkul to be executed as a traitor. The members of the Grand Alliance, still engaged in the war of the Spanish succession, were so impressed with the military genius of the young Swedish King that they tried to buy his alliance. The Duke of Marlborough visited Charles at Altranstadt near Leipzig in Saxony where the Swedo-Polish treaty had been signed. Thus two of the finest soldiers of the age met for the only time. But as Marlborough discerned, Charles XII was intent only on driving the Russians out of Swedish possessions and he marched away to his fate.

Three Swedish armies were available for the Russian campaign of 1708: the main army under the King, which crossed the Vistula in Poland after outmanoeuvring the Russians; a smaller army in Finland; and a Baltic army commanded by Count Adam Ludwig Lewenhaupt stationed in Livonia. What Charles XII's exact strategic plans were is not certain even today. But it seems likely that his original intention was to advance on Moscow directly via Smolensk. The Russians adopted the strategy which was later to be effective against both Napoleon and Hitler. Utilizing the vast spaces of the empire for retirement and scorching the earth which their enemy was to occupy, they avoided battle as long as they could. At first all went reasonably well for the Swedes. They continued across the Berezina river and at comparatively small cost to themselves obliged the Russians to withdraw across the Dnieper. But after that they were bogged down. Everywhere the exceptionally wet weather made the movements of troops and supplies extremely slow. Charles had instructed Lewenhaupt to join him in Russia with fresh troops and supplies. For three weeks he waited on the left bank of the Dnieper for Lewenhaupt's arrival, which was prevented by the abnormal summer weather. So Charles took the decision to march south east into the Ukraine, hoping in the following season to move on Moscow from the south; meanwhile the Ukraine was a fertile land where food, shelter and allies might well be found; for the Hetman of the Dnieper Cossacks, Ivan Stepanovich Mazeppa, had broken with the Tsar and the Tartars might join the Swedes. The Don Cossacks too were in revolt against Peter I. But the majority of the Dnieper Cossacks were alienated by the Swedish demands for supplies, including milk and honey; Lewenhaupt's army was cut off and beaten at the battle of Lesnaja (29 September 1708) and his supply train abandoned. Even when joined by the remnants of that army Charles was left with fewer men than he needed.

After a cruel winter when heavy frosts were followed by a sudden thaw, the Swedes prepared to leave the Ukraine and laid siege to the fortress of Poltava which barred the route to Kharkov and Moscow. The siege was a leisurely one, for Charles XII still had hopes of help from the Tartars or the Turks. But his hopes were not realized and on his twenty-seventh birthday he himself was severely wounded in the foot by a stray bullet; so that when the expected battle with the Russians took place on 8 July 1709 he could not mount a horse. With some difficulty Charles managed to escape across the Russian border into Bessarabia, which was part of the Turkish empire, where he remained in honourable captivity for five years.

The defeat of Charles XII at Poltava had three immediate consequences. The first was that it revived the anti-Swedish alliance between Frederick IV of Denmark, the Elector Augustus II of Saxony and Peter I of Russia. Augustus was re-elected King of Poland, but the Poland-Lithuanian Commonwealth was soon split between the supporters of Augustus and those of the deposed native King Stanislas. The Danes did not find the Swedes as easy to overcome in Charles XII's absence as they had imagined. An attempt by Frederick IV to invade Scania in southern Sweden was halted by a Swedish army under the command of Count Magnus Stenbock at the battle of Helsingborg, but his own attempt to invade Denmark was equally unsuccessful. The second consequence of Poltava was that the Turks were so impressed by the Russian victory over the hitherto invincible Swedes that they themselves feared attack by the Muscovites. Lastly, Peter I, anticipating another Turkish war, tried to appeal to the Balkan Christians to throw off the yoke of their Muslim masters and join the Russians in fighting 'for faith and the fatherland'. The Russian policy of extending their political authority over the Balkans continued to be followed until the twentieth century, although the present ideological bond is Marxism and not Orthodox Christianity.

Under Sultan Ahmed III, who managed to reign for twenty-seven years and was not exclusively devoted to the pleasures of the seraglio, the Turks recovered from their buffetings by the Austrians and their armed forces were strengthened and improved. Thus refreshed, they declared war on Russia in November 1710. Peter, accompanied by his wife Catherine, at once moved into the Turkish principalities of Moldavia and Wallachia (modern Romania) in the spring of 1711, aiming to enlist the aid of the native hospodars or governors and to prevent the Turkish army from crossing the Danube. But the Russian army outran its communications and was short of provisions and supplies. Peter's forces were surrounded and defeated at the battle of Stanileshte on the river Pruth during July. In consequence of this defeat the Tsar was obliged by the treaty of Pruth (July 1711) to give up Azov and Taganrog, won in the previous Turkish war, and also to promise not to interfere in Poland. Further ruptures took place but finally in June 1713 a twenty-five-year peace was signed in Adrianople.

During his captivity in Turkey Charles XII had intrigued for Sultan Ahmed's intervention against Russia, but he had concluded no alliance with his hosts, and the only advantage he obtained from the Turkish victory was the right to return to Sweden unmolested by the Russians. The Turks had no wish to help him further since, after their defeat of the Russians, they were anxious to return to making war on their old enemies, the Venetians, and in fact they managed to wrest back the Morea and capture Corfu. Charles XII reached Stralsund, almost the only Swedish port left in the northern and eastern Baltic, but he was compelled to let it fall into the hands of the Danes and Russians. Then he occupied himself in raising and training a new army which he planned to use against the Danes in Norway. But in November 1718 he was killed by a stray bullet when besieging the fort of Frederikssten which guarded the route from Sweden to the Norwegian capital of Christiania (Oslo). He was succeeded as king by his brother-in-law, Frederick of Hesse, who took the title of Frederick I. As the price of his succession Frederick was compelled to summon the Estates to meet and to abandon the prerogative form of government used by Charles XI and Charles XII.

Though the Turks were victorious over the Venetians, the Holy Roman Emperor, Charles VI, having recovered from his long war against France, decided to intervene on behalf of his former allies. He dispatched his veteran general, Prince Eugene, into Hungary where he crushed the Turks at the battle of Peterwardein, which was fought in August 1716 near the Hungarian-Serbian frontier. In the following year Eugene inflicted an even more severe defeat on the Turks at Belgrade, which surrendered to Austrian arms. By the peace of Passarowitz the Turks gave up much of Wallachia and Serbia to the Austrians, but retained the Morea at the cost of the Venetian Republic.

In September 1721 Frederick I of Sweden brought the war with

Russia to an end. By the treaty of Nystad Sweden retained Finland except for a small area near Peter I's new capital of St Petersburg, and Russia paid an indemnity. But Ingria, Estonia and Livonia were lost to Sweden forever. Earlier Peter had arranged a marriage between his niece and the Duke of Courland, whose land lay west of Livonia. The Duke then conveniently died. Thus the whole of the eastern Baltic came under Russian influence.

Another treaty, concluded in Warsaw in 1716 between Poland and Russia, confirmed Augustus II on the throne but upheld the existing ramshackle constitution which required that the King must consult his diet or Seym where a single deputy could veto a decision. Thus the absolutist powers after which Augustus thirsted were denied him. He did however make sure that Poland did not then become a Russian protectorate.

The net result of all these treaties – Passarowitz, Nystad and Warsaw – was that Sweden and Poland ceased to be great powers. The Poles quarrelled among themselves until in the second half of the eighteenth century their vast country was partitioned among their neighbours. The Swedes, for their part, recognized that the days of the fighting Vasa kings had ended and that they must adjust themselves to a more modest role. Austria, it might have been thought, after defeating both the French and the Turks, largely through the military genius of Prince Eugene, would have henceforward been acknowledged as the leading imperial power in the West with its Habsburg rulers governing, besides their hereditary possessions, Hungary, Transylvania, Bohemia and part of Serbia as well as the southern Netherlands and much of Italy. In fact grave weaknesses were to appear since Charles VI had no male heir. The country that emerged as an unchallengeable great power after the eastern European wars at the turn of the century was Russia. Moreover Peter the Great attempted to strengthen his empire internally as well as externally.

Peter's aim was to reform the administrative machinery of Russia both at the centre and in the provinces and to ensure that the nobility served the state. Following a practice introduced in Sweden and elsewhere, the Tsar substituted what were known as 'colleges' for ministerial departments. Colleges were in effect boards of officials similar to the Board of Admiralty in England where administrative responsibility was collectively shared. On the legislative side he constituted a senate over which a procurator-general presided during the frequent absences of the Tsar. The provinces, which were originally divided into nine unwieldy governments, were in 1719 reorganized into fifty counties each of which was subdivided into districts. Peter also tried to separate the judiciary from the administration. For this purpose the country was divided again, this time into eleven judicial areas. But all this proved too novel and complicated, too contrary to Russian traditions and never really worked. Undoubtedly Peter had hankerings to be an enlightened despot and some impact may have been made upon his mind by the writings of Pufendorf and Leibniz. His ideal appears to have been what has been called 'a police state' in which everyone's functions were defined and where domestic peace and social welfare could be procured. Yet his bureaucracy remained corrupt and uninspired. 'The Tsar pulls uphill alone,' it was said, 'with the strength of ten, but millions push downhill.'

Peter also tried to tidy up the Church. Conscious of the reactionary character of recent patriarchs of Moscow, he replaced them by a synod of ten whose members he nominated. Thus the Orthodox Church was in effect fully subjected to the state. It is extremely doubtful if Peter was a Christian himself; he certainly enjoyed blaspheming. Moreover his wish to develop the economy of his empire postulated toleration for both Protestants and Jews. Again, in order to modernize his empire and to raise the quality of his army officers and civil servants, he tried to impose compulsory elementary education for the children of landowners and to provide technical education for aspiring young men. German and other foreign manuals were translated on his orders. He also sought to create a service nobility not dissimilar from the *noblesse de la robe* in France. State service became compulsory. In 1722 Peter drew up a table of fourteen ranks or grades for military and civil posts in which promotion went by merit. Those who reached the eighth grade automatically became nobility, enjoying the privileges of owning serfs and being exempted from the poll tax. This poll tax had been introduced in 1718 and five and a half million 'souls' (serfs or bound peasants), recorded by periodic censuses, were liable to pay it. Its object was to meet the cost of the upkeep of the army and navy.

Peter's attitude to the economy was empirical. Just as the duties he imposed on his nobility and the taxes he exacted from townsmen and peasants were for the benefit of the armed forces, so the interest that he took in the iron and copper industries was largely motivated by the idea of making Russian munition industries independent of the outside world. A number of state factories were set up, but Peter hardly followed in the footsteps of Colbert. For

example he preferred to promote infant industries by tax exemptions and subsidies. Thus he stimulated the mining of minerals in which his empire, both in Europe and in Asia, was so rich. Peter's attempt to expand the wealth and power of his empire by introducing Western methods of administration and by promoting industrial progress has been admired by modern Russian historians, but with this qualification, that what he achieved was principally at the expense of 'fleecing' the peasants. (His predecessor, Alexis, had been concerned with introducing Western culture into Russia, but Peter was the pioneer of Western technology.) Moreover he only mastered 'bourgeois' ideas to a limited extent and was not even the father of Russian 'capitalism'. 'Peter', wrote the economic historian, Lyashchenko, 'was incapable of changing the existing social conditions. Therefore, while he was fully capable of seeing the negative features of serfdom, he was powerless before his own serf-holding nobility.' A non-Marxist historian, Sir Bernard Pares, wrote: 'Russia was to be Europeanized by the knout.' Furthermore it is fair to say that Peter's policies were always conditioned by the needs of war. Even after the triumph of the treaty of Nystad he would have liked to push forward the Russian frontiers into Poland and south to the Black Sea. But the conquest of the Crimea and the partition of Poland

St Petersburg, Peter the Great's new capital replacing Moscow.

were left to his successors. In the end, he preferred to come to terms with the Turks and the partition on which they eventually agreed was that of Persia. While Peter occupied the Caucasus and the port of Baku on the Caspian sea, the Turks overran Georgia. At the end of his life the Tsar's magnificent constitution declined. Much of his time was spent in his new capital of St Petersburg, which must have cost as many lives as the construction of Versailles. In November 1724 when he was sailing to visit an iron works, he leapt into the icy waters of the Baltic to rescue the victims of a shipwreck. He caught fever and died in February 1725.

The years that followed the death of Peter the Great were called by the Russian historian Vasily Klyuchevsky 'the Epoch of Palace Revolutions'. In 1722 a decree had been issued which allowed each Tsar to nominate his successor instead of his being elected by the Zemsky Sobor. Unfortunately Peter had omitted to name his own successor and in effect the choice was to be determined by the Palace Guard and the group of aristocrats who formed a Supreme Council created by Peter's second wife, Catherine I. She died in 1727 and she was followed by Peter's grandson (whose father Alexis had died in mysterious circumstances during the reign of his own father whom he hated). Peter II died of smallpox in 1730 and the throne passed to Peter I's niece, Anna, Duchess of Courland. Anna died in 1741 and was succeeded by her great-nephew, Ivan Antonavich, an infant who was promptly deposed. The next ruler was Peter I's daughter by his second wife, by name Elizabeth, who governed not ineffectively for twenty years. During this period she found as wife for her nephew a remarkable minor German princess, Catherine, who soon adapted herself to Russian ways and was quickly unfaithful to her husband, Peter III, named Tsar in 1762. His attempt to Prussianize the Russian army, his ridicule of the Orthodox Church, his insulting behaviour to his wife and his planning of an unnecessary war against Denmark combined to make him unpopular in both Church and state. Catherine's lover, Grigory Orlov, and his brother Alexis engineered a conspiracy with the aid not only of the Palace Guard but of two other regiments and Peter III was forced to flee from St Petersburg to be done to death in an outlying village. Catherine was proclaimed Tsarina in St Petersburg cathedral and she announced that she had been obliged to act to save her (adopted) country.

'Who', asked Sir Bernard Pares rhetorically about the events of 1725 to 1762 in Russian history, 'would take this miserable record as the history of a people? Of the six immediate successors of

Peter I, three were women, one a boy of twelve, one a babe of one, and one an idiot.' Certainly many of the reforms of Peter the Great fell by the wayside. The nobility recovered their ancient privilege of doing nothing much for their country. During his short term as Tsar Peter III had 'emancipated' the nobility from serving the state and Peter I's service-aristocracy became ordinary idle nobility. Catherine II was never strong enough to reverse that policy nor did she emancipate the serfs whom she came to fear after peasant rebellions against her. In foreign affairs Russia in the 1730s had engaged in the war of the Polish succession, one of those futile wars which punctuated the annals of the Western world during the first half of the eighteenth century. Augustus II of Poland had died in 1733; Russia, in alliance with Austria, backed his son to succeed him as Augustus III. The France of Louis XV supported Charles XII's erstwhile choice as king, Stanislas Leszczynski, who happened to be Louis XV's father-in-law. As the Russians and Austrians had easy access to Poland and the French had not, Augustus III duly succeeded. The other war which involved Russia was the Seven Years' War (1756–63) waged against the military genius of Frederick II of Prussia from which nothing whatever was gained.

In Sweden-Finland and Denmark-Norway too these were years mostly of peace and political confusion. After the death of Charles XII, who had failed to sustain his victories and had exhausted his kingdom's resources, a reaction against the Vasa monarchy took place in Sweden. Charles XII's brother-in-law, Frederick I, reigned as a constitutional monarch for over thirty years. These years were known as 'the time of freedom'. During the reign a kind of party system developed in the Riksdag, the parties being known as the Caps and the Hats. The Caps were more or less pacific and favoured an English alliance, while the Hats were irredentist, pro-French and anti-Russian. After a short and absurd war with Russia (1741–3) when the Hats vainly tried to regain the lost Baltic provinces and managed only to lose control of Finland, peace was restored by the treaty of Abo, the Swedes surrendering a small strip of Finland to the Russians. In return for this modest peace the Hats accepted a Russian candidate for the succession to the throne, Adolphus Frederick of Holstein-Gottorp, a descendant of both Charles XII and Peter the Great, who became king in 1751 with the title of Frederick II. Frederick's wife, Louisa Ulrika, a sister of Frederick II of Prussia, dominated her husband. Nevertheless the Swedes fought against Prussia during the Seven Years' War but without achieving anything whatsoever. The militarism of the Hats damaged the prestige of Sweden.

In Denmark Frederick IV's successful defiance of Charles XII of Sweden made him popular enough to establish absolutism for the House of Oldenburg. His son, Christian VI, and his grandson, Frederick V, avoided wars and governed a prosperous country. Improved agricultural methods were introduced, commerce expanded and industries developed, especially in Norway. The eventual renunciation by Sweden of its traditional alliance with the Dukes of Holstein-Gottorp enabled the Danish government to strengthen its position in Schleswig and Holstein and by 1773 the whole of these strategic lands were recognized as belonging to the crown of Denmark.

The ending of the great Northern war by the conclusion of the treaty of Nystad (to which the treaty of Abo was an appendage) therefore left northern Europe in comparative peace. The victories and the reforms of Peter I – whatever his faults and mistakes – had ensured the ultimate emergence of Russia as one of the greatest political and military powers in the Western world. During the late eighteenth century Catherine II was to complete the expansion of Russia to the west and the south, which Peter had begun. But Russia was not yet an important industrial nation nor were there any real signs of intellectual or cultural advance such as were to contribute so strikingly to Western civilization in the nineteenth century, especially in literature and music. Indeed in spite of the exertions of two autocrats, Peter I and Catherine II, even as compared with the achievements of the neighbouring Scandinavian kingdoms, the veneer of Western culture in eighteenth-century Russia wore pretty thin.

11 Europe in the Grip of Dynastic Ambition 1715-40

In western and southern Europe the governments that had been fighting against the France of Louis XIV for the best part of twenty-five years might have been assumed to be exhausted. Certainly they had accumulated considerable national debts and so had France after the death of the 'sun king', who confessed in the end that he had been too fond of war. In actual fact it was possibly the wealthy Dutch Republic that had accumulated the largest national debt in return for which it had gained only what was to prove a more or less useless barrier of fortresses in the southern Netherlands. So costly had been the upkeep of the land forces enlisted to attain that end that it had neglected the navy. Still, both the Dutch Republic and the British government had mastered the art of funding national debts, whereas the French had not. Spain, on the other hand, over the future of whose extensive empire war had been fought during the first decade of the eighteenth century, was left in a condition of comparative prosperity. For the French had largely subsidized the war, waged in support of the rights of the French King's grandson, and had supplied most of the soldiers and sailors who fought it.

It is true that the Spanish kingdom had been divided in its allegiance, the Castilians supporting Philip of Anjou, and the Catalans, Aragonese and Valencians adhering to the Archduke Charles. This in fact benefited Philip V when his title to the throne was recognized by the peace treaty. For he was able to do what his predecessors had failed to do and that was to abolish the privileges of Aragon and materially reduce those of Catalonia and Valencia. Furthermore he was no longer burdened with the southern Netherlands, which for years had been more of a nuisance than an asset to the Spanish Crown. The British also gained as they had acquired considerable commercial and colonial advantages from the war of the Spanish succession. Spain in fact was pretty well off as the result of the war.

But it came about that during the twenty-five years that followed the peace settlement the countries that had engaged in the war did not lay down their arms for long but continued to plot and to fight against one another. Apart from the continual colonial rivalries, the other main reason was essentially dynastic. The Emperor Charles VI's son had died and his father was anxious to ensure for his daughter, who was born in 1718, the succession to all the Habsburg dominions. He therefore looked for bargaining counters and was not forthcoming until he obtained them. He refused to recognize the right of the Hanoverians to acquire the British throne after the death of Queen Anne in 1714; he would not renounce his meaningless title of King of Spain; he went on fighting the French in the southern Netherlands until Prince Eugene's defeat at the battle of Denain in 1712 obliged him to make peace.

George I, the Elector of Hanover, a duchy which he left with marked reluctance for London, was naturally anxious to gain the general recognition of his title as king since he was aware that the late James II's son, the Old Pretender, who called himself James III, was still lurking in France and could command considerable nostalgic loyalty in Scotland.

The dynastic interests of Philip V were twofold. First, he would have preferred to be King of France than King of Spain and was therefore the enemy of the Duke of Orleans, the guardian of Louis XV, the five-year-old grandson of Louis XIV, on whose account he had assumed the sole regency in Paris. Philip V was also later to be egged on by his studiously domineering wife, Elizabeth Farnese, to obtain thrones for their two sons in Italy (since Philip already had two sons by his first wife to succeed him on the throne of Spain). The French Regent also had his ambitions. Should the child King die, might he not stake a claim to the French throne rather than his nephew Philip V, who had renounced it?

Finally, it may be said that both Habsburg Austria and Bourbon Spain were dissatisfied powers. The Spaniards of course regretted losing their possessions in Italy – Naples, Sicily and Sardinia – which they had enjoyed for so long. The fact that the King acquired an Italian second wife was a constant reminder of his loss. The Emperor Charles VI, for his part, was bitter because he had been deprived by his allies of the throne of Spain when he had fought there in person and actually been crowned at Madrid in 1706. His acquisition of the southern Netherlands from Spain was to prove of little advantage to him. First, he was obliged to bargain at length with the Dutch over their fortress barrier; secondly, neither of the two maritime powers was going to allow him to exploit the geographical position of the southern Netherlands to

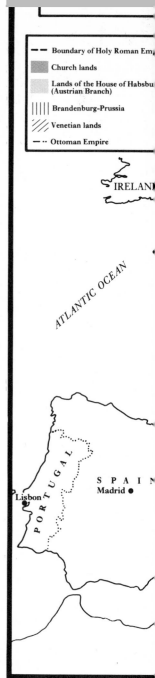

Boundary of Holy Roman Emp

Church lands

Lands of the House of Habsbu (Austrian Branch)

Brandenburg-Prussia

Venetian lands

Ottoman Empire

IRELAND

ATLANTIC OCEAN

PORTUGAL

Lisbon

SPAIN
Madrid

expand foreign trade from either Ostend or Antwerp. Thus the dynastic uncertainties and dynastic ambitions of monarchs – even George I of England wanted to expand the territory of his beloved Hanover – made for complicated diplomatic negotiations and futile wars from 1715 onwards.

To those historians who believe that changes are determined entirely by economic facts or philosophical ideas it must seem strange that, superficially at least, personalities count for much. Take Philip V of Spain for example. In essence he was lazy and happy to leave the government to others. But he combined in awkward measure extreme piety with obsessive sexuality. When his first wife, Maria Luisa of Savoy, died, Giulio Alberoni, the agent of the Duke of Parma in Madrid, recommended his master's daughter, Elizabeth Farnese, as her successor, and after complicated intrigues she arrived in Spain to claim her husband. Elizabeth Farnese was neither well educated nor particularly clever, but she knew what she wanted and in order to ensure it, she hardly ever left her husband's side. The King and Queen never occupied separate beds but shared a four-poster scarcely four feet wide. The day started for them when the curtains of the bed were drawn by the Queen's former nurse or *azafata*. The royal pair then had breakfast consisting of a specially prepared and very greasy gruel. Then they said their prayers at length. While the Queen did tapestry work, affairs of state were discussed. The King next attended the Queen's toilet, one of the biggest functions of the day. After dinner they went out shooting, but the King liked the sport to be arranged in the most comfortable manner possible. So he and his wife were driven out to a pre-selected spot where the peasants had been rounding up game since dawn. Their Catholic Majesties sat in bowers while the game was chased past them to be shot at. A bag of deer, wolves, foxes, hares and even pigeons was the trophy of the day's amusement. The only time the Queen actually left the King was to make her confession, and if she was too long over it the King complained. Such was the unbroken tête-a-tête that enabled Elizabeth Farnese to decide matters of foreign policy; and, at first Alberoni, who became the chief minister of Spain and was awarded a cardinal's hat for his attention to political duties, carried out her wishes. He helped to flutter the diplomatic dovecotes and to find employment for European armies for several years.

France too was governed in accordance with the wishes of an indolent ruler, the Duke of Orleans. He has sometimes been pictured as an extremely ambitious man, but the fact was that he had all the pride of the Bourbons, and it was others who took advantage of this pride to push him on to ignore the will of Louis XIV and instead to constitute himself sole Regent. Naturally the Court reacted against the conduct and the atmosphere of the previous regime which had changed totally once Madame de Maintenon married the old *roué*. When Louis XIV died the government for the time being returned from Versailles to Paris. Instead of appointing ministers who were responsible only to himself, the Regent set up councils to cover different branches of government including finance and foreign affairs. In fact the government fell largely into the hands of two remarkable men, the Abbé Guillaume Dubois, son of a French doctor, who made his way into the Court as a tutor to the nobility, and John Law, son of a Scottish goldsmith, who worked out wonderful but disastrous schemes for paying off the national debt in return for the grant of monopolies. The Regent himself was more interested in the arts, the sciences and the fair sex, than in the burden of governing. He had two sets of mistresses, a higher and a lower grade. The higher grade was led by Madame de Parabère who 'drank like a drain'. The lower grade were said to trot about like little mice among the grander ladies of the Court, and included leading actresses. One of the Regent's most notable contributions to the welfare of Paris was to establish public balls in the Opera House for which tickets were sold at six *livres* apiece. These balls were often attended by the Regent and the Abbé Dubois in suitable disguises. The Abbé was as debauched as his master. The five-year-old King was set examples which ultimately he followed.

The victorious countries in the war of the Spanish succession rejoiced in the peace apart from Austria which was still aggressive and dissatisfied. The Dutch, it is true, had been humiliated during the peace making, but they had at least attained William III's objective in preventing France from conquering the southern Netherlands: that achievement was left for the French revolutionaries in the 1790s. The Dutch also obtained less by way of commercial advantages from the treaties than they might reasonably have hoped. Professor Geyl believed that the treaty of 'Utrecht closed the period of North-Netherland greatness' and thought that its decline was due to internal causes sapping the national spirit. Other historians consider that the Dutch financial supremacy in the West continued well into the eighteenth century, even if by then the Dutch had ceased to be commercially predominant.

During this second Stadholderless period the Dutch had no inspiring leader such as William I or William III of Orange. And in spite of the wish of the Regents to keep out of future wars their fortunes were unavoidably shackled to the continental mainland, while Great Britain was involved only through its Hanoverian kings.

In England George I was no nonentity, although he was hardly popular. Having divorced and imprisoned his wife, he arrived in his kingdom accompanied by his principal mistress, who was nicknamed the 'Elephant and Castle'. He also brought with him some capable German advisers and a couple of intelligent Turkish servants. The idea that his ignorance of the English language lowered his authority has been disproved; he talked to his ministers in French. At first his position on the throne was unstable. Lord Bolingbroke, who had largely engineered the treaty of Utrecht, disappeared into France to become Secretary of State to the Old Pretender. With foreign help the Old Pretender invaded Scotland twice, first in 1715 (he ought perhaps to have tried earlier before George I had settled in) and then in 1719. Each invasion was abortive. In fact the reign of George I was prosperous. Two outstanding Whig ministers, James Stanhope and Robert Walpole, served the King faithfully. Stanhope aimed to make Great Britain respected abroad, Walpole to keep out of wars.

Such was the general situation among the powers that had been the principal combatants in the long wars. As a result of the peace treaties Italy received a new face. The Duke of Savoy was given Sicily to rule; the Emperor Charles VI acquired Milan, Naples and Sardinia. The Republic of Genoa had close relations with Naples and Tuscany, where a high level of baroque culture prevailed. The Republic of Venice was linked with Vienna, but was still menaced by the Turks. The rest of Italy was dominated by the Papal States. Clement XI (1700–21) was a distinguished pope who resisted the spread of Austrian Habsburg influence in Italy which diminished his prestige and damaged his finances. Momentarily it looked as if there would be a revival of the age-old conflict between pope and emperor.

Finally on the other side of Europe Brandenburg-Prussia was emerging as a considerable power. Frederick I, who had gained the title of the first King in Prussia, was a man of discrimination, the patron of arts and letters, while his wife was a friend of Leibniz. Frederick extended liberty of conscience, which promoted trade, but the national finances were affected by his extravagance. His

Frederick William I of Prussia, the military organizer whose work helped to lay the foundations for the expansion of Prussia under his son, Frederick the Great.

successor, Frederick William I, who became king in 1713, was, on the contrary, exceedingly parsimonious. He built up a war chest and an army but managed to keep out of war. 'His court', it has been said, 'was a barrack, his kingdom a combination of the farm-yard and the parade ground, and he viewed both with the eye of the non-commissioned officer and the stud-groom.' He and his grandfather, the Great Elector, paved the way for the expansion of Prussia into Germany which was to begin in the reign of King Frederick II.

The first of the dynastic affairs that endangered peace primarily affected Great Britain and to a lesser extent France. In 1716 Peter the Great of Russia had married his niece to the Grand Duke of Mecklenburg whose duchy lay next to Hanover, while the Danes had previously snatched from the Swedes the territories of Bremen and Verden which lay to the north-west of Hanover. George I was alarmed for the safety of his much beloved Electorate, which had only recently been established as such. At the same time the Regent of France was concerned over the aim of Philip v of Spain to oust him from his office or to deprive him of the chance of the succession if Louis xv (who was sickly) should die. So a defensive treaty was negotiated between the two former enemies, Great Britain and France, to guarantee the Utrecht settlement as far as it concerned them and also 'the succession to the thrones of France and Great Britain'. The Dutch were induced to accede to this treaty, which was signed at The Hague in 1717, and became known as the Triple Alliance. Ultimately Peter the Great withdrew his troops from Mecklenburg and abandoned a scheme in which he was involved with his old enemy, Charles xii of Sweden, to support the Jacobites against the Hanoverians in Great Britain. In 1715 Denmark had sold Bremen and Verden to Hanover. Thus King George i was eminently satisfied.

The second dynastic question that agitated Europe related to the Spanish royal family. During the years 1716–20 Elizabeth Farnese was busily engaged in bearing her husband sons. Don Carlos (the future Carlos iii of Spain) was born in 1716 and the idea soon dawned on his proud mother that he could be found a kingdom in Italy. Philip v, dissatisfied with the small remains left to him in Italy by the peace of Utrecht (he had been allowed to keep part of the island of Elba) decided to invade Italy while the Emperor Charles vi was absorbed in his war against the Turks and was at loggerheads with his former allies. Alberoni, now the chief Spanish minister, had been occupied in improving the economy, putting the royal finances in order and building up the armed forces. So at the end of July 1717 an armada and a sizeable expeditionary army left Barcelona to launch an attack on the island of Sardinia, which by November was completely reduced. This assault on the Emperor in Italy was justified by the somewhat flimsy excuse that the Spanish Inquisitor-General had been ill treated in Milan. The news of the Spanish offensive caused excitement throughout Europe.

James Stanhope, the first of Great Britain's peripatetic Foreign Ministers, sought a compromise which would ensure peace. So did the Abbé Dubois, who visited England in September 1717 where he developed indigestion and gout through attending too many Anglo-French banquets. The proposals agreed were that the crown of Spain should be guaranteed to Philip v and that Elizabeth Farnese's eldest son should have the reversion of the duchies of Parma and Tuscany whose dukes were expected to die childless; Victor Amadeus ii of Savoy was to be asked to exchange

Opposite: Peter the Great, Tsar of Russia, portrayed as a doctor.

Sardinia for Sicily with the Emperor Charles VI, thus improving his strategic position in southern Italy. The Emperor accepted these proposals and acceded to the Triple Alliance, converting it into a Quadruple Alliance in August 1718. The Spaniards, however, could not at first be persuaded to consent to these terms after their easy conquest of Sardinia. Instead they prepared to invade Sicily, while in order to distract British attention they provided an expeditionary force, led by the Duke of Ormonde, which left Cadiz to invade Scotland in the name of James III in the spring of 1718.

But the Spaniards had taken on much more than they could manage. The Spanish warships making for Scotland were sunk by a storm in the Bay of Biscay while the Old Pretender wisely remained in Madrid. Admiral George Byng, who had been sent to the Mediterranean with orders to protect Naples and Sicily, destroyed the main Spanish fleet at the battle of Cape Passaro off southern Sicily. In December 1718 Great Britain declared war on Spain and a month later the French followed. The Duke of Berwick led a French army into Spain where he met with little resistance since the bulk of the Spanish army was away in Italy. By the time Berwick retired into winter quarters the rulers of Spain had had enough. Alberoni, who was unjustifiably made the scapegoat for defeat, was dismissed from office. The terms concocted by Stanhope and Dubois were accepted. In January 1720 Spain adhered to the Quadruple Alliance making it a Quintuple Alliance.

The settlement did not last long. In 1723 the dynastic world was electrified by the death of the French Regent, overcome by his debaucheries, in the prime of life (Dubois, also a *bon viveur,* died in the same year) and by the abdication of Philip V who was in a state of depression because of medical orders to diet and to take exercise after constant overeating, a trait which he had inherited from his grandfather, Louis XIV. But these events made little difference to the diplomatic scene. For Cardinal André Fleury (Louis XV's tutor) who was soon at the age of seventy-three to take over the effective government of France, also wanted, like Dubois, to maintain the peace, while Philip V, whose eldest son by his first wife, Luis I, died of smallpox soon after his accession to the throne, was persuaded by his second wife to resume the government. Elizabeth Farnese, with the help of a Dutch adventurer, Johann Willem Ripperda, who had replaced Alberoni, planned to achieve her expansionist aims for her family in Italy by agreement with the Emperor instead of by fighting him. Charles

Opposite above : Philip V of Spain with his family. Philip was Louis XIV's grandson and his candidate for the Spanish succession on the death of the last Habsburg King of Spain, Carlos II. When Philip left Versailles to take up the Spanish Crown in 1701, Louis exhorted him to be a good Spaniard, but never to forget that he was a Frenchman.

Opposite below : The young Louis XV with his uncle, the Duke of Orleans, who was Regent during the first years of his reign.

187

VI who, though he preferred music, was no fool at politics, was anxious that the inheritance of his possessions, which had been arranged in the constitutional instrument known as the Pragmatic Sanction, should be guaranteed by all the other European powers. (This document determining the succession of his elder daughter to all dominions had been accepted by all the Diets, even by those of Hungary whose right to elect its ruler was not denied.) He also aspired to increase industry and commerce in his territories, particularly by founding an Ostend Company, whose profits would, he hoped, pay for the cost of the upkeep of the southern Netherlands. Philip V of Spain undertook to guarantee the Pragmatic Sanction and to support the Ostend Company in return for the Emperor's investiture of Don Carlos with the duchies of Parma and Tuscany (when they fell vacant) and assistance in the recovery for Spain of Gibraltar. All this was agreed to in the first treaty of Vienna.

The arrangements thus made broke up the Quintuple Alliance, but the original Triple Alliance was unimpaired. The British and Dutch united to force the Emperor to suppress the Ostend Company and when the Spanish government, fortified by the treaty of Vienna, claimed the return of Gibraltar and Minorca, and Gibraltar was subjected to a siege, England and Spain went to war. British seapower was effective in protecting Gibraltar and Cardinal Fleury exerted himself to apply pressure on Spain and the Emperor. By the treaty of Seville, concluded in 1729, Charles VI

agreed to suspend the operations of the Ostend Company; the Spanish rulers abandoned their demands for Gibraltar and Minorca; and the British promised to underwrite Don Carlos's claim to the Italian duchies.

Just over a year later the Duke of Parma at last died without heirs. The Emperor promptly sent troops to occupy the duchy and Elizabeth Farnese called upon the British and French to fulfil the promises made in the treaty of Seville. They did so by means of diplomacy, not war. The British and the Dutch consented to guarantee the Pragmatic Sanction. In return the Emperor allowed Don Carlos, who had now reached the ripe age of fifteen, to take over the duchies of Parma and Piacenza. (This was by the second treaty of Vienna, concluded in 1731.)

When in the autumn of 1732 Don Carlos formally assumed the title of Grand Duke of Parma, the dynastic ambitions of Elizabeth Farnese for her firstborn had been realized at last. The Emperor Charles VI had made good progress also in collecting guarantees of the Pragmatic Sanction for the benefit of his daughter, and it may well have seemed that peace would supervene. Not a bit of it. In February 1733 Augustus II of Poland died and Elizabeth Farnese at once began to fish in troubled waters, seeking a larger catch for her eldest son.

Why the French allowed themselves to become involved in the war of the Polish succession, in which its formidable opponents included Austria and Russia in alliance, is not entirely clear. The explanations usually offered are first that it was the traditional policy of France to fight the Austrian Habsburgs and to isolate them as far as possible by exerting diplomatic influence over Poland and Turkey, and secondly, it is asserted, the French were becoming bored with not having been lately at war. The war policy of Louis XV did not have the approval of Cardinal Fleury who had the sense to see that nothing was to be gained from it. However, the French concluded separate offensive treaties with Spain and Sardinia and sent an army into Italy to attack the Austrians. The 'family compact' between the Bourbons of France and Spain (concluded in the Escorial Palace in Madrid in November 1733) lent valuable aid to the Spanish ambitions in Italy. The Spanish forces were remarkably successful in the campaign of 1734, capturing both Naples and Sicily. But the French under the command of the veteran Marshal Villars quarrelled with Charles Emmanuel of Sardinia and Villars himself died in Milan. Then the French defeated the Austrians twice, once in Parma and once in Guastalla in Modena. In the spring of the following year, Charles VI gave up. Through the mediation of the maritime powers the preliminaries of peace were concluded, although the third treaty of Vienna, as it was called, was not signed until 1738. In that treaty some complicated arrangements were reached. King Stanislas of Poland renounced his throne (although his subjects would have much preferred him to Augustus III) and was compensated by being created Duke of Lorraine on the understanding that, when he died, the duchy would become French. The Duke of Lorraine was awarded the duchy of Tuscany, and the Emperor was assigned Parma and Piacenza, while he retained most of the Milanese except for parts of it allotted to the King of Sardinia for his share in the war. But it was Don Carlos who gained the most. For in return for giving up Parma and Tuscany, he received both Naples and Sicily from the Emperor, who in return merely added another guarantee of the Pragmatic Sanction to his growing collection of autographs. Thus everyone was more or less satisfied. For the French the ultimate reversion of Lorraine was a considerable gain. One significant episode in this so-called war of the Polish succession was that for the first time a Russian army marched west as far as the river Neckar. In the year after the treaty was signed Fleury uttered a warning: 'Russia', he said, 'in respect of the equilibrium of the north has mounted too high a degree of power and its union with the House of Austria is extremely dangerous.' Thus Russian military aggressiveness was recognized twenty years before the formidable Catherine II became Tsarina.

Neither Fleury nor Robert Walpole had wanted the war. Walpole took pride in the fact that no English soldier had been killed in battle for a long time. But now another war loomed ahead. Like the French, the English had grown bored with peace; in the Houses of Parliament members began to clamour for war against Spain because of the constant and violent disputes between British traders and Spanish authorities in the West Indies. English merchants, particularly those belonging to the South Sea Company had long engaged in systematic smuggling into the West Indies and also Central and South America. On the other hand, the *guarda-costas*, licensed by the Spanish governors to stop smuggling, were little more than pirates since they seized any British merchant ship on which they could lay hands. A certain Captain Jenkins had told the House of Commons how his ship had been pillaged and his ear torn off. After that he declared that 'he committed his soul to God and his cause to his country'.

At first the Spaniards attempted conciliation since their forces were fully occupied with the war in Italy. But negotiations for an agreed settlement broke down. Walpole thought that the Spaniards had a good case and did not want to go to war with them since he feared that the 'family compact' of 1733 would bring in the French so that Great Britain would be isolated. Reluctantly he was compelled by political pressure to consent to a declaration of war on Spain in October 1739. In London the mob rejoiced and bells were rung. Walpole, who was then sixty-three and had been a member of the House of Commons for some twenty years, told the Duke of Newcastle, who was Secretary of State for the south, 'It is your war and I wish you joy of it.' He is also reputed to have said in a melancholy way: 'They are ringing their bells now; soon they will be wringing their hands.' The war started off with a bang, for Captain Edward Vernon, who had declared in the Commons that Portobello in Central America, which was a centre of *guarda-costas,* could be captured with six ships was taken at his word by the government; he was appointed an admiral, given six warships and to the general astonishment occupied Portobello in two days. This so-called 'War of Jenkins's Ear' was to be absorbed into a much wider war in the West which was to convulse Great Britain and America for more than twenty years. From these wars two new great powers were to emerge – Great Britain and Prussia.

12 Europe Expanding 1740-63

The period between 1689 and 1815 has been called the second Hundred Years' War between England and France. Though intervals of peace occurred, most of the time these two kingdoms were officially or unofficially fighting one another. But after the peace of Utrecht had been signed the principal conflicts took place in the New World. The acquisition by England of Newfoundland and Nova Scotia brought the French and English face to face in North America. Because of the extent of good unoccupied land and the growth of international trade the population of the Americas was rising rapidly. Emigrants from Europe, including many Scots-Irish and Protestant Germans, settled along the eastern coast of North America; by the middle of the century the thirteen British colonies had a population of a million and a half, while the population of England itself had risen to seven million. The French population was also increasing and it stood at three-and-a-half times the English population. But in the whole of Canada not more than fifty thousand French colonists were to be found. The Spanish colonies in North, Central and South America were also growing, and pioneers were advancing into hitherto empty areas in the south. Both the French and the Spaniards would have liked to confine the British east-coast colonies to an area of not more than two hundred miles inland. Consequently frontier warfare was endemic.

The Spaniards under the Bourbons were more aggressive than Habsburg Spain had been. Philip v's ministers exerted themselves to build a new and up-to-date navy to protect their Atlantic convoys, though it took time to recover from the naval defeat at Cape Passaro. The government of the overseas vice-royalties of the Spanish empire was reorganized. But the Spanish fleet could not hope to challenge the British navy. Indeed the policy of sending regular convoys to Vera Cruz in the Gulf of Mexico was abandoned after 1736. For the defence of the Spanish empire the government in Madrid was obliged to rely on the loyalty of the local inhabitants in the West Indies and South America and on the fortifications of their naval ports in Spain itself to resist assault from the sea. As has been noticed, in order to prevent the illegal trading by British privateers or smugglers, the Spanish government depended on irregular *guarda-costas*. Both the Spaniards and French devoted the larger part of their resources to warfare on the European mainland. The Spaniards were concerned with the affairs of their royal family in Italy, while French wealth was squandered on the unpromising war of the Polish succession.

Great Britain was directly involved in Europe only because its kings (George I and George II) were always anxious over the safety of their Electorate of Hanover. However, Walpole had refused to take part in the war of the Polish succession, even though treaty obligations required him to give assistance to the Habsburg Emperor. The British were becoming increasingly aware of the value of the colonies and the rich trade in sugar, tobacco, naval materials and slaves. Although the British navy was handicapped by the fact that its admirals (except for Vernon) were senile, it still possessed a considerably larger number of warships than either France or Spain and could hope to protect the growing overseas dominions. But the ships themselves were neither as seaworthy nor as heavily gunned as those of their enemies, while the sailors were recruited chiefly by press-gang methods. Still, its warships outnumbered the French by about three to two. It also had widely spaced bases, at Minorca and Gibraltar, in the West Indies and in North America.

The French were the foe most feared by British statesmen on account of their colonies and commerce, replacing their Dutch rivals of the seventeenth century. In 1740 the Duke of Newcastle warned that sooner or later France would dominate both Europe and America. Lord Carteret, a brilliant diplomatist, who served as Secretary of State for the north in the ministry headed by Newcastle's brother, Henry Pelham, which replaced that of Walpole in 1742, once said: 'Look to America ... Europe will take care of itself.' This was not altogether accurate since Carteret himself sought allies and provided subsidies to protect the Electorate of Hanover. Nevertheless the Council of Trade kept a close watch on the affairs of the colonies and urged that fortified posts should be set up at Oswego on the eastern side of Lake Ontario and at Saratoga south of Lake Champlain. The French, however, had not been idle since the peace of Utrecht. They had built a powerful naval fortress at Louisbourg in Cape Breton Island, north of Nova Scotia, and they attempted to keep the Acadians friendly to them through the efforts of Jesuit missionaries. The fortress of Louisbourg was intended to guard the entrance to the St Lawrence river which led to Quebec; a fortress at Crown Point, west of Lake Champlain, was a retort to Saratoga; and later in the century (in 1753) Fort Duquesne was constructed to the west of Pennsylvania. The British for their part granted a charter to Nova Scotia and built a fortified port at Halifax in the south of the island as a riposte to Louisbourg.

Speaking of the war of the Austrian succession in 1748 and the Seven Years' War in 1756 a British historian has observed: 'Each war began as a struggle for power in the New World and each was swiftly complicated by the conflicts of the Old.' Great Britain was at war with Spain in 1739 before the invasion of Silesia by the Prussians set Europe aflame in the autumn of 1740. Again, Great Britain was unofficially at war with France in North America two years before the Seven Years' War broke out in Europe. The Emperor Charles VI died in October 1740 six months after Frederick Hohenzollern became King of Prussia. When Frederick promptly attacked the Austrians in pursuit of an unjustifiable claim to Silesia, the French took the opportunity of supporting him against their old enemies, the Austrian Habsburgs. The British, for their part, were the only people to remain loyal to their pledge to uphold the Pragmatic Sanction and hired Dutch troops and sent money to assist Queen Maria Theresa of Hungary, Charles VI's heiress. Just as the French were delighted to attack the Austrians once again, so the British rejoiced in the opportunity of fighting the French in the West Indies and North America. They hoped to capture Cape Breton Island and to thrust the French away from the region of the Ohio.

Although the French and English were not officially at war until 1744, they were soon fighting each other everywhere. The French had concluded a treaty with Bavaria whose Elector, Charles Albert, craved the imperial crown, which Maria Theresa could not inherit. The British sent a contingent under George II's brother, the Duke of Cumberland, to fight along with their hired Dutch and subsidized German allies on the river Main. This army defeated the French at the battle of Dettingen in June 1743. It was not a decisive victory and the war in Europe dragged on for another five years. Meanwhile in America an expedition of volunteers organized by William Shirley, the Governor of Massachusetts, supported by British warships captured Louisbourg from the French (11 June 1745) and a French relieving squadron was beaten off in the following year. In India the French captured the British trading post at Madras, while British forces failed to take the French post of Pondicherry. By 1748 bad harvests and high taxation induced the French to seek peace.

In eastern Europe Frederick II of Prussia had already twice exacted an agreement from Queen Maria Theresa that he could keep his conquest of Silesia. His acquisition of this formerly Austrian territory was conditionally guaranteed by a treaty concluded at Aix-la-Chapelle. The only other important change was that Maria Theresa allowed the second son of Elizabeth Farnese, Don Philip, to take over Parma and Piacenza as an independent state. Much to the annoyance of the New Englanders, the British government handed back Louisbourg to the French in exchange for Madras in India. Sardinia, which had fought in the war on the French side, received part of the Milanese. Thus after thirty years the Austrian Habsburgs had lost nearly all the territories in Italy which had been awarded them at Utrecht. The war between Prussia and Austria was to be renewed in eight years and the war between France and Great Britain outside Europe scarcely ceased.

The settlement at Aix-la-Chapelle was little more than a truce in both Europe and America. In Europe Queen Maria Theresa, who was showing herself to be a conscientious, compassionate and enlightened ruler, was determined to regain Silesia from Frederick II of Prussia, whom she detested. As a preparation she reorganized her administration, centralizing it as far as she could; she founded a military academy at Wiener Neustadt; she tried to increase her revenues so as to pay the army and supply it more adequately; and, having at last managed to rid herself of the aged counsellors she had inherited from her father, she planned to isolate Prussia diplomatically with the aid of Prince Wenzel Anton von Kaunitz-Rietberg, who first distinguished himself as her ambassador in Paris during the years 1750–3.

While Kaunitz was trying to persuade Louis XV, his witty and intelligent mistress, Madame de Pompadour, and his ministers to change sides and fight Prussia, the Marquis de la Galissonière, Governor of Canada, pursued an offensive-defensive policy against the British North American colonies. Louisbourg was strengthened and military reinforcements arrived in Canada from France soon after the peace treaty had been signed. French colonial aims were clear enough. The objective was to link up Quebec in Canada with New Orleans in Louisiana (founded in 1718) by

Queen Maria Theresa with her husband Francis I and twelve of their sixteen children. Their eldest son eventually succeeded to the Austrian throne as Joseph II, while their youngest daughter, Maria Antonia, or Marie Antoinette, became the tragic Queen of France. Portrait by Martin van Meytens.

way of the three thousand-mile river Mississippi along which forts were erected to keep the thirteen British colonies confined behind the Allegheny mountains. The areas where the colonists were vulnerable were on the frontiers of New York, Pennsylvania and Virginia, but the direct danger to New York from Canada via Lake Champlain and the Hudson river was the most serious. Hitherto the colonists had been on friendly terms with the Six Nations of Indians whose influence was paramount in the Mohawk valley, a tributary of the Hudson, and stretched as far as the Mississippi. With their aid British traders had been able to buy valuable furs and they acted as a kind of buffer against the French.

The colonies of New England were very conscious of the value of these Indians, but when in 1722 a conference was held at Albany with the governors of Pennsylvania and Virginia, who were also menaced by French aggressiveness, no agreement could be

196

reached. However in 1754 William Shirley, the Governor of Massachusetts, who had been responsible for the successful expedition against Louisbourg in 1745, summoned a second conference at Albany and then the commissioners agreed (on the advocacy of Benjamin Franklin from Pennsylvania) to elect a joint council representing seven colonies to deal with questions of Indian trade, defence and unoccupied lands. But the mutual jealousy of the colonies was too fierce to permit of union at this stage. In fact it was on the frontier of Virginia and not of New York that war was first to flare up. The Governor of Virginia dispatched a twenty-three-year-old major of the militia named George Washington to assert the rights of Virginia to two hundred thousand acres of land in the Ohio valley, which they claimed were theirs, against the encroachments of the French. While on a reconnaissance during the previous year Washington had been told by French officers 'in their cups' that 'it was their absolute design to take possession of the Ohio and by God, they would do it'.

In July 1754 Washington, who had now been promoted full colonel, allowed himself to be surrounded by a French force that outnumbered his and on his return to Virginia he quarrelled with the governor and resigned his commission. In the following year, a general named Edward Braddock, sent from England with two regiments of regulars, joined the Virginia militia in a campaign against the French only to be ambushed and humiliated. Braddock himself was killed, while George Washington, who had returned to the fray, had four bullets through his coat and two horses shot beneath him.

While unofficial war was thus being waged on the American frontiers, the British Cabinet in London was trying to make up its mind what was best to be done. For not only were the French on the rampage in America, but the French and English East India Companies were at daggers drawn in India, while disputes were taking place over the ownership of the Windward group of islands in the West Indies as well as over the boundaries of Nova Scotia. After the death of his brother in 1754 the Duke of Newcastle had become Prime Minister. Newcastle was timid, hard-working, vain and (according to Lord Chesterfield) 'as jealous of power as an impotent lover of his mistress'. He had in his government two extremely capable men, Henry Fox (the father of Charles James Fox) who was Secretary at War, and William Pitt, whose grandfather had amassed a fortune in India, as his Paymaster-General. Neither the British nor the French government was enthusiastic

North America in 1763

Thirteen colonies and British possessions before 1763

British acquisitions 1763

Spanish possessions before 1763

Spanish acquisitions 1763

RUPERT'S LAND

NEWFOUNDLAND

Louisbourg

C A N A D A

St Lawrence

QUEBEC (created 1763)

Quebec

Montreal

NOVA SCOTIA

NEW HAMPSHIRE

NEW YORK

MASS

New York

CONN

PENNSYLVANIA

Philadelphia

NEW JERSEY

MARYLAND

DELAWARE

Missouri

VIRGINIA

LOUISIANA

Ohio

NORTH CAROLINA

SOUTH CAROLINA

GEORGIA

ATLANTIC OCEAN

Mississippi

Rio Grande

WEST FLORIDA (created 1764)

EAST FLORIDA

BAHAMA IS

GULF OF MEXICO

Havana

CUBA

VICE-ROYALTY OF NEW SPAIN

WEST INDIES

CARIBBEAN SEA

about a full-scale war for which big fleets and armies would be needed but the coming of such a war was rooted in the past when antagonisms had arisen between the British and French in the New World and between Prussia and Austria in the Old. Since the British government recognized that a general war with France was almost impossible to avoid, the question arose of what was best to be done about it. Newcastle himself favoured containing the French in Europe by the conclusion of subsidy treaties while strengthened British military and naval forces took action in the West Indies and in North America. The problem was complicated by George II's desire to protect his Electorate of Hanover. The first treaty concluded by Newcastle's government was with Russia. By the Convention of St Petersburg (June 1755) the Russian government undertook to maintain an army on the eastern border of Prussia and a naval force in the Baltic to prevent Prussian aggression against Hanover and a promise was also made to lend aid if Great Britain itself were attacked. The Convention alarmed the Prussian King, Frederick II, who envisaged a joint offensive against his kingdom by Russia and Austria. He therefore consented to a defensive treaty with Great Britain to preserve the territorial status quo in Germany.

Though both these treaties were defensive in character and the Anglo-Russian treaty was to prove abortive, they sufficiently alarmed Queen Maria Theresa to implement Kaunitz's scheme for an alliance with France. Thus what is called the *renversement des alliances* was completed and in the Seven Years' War, which began in August 1756, Prussia was allied with Great Britain and Austria with France. What really lay behind these treaties was that the British hoped to protect Hanover from a French attack, while the Austrians wanted the French to secure the southern Netherlands from assault and to intimidate the rest of Protestant Germany while they themselves dealt with Prussia.

Newcastle's foreign policy by no means commanded universal approval in Great Britain. The opposition was led by William Pitt who was reckoned the finest orator in the House of Commons. In a speech which he delivered at midnight on 13 November 1755 he asked the question: 'Why was the present war undertaken if not for the long-injured, long-forgotten people of America? And can you expect to carry on this war by these incoherent, un-British measures instead of using our proper force?' That force was the navy. Nor was Pitt in his speeches at all shy over mixing his metaphors. He compared Newcastle to 'a gentle, feeble, languid stream, and, though languid, of no depth' and in another speech he compared him to a child in charge of a go-cart pushing old George II and his family over the precipice. For such speeches he was understandably dismissed from office.

The timid Newcastle was upset by Pitt's oratorical flights in the Commons, but he was even more concerned by news that the French were threatening to invade England. When he learned that in May 1756 the French had conquered Minorca which Admiral Byng had failed to relieve (a failure for which he was court-martialled and shot), Newcastle resigned. With reluctance George II made Pitt Secretary of State for the south in a government headed by the Duke of Devonshire. But the King disliked Pitt and was sensitive to his criticisms of the policy of protecting Hanover. Six months later, Pitt was dismissed by the King and it was New-castle not Pitt who proved indispensable as the experienced manipulator of seats and votes in the House of Commons. Newcastle for his part thought that he needed the energy and force-fulness of Pitt as his War Minister. George II was old and tired, and gave way. For the next four years Pitt was in effect War Minister and Foreign Minister and the organizer of victory over the French.

William Pitt was educated at Eton and Trinity College, Oxford. After the death of his father he considered a career in the Church but in fact he obtained a commission in the army and thus acquired some knowledge of military affairs. When Sarah, the widow of the great Duke of Marlborough, died in 1742, she left Pitt £10,000 which simplified his career as a politician. But he had been a member of the House of Commons for the best part of twenty years when his supreme opportunity came. All his life he suffered from ill health, chiefly gout, which was intensified by neurosis. However, at the age of forty-seven he found a wife and his health at once improved. At forty-nine he became the effective head of the government. He was a brilliant and indefatigable administrator, and his military studies and knowledge of history stood him in good stead. The old King came in the end to appreciate his abilities and he managed to get along with the King's German mistress, the Countess of Yarmouth. He had an imperial vision and, when he took over the government, his first thoughts were of America to which he at once sent reinforcements. But the year 1757 was one of almost unmitigated disaster for Great Britain.

It is true that the British navy outnumbered that of the French and that in time Pitt discovered far better admirals. But the French

William Pitt, Earl of Chatham, who was in effect war minister and foreign minister in Britain during the Seven Years' War.

were to find an energetic minister in the magnificent Etienne-François, Duc de Choiseul who, with the approval of Madame de Pompadour, replaced the pessimistic Abbé Bernis as Foreign Minister after Bernis had retired to his monastery. Furthermore in men like Marquis Duquesne de Menneville and Louis Joseph Montcalm in Canada, Joseph François Dupleix in India and La Galissonière and the Duke of Richelieu, who together conquered Minorca, the French had daring and patriotic commanders. The French population was about three times that of England so that large armies could be raised. But in America it was mainly a naval war. At first things went as badly as possible for Pitt. John Campbell, the Earl of Loudoun, who had been sent to recapture Louisbourg and thus clear the way up the St Lawrence river,

Frederick II, 'the Great', King of Prussia.

Opposite above: Admiral Vernon taking Portobello in November 1739, during the war of Jenkins's Ear.

Opposite below: Louisbourg beseiged by General Wolfe, supported by the fleet under Admiral Boscawen. In July 1758 the city fell and was dismantled.

quarrelled with the colonists and proved more adept at penning lengthy dispatches in his own handwriting and organizing the planting of cabbages than he did at fighting. Admiral Francis Holburne, who sailed to Louisbourg to support Loudoun's army, looked into the harbour and finding the French had one more warship than he had, decided by agreement with Loudoun to abandon the attack. Later in the year after his fleet had been reinforced, Holburne managed to lose most of it in a hurricane off Cape Breton. At the same time Colonel Montcalm had taken Fort William Henry, south of Lake Champlain and was threatening Albany in New York. In Europe the French successfully advanced into Westphalia outflanking the southern Netherlands. When in the same year George II's son, the Duke of Cumberland, who had been ordered to protect Hanover with an 'army of observation' (Frederick II, having lost all interest in doing so, was engaged in fierce war in Bohemia), capitulated to the French Pitt was in despair. 'The empire', he wrote, 'is no more, the ports of the Netherlands betrayed, the Dutch Barrier an empty sound, Minorca and with it the Mediterranean lost and America itself precarious.'

But soon the tide turned. Frederick the Great (as he was now called) defeated both a French army and an Austrian army at the end of the year. Loudoun and Holburne were replaced. George II recognized that Pitt possessed a gift for finding good officers; when one of his courtiers said that James Wolfe was mad, he retorted 'then I wish he would bite some of my other generals'. Pitt selected James Wolfe, James Abercrombie and Jeffrey Amherst to combine in a triple offensive against Canada. Wolfe was to sail up the St Lawrence, Abercrombie to advance up the Hudson, and Amherst to move down the St Lawrence by way of Lake Ontario. In 1758 Pitt organized attacks on the French Atlantic coast to keep their fleet at bay. In America Fort Duquesne on the Ohio fell at last to a British force and was renamed Pittsburg. Although in 1759 the French made preparations for the invasion of England Pitt did not lose his nerve. He relied on the Channel fleet and the militia to defend the island base and continue to pursue an offensive policy. The British navy reasserted the command of the seas. Two victories were won, the first off Lagos in Portugal and the second off Quiberon Bay in Brittany. So the campaign in Canada was able to go forward without interruption. General Wolfe, supported by Admiral Edward Boscawen, who had taken over from Holburne, occupied and dismantled Louisbourg in July 1758, so that in the following year Wolfe was able to

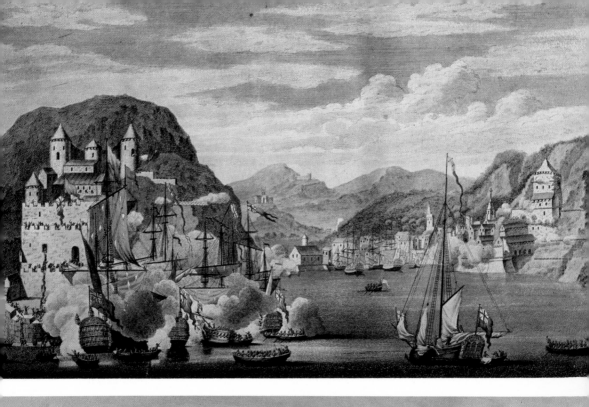

carry his forces up the St Lawrence to surprise and capture Quebec. Both Wolfe and Montcalm were killed in the fighting. In that same summer Amherst took the French forts near Lake Champlain. Thus a year later he was able to capture Montreal. So Canada was conquered.

British seapower also ensured the defeat of the French – and later of the Spaniards – in the West Indies. The French possessed two large and valuable sugar islands in the Antilles which had a bigger output than Jamaica and useful harbours. But for their security they were dependent on the French navy and after its defeats in battle the British were able to do more or less what they liked; Guadeloupe fell in 1759 and Martinique in 1762. The British also occupied Dominica to the north of Martinique in 1761 and two of the disputed Windward islands, St Lucia and Grenada, in 1762. The planters in Jamaica had ambivalent feelings about the capture of these French islands because they feared that if they became permanently British their own sales of sugar would be undercut.

Far away in India British seapower also asserted itself. The principal trading posts of the British East India Company were widely scattered at Bombay in the south west, at Madras in the Carnatic, and at Calcutta in Bengal. The French were mainly concentrated in the Carnatic and the Deccan to its north, which was cut off by mountains from the sea. The French Governor of India, Joseph Dupleix, was exceedingly optimistic about his chances of defeating the British and thought he could raise enough money in India to pay for the war. But the British had two able generals in Robert Clive and Eyre Coote and were periodically supported from the sea. Though, to begin with, they suffered setbacks when the Nawab of Bengal, Siraj-ud-Daula, took Calcutta in 1756 and when Madras was threatened by the French, Clive soon defeated the Nawab at the battle of Plassey and by 1760 the English gained the upper hand in the Carnatic. Not only was Madras relieved but, after the French and their allies had been beaten at the battle of Wandewash in January 1760, and Pondicherry, the most valuable French trading post, was captured a year later, the whole of the Carnatic came under British control.

The French failures in Canada, the West Indies and India were principally caused by the shortcomings of their navy and by the fact that many of their soldiers were absorbed in Germany. To the surprise of Frederick the Great, the French sent two armies amounting to some hundred and fifty thousand men into Germany

Opposite above: After the fall of Louisbourg, Wolfe took his forces up the St Lawrence river and after scaling the heights of Abraham, captured Quebec. In the fighting, both Wolfe and the French commander, Montcalm were killed. A hand-coloured engraving of the taking of Quebec.

Opposite below: In 1759, both the Toulon and Brest fleets put to sea to try to break the English blockade. Boscawen destroyed the Toulon fleet at Lagos, while Hawke smashed the Brest fleet in Quiberon Bay, off the Brittany coast. This painting by Richard Wright shows the gales which lashed the opposing fleets at Quiberon Bay.

in 1757 while his own army was only about the same size. But he had also to contend with the Austrians and the Russians, who attacked East Prussia in the same year. Frederick spoke of dying with his sword in his hand. In fact that did not prove necessary. For he defeated the French at Rossbach, the Austrians at Leuthen, and the Russians at Zorndorf. He found the Russians his toughest opponents and they inflicted a defeat upon him at the bloody battle of Kunersdorf near Frankfort-am-Oder in August 1759. The astonishing defiance by the Prussians of all their enemies involved the French in further commitments rather against their wishes.

When the Duke of Choiseul became the French Foreign Minister in November 1758 he tried to reduce the French treaty obligations to Austria and an agreement was reached at Versailles which cut down the subsidies to Austria and withheld French forces from Bohemia. Nevertheless the French were still obliged to keep an army of a hundred thousand men on the Rhine and in fact two years later the French army in Germany reached a hundred and sixty thousand men. Choiseul's ambitious scheme for the invasion of England collapsed and the French navy was

everywhere defeated. Choiseul was left with only one hope and that was to enlist the support of the Spaniards, though the combined fleets of France and Spain did not exceed that of the British. Carlos III, the eldest son of Elizabeth Farnese, who had just come to the throne of Spain, was anti-British and the Spanish merchants and colonists had many grievances to air. William Pitt tried to prevent the Spanish entry into the war by offering to surrender Gibraltar in exchange for Minorca, but negotiations broke down and in August 1761 a 'family compact' was concluded between Spain and France. Pitt wanted immediately to launch an offensive against Spain, but the rest of the Cabinet, headed by the Duke of Newcastle, refused to concur and in October 1761 Pitt resigned. The British were then compelled to declare war on Spain at the beginning of 1762 and promptly illustrated their command of the sea by capturing Havana in Cuba and Manila in the Philippines far away in the Pacific. Having played his last card, Choiseul was forced to sue for peace.

Meanwhile the situation of Frederick the Great, who had been obliged to withdraw from Bohemia and Saxony in order to defend Silesia and the hereditary possessions of his family and had appeared to be in desperate straits, was suddenly and surprisingly

The capture of Havana in Cuba by the English fleet in August 1762.

saved by the death of the Tsarina Elizabeth in January 1762; she was succeeded by her nephew, Peter III, who at once made peace with Prussia. The settlement between Great Britain and France was concluded separately from that between Austria and Prussia, in Paris. In this treaty the main points were that the British were allotted the whole of Canada, of North America as far west as the Mississippi, and the Spanish territory of Florida, which the French agreed to replace by handing over Louisiana to Carlos III. In return the French West Indian islands were returned and Belle-Isle off Newfoundland (which the British had taken in 1761) was exchanged for Minorca. Thus British power in North America stretched from Hudson Bay to Florida and from the Atlantic to the Mississippi with virgin lands waiting to be settled. Pitt in opposition criticized the treaty; for he would have gone on fighting until the French were completely crushed. It was also plausibly argued that the surrender of Guadeloupe and Martinque was a grave mistake. The English admiral Rodney thought they ought to have been retained for strategic reasons; the West African slave traders regretted the loss of a profitable market; while British business men urged that economically the West Indies were of more value to the Crown than Canada whose snowy wastes had hitherto yielded only furs.

It is fascinating to speculate what would have happened if the British had left Canada to the French and had seized the whole of the West Indies including Cuba. The might-have-beens of history are and no doubt should be resistible. Still, if the endemic frontier wars between the French Canadians and the North American colonists had continued and if the British had secured alternative naval bases in the West Indies free from French or Spanish opposition, one wonders what might have happened during the American War of Independence and what would have been the future history of the Western world.

13 Eighteenth-Century Britain: the Road to Power

The territories acquired by Great Britain in America, the West Indies and the Mediterranean as a result of the conclusion of the treaty of Utrecht and, fifty years later, by the signature of the treaty of Paris, converted the kingdom into a great power, indeed the predominant power in the Western world. At home it obtained a stable and balanced administration. Its form of government was known as a 'parliamentary monarchy' which prevailed while much of the remainder of Europe was ruled by more or less enlightened absolutism. César de Sassure, a Swiss traveller who paid a long visit to England about the time when George II was peacefully succeeding his father George I, wrote: 'England undoubtedly is, in my opinion, the most happily governed country in the world. She is governed by a King whose power is limited by wise and prudent laws, and by Parliament. . . .'

Charles II and James II had attempted to rule without Parliament or to mould Parliaments which would fulfil their wishes. After the Bill of Rights, passed on the accession of William and Mary in 1689, laid down that 'parliaments ought to be held frequently', that the election of members ought to be free and that 'freedom of speech and debates and proceedings in parliament' ought not to be questioned in any court of law, Parliament became an essential and unchallengeable part of the British constitution. It is true that the Triennial Act of 1694 required only that Parliament should meet once in three years (and that a new Parliament must be elected every three years) but in fact henceforward Parliament met every year. In 1697 a Civil List was introduced to pay all the expenses of the royal household, but the sums of money needed to support the armed forces had to be voted by the House of Commons. Thus as a contemporary, Dr Gilbert Burnet, remarked, 'it was taken as a general maxim, that revenue for a certain and short term, was the best security that the nation could have for frequent parliaments'.

Another limitation on the rights of monarchy was that the king was no longer permitted to dispense with or suspend the operation of acts of Parliament as James II had done for the benefit of non-conformists to the Church of England. A clause in the Bill of Rights declared that 'the pretended power of suspending laws ... without the consent of parliament' was 'illegal'. By the Act of Settlement, passed in 1701, which provided for the succession of the Hanoverians, who were descended from James I, if Princess Anne had no heirs, it was also laid down that the judges were to be secure in office as long as they behaved well and that they could not be removed from office except by an address to the king from both Houses of Parliament. Finally, the Bill of Rights stipulated that no monarch might be a Roman Catholic, while the Act of Settlement stated more specifically that he was required to be a member of the Church of England.

Since Parliament's rights were thus strengthened at the expense of the monarchy and since Parliament was in session every year, the king's principal minister was required to act as a mediator between king and Parliament. This conception of mediation evolved slowly. Althought in the reign of Queen Anne, Sidney, Earl of Godolphin and Robert Harley, Earl of Oxford, neither of whom were fundamentally party men, were thought of as the chief ministers of the Crown, it was not until the long tenure of office as the First Commissioner of the Treasury by Sir Robert Walpole (1721–42) who, like his successor Henry Pelham, sat in the House of Commons, that the idea of there being a clearly defined Prime Minister, responsible to king and Parliament, was firmly established. At the same time a Cabinet or Cabinet Council, attended by the principal officers of state, who advised upon policy, came to meet regularly under the First or Prime Minister. William III and Queen Anne frequently presided over their own Cabinets, but the first two Georges did not. Nevertheless the king ordered what questions were to be considered by Cabinet meetings and its recommendations were reported back to him. But Cabinet ministers then had no corporate responsibility for their advice, though for a long time Walpole was able to keep them together effectively. Furthermore, as has happened throughout modern British history, the real decisions were frequently taken by a small and efficient 'inner Cabinet' rather than by the bigger and more formal body which might not be able to reach agreement quickly. Walpole, by dining and wining with the most influential of the king's ministers, was generally able to prepare the way for

William and Mary, depicted as the champions of parliamentary liberty and the Bill of Rights: from an engraving by de Hooghe and C. Allard of 1689.

an agreement by an inner group which then had little difficulty in imposing its views on the larger Cabinet. Thus without any specific enactments two permanent British institutions – the office of Prime Minister and the efficient Cabinet – were born in the eighteenth century.

But neither of these institutions was absolute. The smooth functioning of government also required the co-operation of members of Parliament, the leaders of the Church, the organs of local government – the Lords Lieutenant and the justices of the peace – and the monarch himself. In spite of the restrictions imposed on the monarchy after the revolution of 1688, its authority remained considerable. The monarch still appointed all civil servants and paid them out of his own funds; as Supreme Governor of the Church of England he also nominated bishops and higher clergy; he declared war and made peace; he laid down or approved the lines of foreign policy; he selected all his ministers and house-hold officials; he summoned and dissolved Parliaments when he liked; in theory he could veto any legislation of which he did not

Sir Robert Walpole (standing in the foreground) addressing the Cabinet Council: from a painting by J. Goupy.

approve. Finally the Court remained the centre of political and social life. Indeed it was the comparative drabness of the Court under George I, who preferred Hanover to St James's, which enhanced the influence of Robert Walpole as Prime Minister since he enjoyed entertaining on a lavish scale.

Thus the powers of the king of England remained very great and the effectiveness of the government rested on intangible and unwritten conventions of the constitution. Walpole was a genius at manipulating Parliament through the exercise of royal patronage and at persuading the King to agree to what he wanted. Walpole once explained privately that it was fatuous to 'gain the King' by indulging him 'in all his unhappy foibles'; what a Prime Minister needed to do was to employ 'address and management' as 'the weapons' with which to fight; for 'plain truths' would not 'be relished at first'; and all advice that was offered must be carefully 'dressed up'. When George III came to the throne in 1760 at the age of twenty-two he possessed a deep puritanical sense of his duties and responsibilities and was resolved to promote clean government and not to be managed. According to his favourite, John Stuart, Earl of Bute, whom he appointed Prime Minister in 1762 (although he had no following in the House of Commons) the King was determined 'never upon any account to suffer those ministers of the late reign who have attempted to fetter and enslave him ever to come into his service while he lives to hold the sceptre'. The young King's stubbornness and resolution not to be 'managed' by anybody brought to an end a long period of political and social stability in England and contributed to the causes of the American Revolution.

Two factors which assisted British imperial and economic progress in the first half of the eighteenth century were the union of England and Scotland and the improved direction of the national finances. Scotland was a relatively poor country, with a population of about a million who wove textiles with which to clothe themselves and grew barley and oats out of which to manufacture ale and porridge – the staple items for their consumption. Their exports consisted chiefly of food such as cattle, salmon and herring, though they had to compete with the energetic Dutch when it came to fishing in the North Sea. What they lacked in wealth, they made up in national pride. Their tradition was one of enmity towards England. Scottish armies had fought for both Charles I and Charles II against the English Parliament; they had resented the rule of Charles II's Commissioner, John Maitland, Earl of Lauderdale, and were no enthusiasts for William and Mary whom they treated as elected not hereditary sovereigns. The lowlands were almost entirely Presbyterian; in the sparsely populated highlands religions were mixed and the conditions of life primitive and sometimes superstitious. The Scots had an ambivalent attitude to the House of Stuart. The Stuarts had reigned in Scotland for centuries before they came to England and until the reign of Charles I, came to accept that Presbyterianism was the dominant religion of the land. On the other hand, James VII of Scotland (James II of England), his son and his grandson, the Old and Young Pretenders, were ardent adherents of Roman Catholicism, the bane of the Presbyterians.

At the beginning of the reign of Queen Anne her ministers

insisted on the necessity for union with Scotland, but the project needed careful handling, first because of the Scots' envy of the English and the English contempt for the Scots and, secondly, because the Scots had sour memories of their union with England at the time of the Cromwellian Protectorate when they had been held down by an English army of occupation. Queen Anne's ministers wanted the union largely because the Queen's health was precarious and it was thought unlikely that any of her many children would grow up to survive her. Thus the hereditary Protestant Stuart line was likely to come to an end. Instead of the personal union brought about by the two kingdoms sharing a sovereign, a constitutional union established by treaty would be substituted. The Scots valued their independence and a freely chosen Parliament, which met at Edinburgh in 1703, soon passed an Act of Security which laid it down that the Scots would not on the death of Queen Anne recognize the same successor to the throne as in England unless a union satisfactory to them had by then been negotiated. The English Parliament retorted with an Alien Act which stated that if the Scots refused to accept the same king as the English did, they would be prohibited from selling their principal exports either in England or in Ireland. Thus the Scots feared that they would lose their livelihood while the English dreaded a civil war in which the French, as often before, might side with the Scots. Having each made their gestures, the two parties got down to business and a treaty of union was completed. The Scots agreed to recognize the Hanoverian succession, to obey the rule of the Parliament at Westminster, and to pay their share of joint taxation. In return the Scots were allowed to send forty-five members to the House of Commons and sixteen representative peers to the House of Lords. The English also gave nearly £400,000 to the Scots which enabled them to pay off their national debt and to repay those shareholders who had lost money in a speculative attempt to establish a colony at Darien in Central America. Thus the treaty improved the financial and trading position of the Scots. Furthermore the security of the Presbyterian religion was guaranteed. What the Scots lost, however, was political independence. The Edinburgh Parliament was abolished. Many Scots considered that they had sold their birthright for a 'mess of pottage'. England was to benefit from the enterprise of the Scots in business, in politics, in soldiering and, in the long run, also from Scottish prose and poetry, philosophy and theology, for the Scots had long been a highly-educated people.

The Scottish resentment at the loss of their independence was reflected in the support given to the Old and Young Pretenders when they tried to invade the British Isles with foreign help. The attempt of 1715 came too late because Louis XIV of France had accepted the Hanoverian succession in the treaty of Utrecht and George I had peacefully ascended the throne of England. The Jacobite leader, the Duke of Ormonde, twice tried vainly to effect a landing in Devonshire while an invasion of England from Scotland was defeated at Preston on 13 November. On the same day a drawn battle was fought at Sheriffmuir, north-west of the Firth of Forth, in which the highlanders distinguished themselves. The English had hastily to bring over a Dutch expeditionary force. James Edward, the Old Pretender, did not reach Scotland until after these two battles had been fought and by February 1716 he had left. By 1745, when England was again at war with France, the Old Pretender, now in his late fifties, sent over his son, Charles Edward, who was twenty-five. The Young Pretender's youth and charm invoked loyalty in Scotland, but after invading England and capturing Carlisle in November 1745 he found little support in a prospering kingdom and withdrew after he reached Derby. For a time the Jacobites were victorious in Scotland and captured Aberdeen. But the Duke of Cumberland with a superior

The highlanders fighting for Charles Edward Stuart being cut to pieces by Cumberland's troops at the battle of Culloden.

215

London in 1711, from an engraving by Johannes Kip. St James's Palace can be seen in the right foreground and Wren's Church of St James, Piccadilly, in the centre left.

army of professionals beat the Young Pretender at the battle of Culloden and ruthlessly pursued and executed Jacobite fugitives. Yet it was symptomatic of the romantic devotion that Charles Edward inspired that he was able to wander about the highlands and western isles for five months before escaping to France. The last days of the Young Pretender, who died in 1788, were pathetic. Henceforward highland soldiers were to serve Great Britain with brilliant courage.

The union with Scotland strengthened the security of the British Isles. But the principal reason why Pitt was able to build up the first British Empire was that the kingdom had a viable system of public finance. At the outbreak of the war with France in 1702 the

216

national debt had amounted to £12,800,000. By the end of that war it had trebled and by 1763 it increased to £132,000,000. By then, however, satisfactory methods of funding the debt were worked out, not only by the Bank of England but by large companies such as the East India Company and the South Sea Company, which after a desperate gamble in the 1720s to exploit the opportunities of trade with the Spanish Empire, became a holding company for government stock. In 1758 the British government experienced no difficulty in borrowing eight million pounds from the City of London to meet its needs in war, whereas in the seventeenth century it had found it hard to borrow even fifty thousand pounds. Sir Robert Walpole was a capable financier. Indeed his reputation was based on the way in which he had restored the kingdom's financial position after the wave of speculation known as the South Sea Bubble. The government's income was founded on three main pillars: a land tax, an excise which fell chiefly on beer, and customs duties imposed on rising imports. The customs duties raised less than they might have done because of widespread smuggling, while Walpole's attempt to extend the scope of the excise met with resistance in Parliament. The land tax was lowered in time of peace, but was an invaluable resource in war. Walpole was skilful though hardly enlightened about taxation. His ideal was to reduce or abolish the land tax which hit country gentlemen like himself. He let it be known that he preferred an excise on salt to one on candles on the ground that the former would fall chiefly on the poor. 'He believed,' writes his biographer, Professor John Harold Plumb, 'in taxing the poor; it kept wages low, and low wages encouraged the working man to work.'

Though the gap between rich and poor was still wide – Walpole spent more in a year upon his wigs than he paid his footman – the mass of the English people were undoubtedly better off in the eighteenth than in the seventeenth century. Naturally it is dangerous to generalize. In London many horrible slums and grinding poverty were to be found; since few manufacturing industries were concentrated in the capital, the bulk of the people were engaged in service industries and were liable to suffer from unemployment or underemployment. On the other hand, as the population drifted into the midlands and north to work in the coal and metal industries or in textile manufacture, an impression of southern depopulation was created. In fact higher wages were paid in London than elsewhere. Outside the capital many of the men employed in industry still had small landholdings in which they worked at harvest time. The hours of labour were long and tiring with few holidays, while conditions were often unhygienic. Craftsmen might earn as much as three shillings a day and Daniel Defoe related that when he offered ordinary labourers nine shillings a week they said that they could get more by begging. The price of bread was twopence a pound and cheese and meat about four pence a pound so that the wage earner fortunate enough to have regular work must have been relatively well off. Defoe thought that most people were able to eat fresh meat (which they hardly did in the seventeenth century) and buy strong beer. 'We see their houses and lodgings tolerably furnished, at least stuffed well with useful and necessary household goods; even those we call poor people, journeymen, working and pains-taking people do thus; they lie warm, live in plenty, work hard and need know no want.' In another pamphlet Defoe wrote: 'English labouring people eat and drink, especially the latter, three times as much in value as any sort of foreigners of the same dimensions in the world.' He believed that despite laziness and improvidence they were more prosperous even than the average Dutchman.

Sassure, as a serious-minded Swiss, was shocked at the amount of drinking that went on in England. 'Though no wines are grown in England,' he noted in 1727, 'it is no hindrance to drunkenness, for in the daytime the lower classes get intoxicated with liquor and beer, and the higher classes in the evening with Portuguese wines and punch.' Sassure also asserted, like Defoe, that the English tended to be lazy and yet to live comfortably. He observed that servant-maids wore silk on Sundays and holidays and were 'almost as well dressed as their mistresses' and that 'even women of the lower class do little needlework'. It has been estimated that in 1722 thirty-three million bushels of malt were used for brewing, representing a thirty-six-gallon barrel of beer for every man, woman and child in the population. One could be 'drunk for a penny and dead drunk for twopence'. Until legislation restricting gin traffic was passed in the middle of the century, gin was incredibly cheap and about seven-thousand 'dram-shops' existed in the capital alone. Farmers often gave their labourers free beer and cider. 'Would you believe it,' Sassure asked one of his correspondents, 'though water is to be had in abundance in London, and of fairly good quality, absolutely none is drunk? The lower classes, even the paupers, do not know what it is to quench their thirst with water.' It is said, he added, 'that more grain is consumed in England for making beer than for making bread'. But he also noted the consumption of non-alcoholic drinks. For after remarking that 'Englishmen are great drinkers' he drew attention to the great popularity of coffee-houses, where chocolate and tea were also served, and he asserted that many working men regularly started their day by going to coffee-houses to learn about the latest news.

What of the wealthier ranks and orders of society? The clergy were neither overworked nor greatly underpaid. After the Puritan outburst of the mid-seventeenth century and the teaching of Locke and others at the end of the century religious enthusiasm waned. Bishops were generally wealthy and, at the other end of the scale, curates were modestly paid, earning less than a skilled craftsman. The vicars and rectors appointed by patrons who were often the squires of the neighbourhood, were adequately housed and were not unduly busy. Sassure thought that 'the greater number of the priests were stout and ruddy and their comfortable appearance convinces you that they lead pleasant and not fatiguing lives'. Even the nonconformists, after they had secured toleration, were less enthusiastic than their ancestors had been. The behaviour of the Quakers or Shakers struck foreigners as odd but not because they pulled down preachers from their pulpits as in George Foxe's time. They became an exclusive sect and sometimes made a lot of money by dedicating themselves to commerce. It was not until the Wesleyan movement arose in the middle of the century that revivalism, based on 'plain old Bible Christianity', was again brought home to the masses.

Though agriculture was still the most important occupation in the first half of the eighteenth century, both commerce and industry were expanding. Foreign trade was buoyant and besides the re-export of a variety of goods, brought in by the great trading companies, invisible exports were obtained from shipping services, insurance and the like. Duties on exports were reduced or abolished and the coal industry, which now flourished in both England and Scotland, found many foreign buyers. Although English roads were as yet unmetalled, goods were carried from one part of the kingdom to another by coastal shipping which had an ample choice of ports. Merchants had never been looked down upon in England and the big capitalists like Sir James Bateman or Sir Gilbert Heathcote, who were both bankers and exporters, could easily buy their families into the landed aristocracy. Sassure thought it worthy of remark that 'men of good family and even of rank' might 'become merchants without losing caste' and he maintained that some

English merchants were far wealthier than many sovereign princes in Italy or Germany.

Yet in spite of the growth of commerce and the willingness of the great landed proprietors to marry their sons to merchants' daughters, the peak of English society was still represented by a closely knit oligarchy. Foreigners were impressed by the huge houses and vast estates that they saw everywhere in the land. Magnates like the Devonshires, the Newcastles and the Bedfords formed a Whig aristocracy which was always at the heart of the government. Every year they would build new houses and buy new estates. They sent their sons on expensive grand tours of Europe. They increased their wealth by investing in commerce or industry and by speculative building. They also had first claim to offices out of which fortunes could still be made. They served in the Cabinet, they ruled their counties as Lords Lieutenant, they saw that their relatives were elected to the House of Commons and they had a conscious sense of being the governing class. Their wealth and their background gave them immense influence. There was no 'crisis of the aristocracy' in eighteenth-century England. Thus the Whig aristocracy that governed Great Britain in the first half of the century differed in two respects from other Western nobilities. In the first place, they did not form an exclusive self-contained group. Secondly, they had advantages but no privileges; they paid their full share of taxation and served the kingdom in peace and in war. They had little or nothing in common with the French privileged classes or the idle Russian nobility.

How far were the wealthier classes in England aware of their social responsibilities? It has been stated that 'after 1660 the great impetus of private charity fell off' and that the only help given to the poor was that provided by local rates and unpleasant work-houses. In fact no lavish historical research into this subject has been applied to the early eighteenth century as to the early seventeenth. What is unquestionable is that after the reign of Charles II, which was reputed to have been notable for its debaucheries, a reaction took place in the reigns of William III and Queen Anne; movements were started to reform manners and extend faith. The Society for Promoting Christian Knowledge was particularly active in setting up and co-ordinating charity schools. By the end of Anne's reign some seventy thousand children were attending such schools and by the middle of the eighteenth century thousands had been established, paid for by private gifts, which taught reading, writing, and sometimes arithmetic and handicrafts. This

teaching, writes Dr W. A. L. Vincent, 'was regarded as a remedy for ignorance and vice and a safeguard against sedition and disloyalty. Industry and sobriety, obedience and gratitude, were qualities looked for in charity children when they left the schools.' The children were often provided with clothing and, after their education was completed, apprenticeships were arranged for them. But in parts of Great Britain at least, genuine idealism was the motive and teachers were volunteers. Village schoolmasters, who were badly paid, did their work out of a sense of Christian duty. Sassure observed that 'most parishes in London and in the country have hospitals for the sick, the poor and the aged; also charity schools where poor children are fed, taught and clothed' and proceeded to name some of these institutions, including Christ's Hospital and the Merchant Taylors' School. As G. M. Trevelyan has written, 'the movement towards philanthropy instead of persecution as an outlet for religious enthusiasm, was one of the characteristic fruits of the Revolution [of 1688]'. In the larger towns including London, Bristol and Norwich hundreds of charities are known to have existed, most of which established, besides the elementary schools, almshouses for old people and funds to give relief to the poverty stricken. Indeed it may be doubted whether anywhere else in Europe were the poorer classes afforded such care.

The south front of Chatsworth in Derbyshire, built by William Talman for William Cavendish, 4th Earl of Devonshire in 1684.

221

The celebrated English actor, David Garrick, as King Lear.

In higher education a decline set in after the great period for the founding of grammar schools in the sixteenth and seventeenth centuries. The comparative number of schools established fell off; some were converted into elementary schools; and at others the attendance was reduced. Nine schools, including Eton, Harrow and Winchester, became known as 'public schools' and were the exclusive preserve of the gentry and well-to-do. At these schools the curriculum consisted largely of Greek and Latin, which were chiefly needed for making speeches in Parliament. A contemporary believed that 'a girl which is educated at home with her mother is wiser at twelve than a boy at sixteen who only knows Latin'. The Universities of Oxford and Cambridge were still geared, officially at any rate, to classics and theology. Just as little or no history was taught in the grammar schools, so also when George I founded Regius Chairs of History at the universities it is not known that the holders gave any lectures. Nonconformists were excluded from these English universities, but they could go to Scotland or the Dutch Republic, where higher education was more enlightened and less exclusive.

Literature, as in France, was by no means dependent on the patronage of the English Court; indeed Queen Caroline, the wife of George II, was the only royal benefactor to men of letters. But the statesmen of the early eighteenth century were patrons of

222

authors, since they could use them to report upon the state of the nation and to compile pamphlets on behalf of their policies. Jonathan Swift, Daniel Defoe, Joseph Addison and Richard Steele were all beneficiaries of this type of patronage. But at the same time newspapers and periodical magazines, coffee-houses and book-sellers all advertised literary wares. Steele and Addison produced *The Tatler* and *The Spectator*, while later Dr Johnson edited *The Rambler*. A taste for fiction grew up and even if *Gulliver's Travels* and *Robinson Crusoe* inculcated moral lessons, they could be enjoyed simply as adventure stories. The memoirs of society figures such as Horace Walpole and Lord Hervey commanded attention, while, owing to the initiative of publishers, the first dictionary of national biography, *Biographia Britannica*, began to appear in 1747 and the first national encyclopedia was edited by Ephraim Chambers in 1728. The age of the novel established the names of authors like Samuel Richardson, Henry Fielding and Tobias Smollett. On the whole, translated into modern terms, these authors were not badly paid (they are seldom generously paid even today). The first copyright act was passed in 1710, though it secured literary copyright for a period of only fourteen years.

If English literature flowered in the eighteenth century, the theatre, though it no longer had to rely purely on the patronage of the Court, was much less distinguished than in the days of Shakespeare and Marlowe. David Garrick, the leading figure in the eighteenth-century theatre, though he claimed that it was his 'chief wish' to 'lose no drop of that immortal man', mangled Shakespeare's plays, while his friend Dr Johnson believed that 'many of Shakespeare's plays are the worse for being acted'. The actor-manager of Drury Lane selected tragedies that would enable him to display 'the expression of strong but sudden effects of passion'. Such titillation delighted the middle classes who, after the cleansing of the drama (following the amoral Restoration comedy) flocked to the theatre and had unsophisticated tastes. Only the Italian Opera House in Haymarket was left as the exclus-ive rendezvous of the aristocracy. Thus the drama was debased or doctored to allow for an essentially actor's theatre, just as the heroic couplets of that genius Alexander Pope set a fashion which, when copied by imitators, had neither his economy of diction nor his flow of epigrammatic ideas.

Such, broadly, was the character of British society and culture in the years before George III became king. The aristocracy was neither caste-ridden nor irresponsible. The rapid development of commerce meant that a powerful middle class was coming into existence and that the standard of living was rising. The tenantry were free and adequately fed. Parliament, though far from democratic, was a microcosm of the nation, which could make itself felt in times of crisis. The monarchy, though still wielding much authority, was held in check both by Parliament which met yearly (and had to be changed by a general election, first, every three years, and then, after the Septennial Act of 1716, at least every seven) and by a completely independent judiciary. Also the press was free and literary genius was honoured. Because the British were offshore islanders and had the best navy in the world, they built an empire, managed to preserve a balance of power in the Western world, and feared no man. They did not dominate Western civilization as the French had done in the seventeenth century or the Spaniards in the sixteenth and no doubt they were less enlightened and less educated than nations in modern times. But compared with their own world in their own times, the British were an advanced and civilized people. Because their political revolutions lay behind them and an industrial revolution lay ahead, they were able by the turn of the century, though losing one empire, to create another.

14 Western Society and Economic Growth in the Eighteenth Century

Commerce and shipping in Great Britain expanded after the signing of the treaty of Utrecht and industries like coalmining, ironfounding and the manufacture of woollen cloth, as well as of the new cotton textiles, were active. Nevertheless at least three-quarters of the population was still dependent, directly or indirectly, on agriculture during the next fifty years of the eighteenth century; this was equally true of nearly the whole of the Western world. It used to be widely believed that Great Britain experienced an 'agricultural revolution' about 1760 and that it was followed within twenty years by an 'industrial revolution', which enabled the British to lead the fight against Napoleon and become by the reign of Queen Victoria the richest nation in the world. Modern historical research has modified such beliefs. In general it is agreed that the employment of the word 'revolution', implying, as it does, swift and sudden changes, is inappropriate to economic growth. The most that can be said is that a quickened pace of development is to be detected around 1760; the evidence consists of a lengthening catalogue of industrial patents and the increase in enclosures of land put through by private acts of Parliament. One agrarian historian has indeed argued that a revolution had begun in the seventeenth century since new crops and rotations were then introduced. Another expert has contended that agriculture became more productive during the first half of the eighteenth century, which was, on the whole, a time of good harvests, and that while the British population's standard of living and real wages rose, the kingdom could yet afford to sell thirteen per cent of its grain abroad (whereas, by contrast, the Dutch Republic imported thirteen per cent of its food).

In general it is accepted that whatever agricultural improvements can be assigned to the eighteenth century, nearly all of them can be traced back to activities many years earlier, though they took a century to reach their full fruition. To give one example,

Robert Bakewell of Leicestershire, who pioneered the improved breeding of sheep and cattle. His new Leicestershire breed of sheep attained within little more than half a century an international reputation, while the new Leicestershire long-horn cattle became almost as famous. Painting by John Boultbee.

although the potato was discovered in the sixteenth century, it was not until the last quarter of the eighteenth century that it was commonly grown in open fields to serve as a cheap food for the poor. Such celebrated English writers about agriculture as Jethro Tull, the importance of whose book on horse-drawn hoeing has been exaggerated, 'Turnip' Townshend, once the colleague of Robert Walpole in the Cabinet, who retired to his estates in East Anglia to preach the value of growing root crops and clovers, and Robert Bakewell, who was a specialized sheep breeder, propagated methods of technological progress, but it seems that only a few enlightened landlords obeyed their teaching. Big estates prospered almost everywhere in the Western world where labour was relatively cheap, not so much because their owners were shrewd agriculturalists but simply because they could benefit from the advantages of large-scale production. For example, whereas small producers of tobacco in the Chesapeake earned only a modest competence, big planters owning slaves were richly rewarded by a growing market.

Furthermore it has been questioned whether the British have any right to claim that such ideas as a four-to-six rotation of crops, the use of turnips to feed cattle during the winter, and convertible husbandry (allowing arable land periodically to be turned over to pasture) originated with them at all, but were in

226

fact the adoption of practices which slowly percolated through from the Netherlands and parts of Germany. Certainly western Europe as a whole may be contrasted with Europe east of the Elbe in that different social systems prevailed. In the west tenant farming still largely prevailed and because primogeniture or entails or strict settlements of land were usual, many large estates existed in which landlords might or might not stimulate improved agricultural methods to raise yields and rents. In England, landlords as a rule cultivated sufficient land to supply their household needs but kept in touch with their tenants' problems through stewards or bailiffs. In France, also, the privileged classes, who owned about a third of the fertile land in the kingdom, rarely cultivated it themselves but used it for hunting and other rural pleasures and leased the rest of it to tenant farmers who sometimes had to hand over as much as half their produce by way of rent; but they and other customary tenants (known as *censiers*) would also have to meet taxation demands, undertake work on the roads, and pay tithes to the Church. The relationship between tenant farmers and their landlords varied in different parts of the country; for example, the landlords in Picardy and Artois owned large blocks of land and therefore favoured consolidating their property and adding common or wasteland to it by enclosing it with wooden fences, while in Dauphiné, where the nobility owned less land and used it mostly for hunting, they preferred to receive payment from the peasants for grazing rights and were therefore opponents of enclosure.

In Spain it has been estimated that a third of the cultivatable land belonged to four great noble houses. Such hereditary landlords (whose property was strictly entailed) were largely absentees, who lived at court or in towns, and were rarely improving landlords. Here too *métayers* or share-croppers with very modest incomes were to be found. Although much Spanish soil is infertile, as late as the present century seventy per cent of the population was engaged in earning a meagre living from agriculture.

The situation was somewhat different in the Netherlands and the Scandinavian kingdoms. There the landlords aimed at efficient production. In Denmark they sought export markets for their grain, cattle and dairy products, while in Sweden many of the landlords were practical farmers themselves. This was true also of parts of Prussia where the nobility cultivated their land for profit. Many farmers were tenants on the royal domain where the Crown bailiff fixed annual rents. The burdens of the peasantry here were not oppressive and consequently a thriving rural class was emerging. In East Prussia, however, where the landed proprietors combined ownership with feudal jurisdiction, the lot of the peasant was hard; he often had to devote three or more days' work a week to the cultivation of the fields belonging to his lord, who held him more or less at his mercy. In western Europe in general during the first half of the eighteenth century a tendency existed for ploughland to be converted into pasture, while in France, Spain and elsewhere the cultivation of vineyards spread at the expense of cereal growing. The reason for these developments was the low prices earned by grain during the period. After 1755 the tendency was reversed and enclosures, aimed at getting rid of the old arable strip system in order to improve farming by more intensive husbandry, became common. Historians are not in agreement over whether the low grain prices in the early eighteenth century were beneficial to the mass of agriculturalists or not. Certainly those who were dependent for their incomes on the sale of grain were worse off, but, on the other hand, one has the strong impression that as food cost less the standard of living of many ordinary people rose.

In Europe east of the Elbe landlords took an active interest in exploiting the value of their holdings. They increased the size of their domain farms by reclaiming waste and by reducing the size of their tenants' property. In Russia large landowners became capitalist entrepreneurs and the treatment of their serfs led to

French harvest scene from *Le Nouveau Theâtre*, 1723, by Liger. The early eighteenth century was in general a prosperous period for the French peasants.

social unrest and revolt. In Poland, Pomerania and Silesia vast latifundia (that is to say, centralized domain lands) were to be found fringed by increasingly smaller servile holdings. In Hungary, where the nobles were both numerous and privileged, they ruled as feudal masters, employing their serfs to grow grain or tend cattle on huge estates already established under the Turks and continuing in existence after the wars at the end of the seventeenth century. The Austrian Habsburg monarchs were, for the most part, enlightened rulers and although they were able to exert little influence over the Magyar aristocracy, they succeeded in reducing the feudal burdens of peasants in the other regions of their empire. In general the servile peasantry of eastern Europe could scarcely be expected to give of their best and increase the productivity of the soil. So agriculture was stagnant.

In France and North America, on the other hand, whatever their legal and social obligations may have been and however primitive their methods of cultivation, small farmers at least had the inspiration of working their own land and seeking, whenever the weather permitted, to enlarge their output. Indeed the farmers of North America were unique in that outside the southern plantations they nearly all owned their own land. And in spite of the growth of commerce and industry North America was still essentially rural and contained scarcely any big cities.

To sum up, while the Western world, particularly west of the Elbe, enjoyed considerable prosperity in the first half of the eighteenth century, nevertheless, judged in modern terms, it is unrealistic to speak of an 'agricultural revolution'. Even in relatively advanced countries such as England and Denmark yields from the land were low by present standards. Mechanization was not to be introduced until the twentieth century, at which time an extraordinary transformation of agriculture took place through much of the Western world.

How great was the political influence of the nobility and gentry during the eighteenth century? Unquestionably it was by and large an aristocratic world in which the owners of large estates, because of their economic and social position, exerted real power in the provinces even when they spent much of their time in the capital. In England, for instance, the magnates might pass 'the season' in London or in the county capital or a resort like Bath before returning to their estates about the end of June. The Lords Lieutenant of the counties in effect selected the local magistrates and often determined the choice of members of Parliament. So it was said that England was governed by 'a Venetian oligarchy'. In France the nobility could be divided into three categories: the hereditary nobility, the *noblesse de lettres*, whose members paid a fee for the registration of their status, and the *noblesse de dignité*, which embraced leading lawyers and local officials. Up to the middle of the century and possibly as late as 1770 the position of the French peasant – although naturally varying from district to district – was quite good. Professor Mandrou has pointed out that good harvests enabled the peasants to build up surpluses which they could sell in the towns, while their own health was improved since they enjoyed a better diet and did not suffer from malnutrition. Consequently the population increased and reached some twenty-five million ten years before the Revolution. This prosperity of the peasants made them all the more conscious of the disadvantages to which they were subjected by the privileges of their landlords. These included their right to pre-empt peasant production, their exemption from land tax (*taille*) and their ability through the accumulation of capital from rents and other dues to dictate the course of production. On the other hand, as Professor Robert Roswell Palmer has noted, they did not possess the wide powers, almost of life and death, wielded by the landlords in eastern Europe. It was a discontented but by no means subservient nor poverty-stricken peasantry which, allied to the rising urban classes, ultimately brought about the French Revolution.

Not only in France but also in Spain and Denmark the aristocracy spent little time on their estates but congregated at Court as hangers-on to the monarchy. Similarly in many of the smaller German principalities the nobles enjoyed social prestige but little real political power. In Russia, Prussia and Sweden, however, the nobility exerted considerable influence in public affairs, as also in Hungary. In Prussia they occupied high offices in the army and in the bureaucracy. In Sweden, after 1720, they ruled the government because they constituted the first Estate in the Diet. In Hungary, where they paid no taxes, they manned the most important offices of state. Though their power was reduced in Austria after Queen Maria Theresa had established herself upon the throne, the landed gentry continued to direct local justice and administration. In Poland the first half of the century was a golden age for the nobility who controlled the policy of the kingdom. In Russia the obligation of the nobleman to serve the state in war and peace, insisted upon by Peter the Great, remained effective until the accession of Peter III in 1762.

Although therefore the political influence of the aristocracy and landed gentry varied from country to country, it undoubtedly remained considerable even where monarchs were claiming to be absolute, for they could not afford to antagonize their wealthier nobles. But in countries where a middle class was emerging and increasing some check might be imposed. An upper middle class flourished not only in England and France but also in the United Netherlands, most parts of Italy and Switzerland and in many German cities. This class might consist of professional men such as lawyers, journalists and doctors or commercial but not industrial tradesmen. France and England both experienced a spectacular increase in foreign trade – mainly but not entirely in Europe – after 1713. The United Netherlands was chiefly governed by merchants or retired merchants known as 'patricians'. Patricians were also to be found in Switzerland, while in Prussia and Austria a class of civil servants or 'bureaucrats' was evolving and was appreciated by monarchical governments. As Dr Lindsay has pointed out, the emergence of a full-time professional civil service in the Habsburg dominions was hastened by the military successes achieved by the bureaucratic state of Prussia after 1740. Only in England did the nobility and middle class or '*bourgeoisie*' habitually intermix.

The growth of international commerce and the evolution of more sophisticated methods of public and private finance as well as the comparative prosperity of agriculture in western Europe

Anglo-French trade: French wine and silks arriving in the London docks, from an anti-French cartoon of 1757 by L. Boitard.

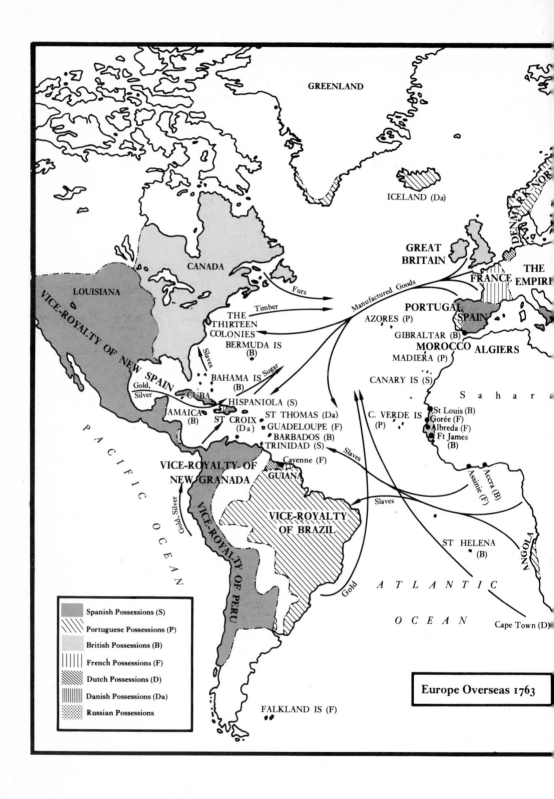

GREENLAND

ICELAND (Da)

DENMARK-NOR
(partial)

CANADA

GREAT
BRITAIN

THE
FRANCE EMPIRE

LOUISIANA

VICE-ROYALTY OF NEW SPAIN

Furs

Timber

Manufactured Goods

PORTUGAL

SPAIN

THE
THIRTEEN
COLONIES

AZORES (P)

GIBRALTAR (B)

MOROCCO ALGIERS

BERMUDA IS
(B)

MADIERA (P)

Slaves

CANARY IS (S)

BAHAMA IS
(B)

Sugar

Gold,
Silver

CUBA

S a h a r a

JAMAICA
(B)

HISPANIOLA (S)

C. VERDE IS
(P)

St Louis (B)
Gorée (F)
Albreda (F)
Ft James
(B)

ST CROIX
(Da)

ST THOMAS (Da)

GUADELOUPE (F)

BARBADOS (B)

TRINIDAD (S)

VICE-ROYALTY OF
NEW GRANADA

Cayenne (F)

GUIANA

Slaves

Accra (B)

Assinie (F)

Gold, Silver

VICE-ROYALTY OF BRAZIL

Slaves

ANGOLA

ST HELENA
(B)

PACIFIC OCEAN

VICE-ROYALTY OF PERU

Gold

A T L A N T I C

O C E A N

Cape Town (D)

▨	Spanish Possessions (S)
▨	Portuguese Possessions (P)
▨	British Possessions (B)
▨	French Possessions (F)
▨	Dutch Possessions (D)
▨	Danish Possessions (Da)
▨	Russian Possessions

FALKLAND IS (F)

Europe Overseas 1763

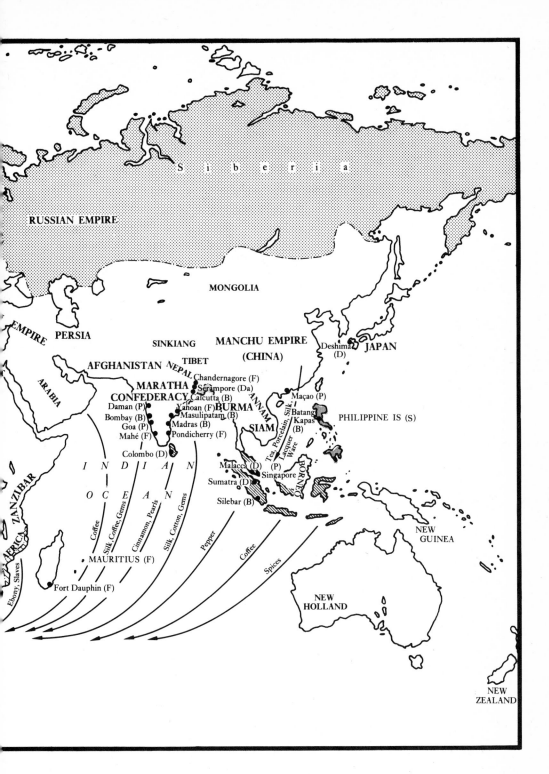

RUSSIAN EMPIRE

S i b e r i a

MONGOLIA

EMPIRE PERSIA

SINKIANG

MANCHU EMPIRE
(CHINA)

Deshima
(D)

JAPAN

TIBET

AFGHANISTAN NEPAL

Chandernagore (F)
Serampore (Da)

MARATHA
CONFEDERACY

Calcutta (B)

Maçao (P)

ARABIA

Daman (P)

Yanoan (F)

BURMA

Batang
Kapas
(B)

PHILIPPINE IS (S)

Bombay (B)

Masulipatam (B)

Goa (P)

Madras (B)

Mahé (F)

Pondicherry (F)

SIAM

ANNAM

Tea, Porcelain, Silk,

Colombo (D)

Lacquer Ware

I N D I A N

Malacca (D)

(P)

BORNEO

Singapore

O C E A N

Sumatra (D)

Silebar (B)

NEW
GUINEA

Coffee

Silk, Coffee, Gems

Cinnamon, Pearls

Silk, Cotton, Gems

Pepper

Coffee

ZANZIBAR

AFRICA

MAURITIUS (F)

Spices

NEW
HOLLAND

Ebony, Slaves

Fort Dauphin (F)

NEW
ZEALAND

all contributed, if slowly, to the coming of what it is customary to call the Industrial Revolution. Although at first the public in Great Britain and France were over-optimistic about the results of the expansion of trade, particularly in the New World, as witnessed by the collapse of the South Sea Company in England and of John Law's Mississippi Company and his other financial schemes in France, in fact thse anticipations were basically correct. The French wine exporting trade flourished; the Dutch continued to monopolize the products of the spice islands; the British sold textiles and re-exported sugar and tobacco, Liverpool and Glasgow growing as ports; Spain sold merino wool to manufacturing countries while Portugal exported port wine and madeira. The Dutch share in world commerce diminished, but they still financed international trade. The French were handicapped by insufficient shipping, but the British thought it worthwhile to maintain a large navy to protect their trade routes. Most western European statesmen continued to believe that exports must exceed imports, for otherwise payments would have to be made in bullion and the nation would become poor. This 'mercantilist' dogma continued to prevail until the middle of the century and its application caused much resentment in British overseas possessions. Still, despite the absence of precise statistics, one can say that trade was buoyant and created a demand for many kinds of products.

It is not easy to explain the intensive industrialization of the Western economy, first and foremost that of Great Britain, towards the end of the eighteenth century. Partly, it is clear, it was owing to the remarkable earlier expansion of commerce. But was this commercial expansion linked to the development of the agrarian economy? If so, the link appears to be subtle and indirect. The relatively low prices paid for grain because of good harvests had brought about a shift away from grain growing to using land for the breeding and feeding of cattle. In much of England, as well as in France and the Dutch Republic, pastoral areas were thought to provide more employment than grain lands. In most parts of England a dual economy prevailed. For instance, woollen cloth was normally produced by farmers, peasants and agricultural labourers who spun or wove in their own houses except during harvest time. In Derbyshire a small farmer might have cows and pigs and at the same time work in the lead mines. Those who combined industrial work of one kind or another with farming were relatively well off and felt secure. Towards the end of the

The port of Marseilles in 1754, painting by Joseph Vernet.

seventeenth century Richard Baxter noted the difference in earnings between agricultural workers in pastoral regions and what he called the 'racked poor' who toiled on arable land from which both smallholders and small tenants were rapidly disappearing. Indeed this dual economy gave men a varied and independent life, which they were reluctant to leave. Thus it was difficult for a capitalist entrepreneur to concentrate workers in factories (instead of distributing his work in labourers' cottages). Thus he had to offer higher wages; yet it is interesting that even in the middle of the eighteenth century industry was still essentially rural.

Nevertheless the enclosure movement, which did not really get under way until about 1760 and was sometimes aimed at turning arable land into pasturage and sometimes at promoting more efficient systems of arable farming with changed rotations and new fertilizers, did have the effect of driving out cottagers who had previously cultivated a few strips in the open fields in order to supplement their earnings from part-time work. But such unfortunates did not necessarily move into industry; they might simply become vagrants. The more enterprising were able to emigrate to North America where they could buy land cheaply and resume the life of husbandmen. Thus no obvious connection can be traced between agricultural developments and the growth of industry. It has however been plausibly argued that because British and French peasants were relatively prosperous in the first half of the eighteenth century, when their food cost them less, they provided a domestic market for manufactured goods which had not previously existed except for luxury goods in demand from the upper classes of society.

What were the other factors that made for industrialization? One, it has been suggested, was a rise in population throughout the Western world, though it can equally be maintained that it was the growth of industry that led to the increase in numbers. Yet while populations almost everywhere were growing, industrialization took place only in Great Britain, France and parts of Germany. Secondly, profits made from commerce and the exploitation of large landed estates meant that more capital became available for investment. For instance, the second Duke of Bridgwater, who, during the Seven Years' War and afterwards, invested large sums in coalmining, turnpike roads and canals, derived his capital chiefly from rents. It is true that much investment went into government funds, which provided gilt-edged security, but still that accustomed people to the idea of saving and investing. But since the rate of interest decreased – that on British consolidated stock was reduced to three per cent in 1757 – those who had money to invest were attracted by more profitable, if also more speculative opportunities, even when their fingers had been burnt in the South Sea Bubble during the second decade of the century. As Professor Thomas Ashton has observed, 'the deep mines, solidly built factories, well-constructed canals, and substantial houses of the industrial revolution were the products of relatively cheap capital', not, one may add, relatively cheap labour. In fact a French inspector of manufactures, writing in 1760, reported that the English 'try by machinery to diminish the price of workmanship by doubling the work done if they can'.

The characteristics of the Industrial Revolution were first, mechanization, secondly, the concentration of workmen in factories, and, lastly, the use of steam power to replace human and animal strength. None of these processes was far advanced by the middle of the eighteenth century. Technological inventions had little to do with the scientific discoveries of the seventeenth century. Indeed modern economic historians have maintained that most of them were 'modest rudimentary contrivances' and that much eighteenth-century technology was merely a development of ideas that can be traced back to Leonardo da Vinci and even to the Middle Ages. Water-driven plant for milling grain or for metallurgy had long been in common use. The most notable advances in the first part of the eighteenth century were in cotton, coal and iron. The cotton industry was relatively new. In the seventeenth century it had centred in the Manchester area and consisted mainly in the manufacture of fustians, a fairly heavy cloth with linen warp and cotton weft. The Chetham family, with whom its origins are associated, sold fustians in domestic markets only. The manufacture of pure cotton goods took place earlier in Switzerland, France and possibly in Holland. In 1733 a Lancashire clockmaker, John Kay, invented the flying-shuttle which enabled the weaver to work on a broader loom and doubled his output. In consequence of its use a shortage of yarn developed, but it was not until 1770 that a Blackburn weaver named James Hargreaves invented a hand-machine known as a 'jenny' which speeded up the process of spinning. The invention of the flying-shuttle and the spinning jenny caused riots in Lancashire on the ground that they threw men out of work. In the 1770s Richard Arkwright, a Preston barber, invented a 'frame' which speeded up the spinning process

Cartoon by William Hogarth drawing the contrast between the industrious and idle prentice weavers at their looms.

237

The Iron Forge by Joseph
Wright of Derby.
Wright's paintings of
scientific and industrial
subjects are especially
effective because of his
dramatic use of light.

and enabled cheap calicoes to be manufactured. He established a
water-driven factory where he employed six hundred workers,
mostly children, in 1771. But cotton mills, using these power-
driven machines, did not become common until about 1780.
Twenty years earlier Great Britain was importing two and a half
million pounds of raw cotton which was worked up by hand in
cottage homes or small shops.

Coalmining, unlike cotton, was an old-established British
industry. Coal was used in manufacture as well as to provide
domestic fuel during the reign of Queen Elizabeth I. By the
eighteenth century most of the outcrops were exhausted and shafts
had to be sunk to reach the coal. Difficulties were caused by the
accumulation of gas and water in the pits. The invention by
Thomas Newcomen, a Devonshire ironmonger, of a pumping
machine to draw off the water was rapidly adopted by nearly all
the collieries, but it was not until 1776 that a much superior and
more economical machine, perfected by James Watt, came into

238

commercial use and inaugurated the age of steam. Demand for coal both at home and abroad doubled between the beginning and the middle of the eighteenth century. Nevertheless the rate of technological progress was relatively slow. Mining was a hazardous occupation; although miners were reasonably well paid, the relations between the mine-owners and their workmen were primitive and harsh.

Coal gradually came into use in ironfounding, which, like coal mining, was an old British industry. Iron was manufactured by smelting ore in a blast furnace heated by charcoal (burnt wood). The molten metal was then run into 'pigs' – oblong moulds – from which castings or wrought iron bars could be manufactured. These then went into slitting mills to provide the raw material out of which pots and pans and dozens of other things could be made. It was Abraham Darby, a Quaker ironfounder, who first thought of employing coke (made from coal) for smelting ore. His works were in Shropshire where there was easy access to the kind of coal which produced a coke suitable for blast furnaces. Whether because Darby was reticent about his achievement, because the new process had to undergo a long period of trial and error or because the material was suitable for only certain types of iron – castings rather than iron bars – it was not for forty years after Darby had begun experimenting with his discovery that it came into general use. In 1760 Great Britain had only seventeen blast furnaces that employed coke for smelting. Though charcoal was also used in steel manufacture, the process was so expensive that it was not until the nineteenth century, after further inventions, that steel began to replace iron for many purposes.

Industrial progress was not confined to Great Britain. The Dutch also had capital to invest in the applications of new inventions. In France, Prussia and Austria the royal governments were conscious of the need to support manufactures. Between 1740 and 1789 generous subsidies were distributed in France to stimulate new industries. It has been suggested that technological ideas often came originally from France only to be developed in practicable terms in England. The French tried to tempt British and Dutch workmen to come to France. John Kay spent several years of his life in France and demonstrated the value of his fly-shuttle in Normandy. Kay died in France where he had been well treated because the government did not wish 'to disgust foreigners from bringing their industry into the kingdom'. Newcomen's pump was also used in other countries which had coal mines.

One can see then that the eighteenth-century industrial advance was a slow business rather than a revolutionary one. The idea that the simple inventions of men like Newcomen, Darby and Kay set the world alight has been abandoned. If it is accepted that Great Britain led the way in the Western world towards the modernization of industry, other explanations must be sought. One view is that private enterprise or lack of government intervention was an advantage, driven home by Adam Smith, the Scottish philosopher, in *The Wealth of Nations*, first published in 1776. Other governments paid out subsidies and upheld monopolies so that in theory their manufacturers should have been better off than their British counterparts. David Landes has written that 'what distinguished the British economy ... was an exceptional sensitivity and responsiveness to pecuniary opportunity. This was a people fascinated by wealth and commerce, collectively and individually.' Others, however, have claimed that the British were outstandingly inventive. Writing in 1757 Josiah Tucker thought that although the Dutch were superior in their application of water mills for sawing timber, 'in regard to mines and metals of all sorts the English are uncommonly dexterous in their contrivance of the mechanic powers'. But one inclines to the conclusion that it was neither laissez-faire nor the possession of workmen who hit on labour-saving devices during the first half of the eighteenth century that explains British industrial progress. It owed more, as has already been suggested, to the availability of capital for investment, to the new markets provided by a prospering agriculture, to the necessity of finding mechanical means to reduce the need for well-paid labour, and to the genuine improvement in transport and shipping. These were the things which made Great Britain into a wealthy kingdom and the heart of a widespread empire before the American Revolution took place.

15 Western Science and Philosophy in the Eighteenth Century

The first three-quarters of the eighteenth century was to produce fewer intellectual and artistic geniuses than the seventeenth century, but it was a period during which the climate of intelligent opinion about science, philosophy and religion was changing throughout the Western world. During the seventeenth century it had been accepted only reluctantly that the world was but one planet in the universe, following the discoveries of Nicolaus Copernicus, Galileo Galilei and Johann Kepler. But in his *Essay on Man*, published in 1733, Alexander Pope could write:

> See worlds on worlds compose one universe
> Observe how system into system runs,
> What other planets circle other suns,
> What varied beings people every star,
> May tell why Heaven has made us what we are.

In spite of the general realization that the earth was a small planet rotating round the sun, and that life on the globe obeyed mechanical laws, most thinkers had an optimistic belief both in the use of reason and in the value of empirical research. Not all thinkers were optimists – indeed two men of genius, Voltaire and David Hume, inclined to pessimism. Voltaire mocked at excessive optimism in *Candide*, a novel sparked off by the earthquake which destroyed most of Lisbon in 1755 – a frightful disaster in the best of all possible worlds, Voltaire called it – undermining confidence in a beneficent deity or order of nature. Neither the Church nor the state was henceforward able in practice to hinder free and untrammelled inquiry into the realities of life. After 1757 the Papacy ceased to ban books on the rotation of the earth. But a censorship of books in France still existed so that authors with daring ideas preferred to publish them anonymously or to wrap them up, as did the sceptic Bayle, in his *Dictionnaire historique et critique* (1697). The result was that a battle against religious dogma, political tyranny and moral hypocrisy was started. The weapons used included satire, an example of which was to be found in Charles de Montesquieu's *Lettres Persanes* (1721) giving an imaginary view of the West as seen from the harem, and the popularization of the findings of seventeenth-century authors such as Francis Bacon, Isaac Newton and John Locke.

Possibly John Locke, who died in 1704, although scarcely a consistent thinker, was the strongest influence upon eighteenth-century thought both in France and in America, not only because of his two treatises on government but because of the views that he put forward so modestly on the nature of knowledge in his *Essay Concerning Human Understanding*. His teaching, that the mind was a white paper on which experience wrote, gradually ousted René Descartes's belief in innate ideas; but Locke in fact assumed the existence of the mind by intuition and considered that reflection not sensation was needed so that the mind could soar beyond simplicities into complexities of thought; however, he was doubtful that ultimate truths could ever be discovered. Thus Locke inaugurated the philosophical scepticism which was so characteristic of the mid-eighteenth century, for he dealt in probabilities rather than certainties. Pierre Coste, a French Protestant, who was with Locke when he was dying, had translated the *Essay Concerning Human Understanding* into French in 1700 and it was widely read.

Both Montesquieu and Voltaire visited England in the early eighteenth century and drank at the fountain of Locke's wisdom. The English statesman Henry St John, Viscount Bolingbroke, wrote to Voltaire recommending him to read Locke's *Essay* in preference to Descartes. Voltaire discussed Locke in his *Lettres Philosophiques* which were published after he returned from two years in England. He said of Locke: 'Plenty of reasoners have given us the story of the mind; at last a wise man has arrived to give us its history.' Voltaire did not read Locke's two *Treatises on Government*, but Montesquieu had done so and was influenced by them. Another French Protestant, René Rapin-Thoras, also disseminated British political ideas and practices in books written in French, while the Abbé Condillac, born in Grenoble, the son of a *noble de la robe*, published a book in 1746, with its title copied directly from Locke's *Essay*, in which he expounded Locke's theories of sensational psychology and rejected the metaphysical systems of philosophers like Descartes in favour of empiricism. 'What [he wrote] could be more ridiculous than that men, coming out of a profound sleep, and finding themselves in the middle of a labyrinth should lay down general principles for finding the way out?' In fact what Frenchmen like Montesquieu, Voltaire and Condillac admired in Locke was not so much his precise philosophical theories as his common-sense and his willingness to base his conclusions on observation and experiment.

Montesquieu who, like Condillac, came from the *noblesse de la robe* in southern France, aimed to combine rationalism and empiricism in his greatest book, *De l'Esprit des Lois* (1748) which rejected fatalistic religious beliefs and dismissed the divine right of kings. Montesquieu set out to produce a comparative study of political institutions and social customs throughout the earth and to compare them in the light of different climates and geographical situations; he showed, for example, that a case might be made out for slavery. He has been described as the father of modern sociology and indeed he tried hard not to make moral judgments. In fact, however, he favoured republicanism rather than despotism, which he thought corrupted itself, and although he did not, as has sometimes been said, advocate the separation of powers, he thought it was necessary that power should check power and he drew an idealistic picture of England, saying that it was 'the one nation in the world which has political liberty as the direct object of its constitution'.

Most Western thinkers in the early eighteenth century were deists, that is to say they adhered to natural religion which did not depend on divine revelation. It was curious that in the year 1726 when the youthful printer from Philadelphia, Benjamin Franklin, was leaving London, Voltaire was arriving. Both of them were to be leading deists. Franklin had read the works of the English deists, the third Earl of Shaftesbury and Anthony Collins, a friend of Locke, when he was still a boy, and openly rejected his father's Calvinism. Voltaire was much more cautious in expressing his religious opinions, but once in a private letter he admitted that he was a deist and defined deists as philosophers who adored God as the supreme being, but were free from all superstitions. However, Voltaire feared that too public an opposition to the Christian faith might damage the causes in which he believed, such as toleration and the reform of institutions, by involving deists in condemnation as sceptics and atheists.

Denis Diderot, who was twenty years younger than Voltaire and led a precarious Bohemian life in the Latin quarter of Paris, was converted to deism after he translated Shaftesbury's

Principles of Moral Philosophy for a French bookseller. Later he became interested in the question of what would happen to a blind man if he regained his sight. Would his reactions sustain Locke's sensational psychology? In 1749 Diderot wrote a book, *Lettres sur les aveugles*, in which he embroidered on the little he knew about a blind professor of mathematics at Cambridge. He invented a dying speech for him in which he was made to say: 'If you want to make me believe in God you must make me touch him ...' The year after this a book appeared in London entitled *Man a Machine*, which was in fact the translation of a pamphlet published in French two years earlier at Leyden. The author was Julien de la Mettrie, a surgeon. Like Diderot, La Mettrie had been fascinated by the moral and psychological behaviour of the deaf and the blind, but his book was frankly atheistic, denying the existence of the soul. Professor Alfred Cobban has observed that just as Leibniz spiritualized matter, La Mettrie materialized the psyche. When the author became known, he had to flee from France to Prussia where he received the protection of Frederick the Great, and was to die shortly afterwards. About ten years later another doctor, Claude Adrien Helvétius, whose father treated the French queen and was of Swiss descent, produced a book called *De l'esprit*, which has been described as in effect La Mettrie's pamphlet 'blown out to the size of three volumes and written in pompous turgidities, instead of the pithy epigrams of La Mettrie'. Helvétius, who was well-to-do, lived a life of gallantry and self-indulgence and in a posthumous work pronounced that 'pleasure and pain are, and will always be, the only principles of action'. Finally, the Baron Paul Henri d'Holbach, whose family had migrated to Paris from the Palatinate, and who wrote more than thirty books, mostly rather tedious, put the case for atheism and materialism and maintained that the soul was an obscure function of the body which could be anatomized. Like Helvétius, he preached utilitarianism, which later was to be so influential in England as a guide to political and moral action in the hands of Jeremy Bentham and James Mill and his son, John Stuart Mill. As we can see, genuine atheists were to be found in eighteenth-century France.

Most of the French writers of polemics were not really original thinkers: they were derivative popularizers, translating the ideas of Descartes and Leibniz, Locke and Newton into simpler language for the benefit of the bourgeoisie. They had their counterparts elsewhere. In Germany Christian Wolff was a disciple of Leibniz, in Italy Francesco Algarotti explained

Les philosophes at table: amongst those shown are Voltaire, d'Alembert, Condorçet and Diderot.

Newtonian physics, as Voltaire also did in France. But basically the outlook was French. Most of these authors (except Helvétius and d'Holbach) exemplified the French gift for lucid prose, witty writing, irreverent attitudes and encyclopedic knowledge. They were more concerned with science than history, with ethics than religion. For the most part, they believed that the lot of mankind could be bettered through reason and education. Their hearts, it can be said, were in the right place. But they were neither philosophers nor political scientists. The term that is usually applied to them is *philosophes*, though possibly encyclopedists is more accurate; for most of them contributed to the *Encyclopédie*, edited by Diderot and Jean d'Alembert, which was started in 1751, finished by 1765, and expounded the nature of science and arts; these, they thought, were more likely to do good to mankind than the Catholic religion.

The two most distinguished philosophers in this period were British – or, to be more precise, an Irishman, Bishop George Berkeley (who once visited California, where a town was named after him) and a Scotsman, David Hume, who met the *philosophes* but did not get along well with them. Berkeley was a Christian, Hume was not. But both of them were empiricists and began a transformation of philosophy where Locke left off. Berkeley took the point made by Locke that knowledge of the outer world is derived only from sensations, but went on to argue that what is perceived is sensible qualities not material things: the body is

Coupe sur la largeur

Echelle de 4 Toises

Section of a corn mill from the *Encyclopédie*, edited by Diderot and d'Alembert.

therefore a complex of ideas. However, for the existence of bodies, that is to say, complex ideas, one has to rely on intuition or inference. Yet different people perceive different things in different ways. Therefore there can be no objective reality. So Berkeley disposed of the existence of matter. The ideas which constitute the active world are a system willed by God: that is why a tree 'continues to be, when there's no one about in the quad'. Thus Berkeley opened the road from empiricism to idealism.

246

This kind of argument took Hume in a different direction. He agreed that knowledge is derived only from sensations, which he called 'present impressions'. Our impressions, he said, are the only things about which we can have certainty; any other knowledge is merely probable. Two impressions may regularly and rapidly follow one another, but no evidence exists to show that they will always do so. So we can only state what we perceive through impressions. We can have no certain knowledge of what things are or how they work. Hume's extremely logical thinking about the character of knowledge has been called alternately scepticism, positivism, and 'honest empiricism'. He did not, however, deny that in practice in daily life one has to rely upon beliefs that are obtained from ordinary experiences. Thus Hume had no truck with metaphysical arguments, for it is impossible to prove the reality of God.

It would be wrong to suppose that these highly subtle logical arguments had much influence on contemporaries, though, in the long run, they contributed to 'idealism', the belief that the object of external perception consists of ideas – a belief which was later to be employed to justify the corporate state – and 'positivism', a philosophical system which recognized only clear facts and observable phenomena. Hume's *Treatise of Human Nature*, which he wrote while living in France, made little impact on society; he said 'it fell still-born from the press'. He turned to writing a history of England which was a masterpiece of Tory prejudice and intellectual conceit. It was not until 1781, when Immanuel Kant published his *Critique of Pure Reason* that an important philosopher tried to reconcile empiricism with idealism and he gave birth to a category of ideas that dominated European philosophy until the twentieth century. Meanwhile in Germany the metaphysical monody of Leibniz as interpreted by Christian Wolff, who was a polymath, continued to prevail. Hume wrote a book on miracles, for which he said adequate evidence could never be discovered: to that extent his outlook linked up with that of the French *philosophes*. Indeed he himself has sometimes been described as a *philosophe*. In fact his arguments were more logical and more profound than theirs, though less useful.

Hume, it has rightly been said, for all his philosophical scepticism, was regarded in his own time as a more respectable figure than the *philosophes*. For their views, as demonstrated in the *Encyclopédie*, were aimed at and penetrated to an intelligent middle class. Yet they too had a highly respectable background. As early as 1695

David Hume, the empirical philosopher and author of *Treatise of Human Nature*. This portrait was painted by a fellow Scotsman, Allan Ramsay.

247

the French *Académie Royale des Sciences* had commissioned René de Réamur, an extremely versatile scientist, to compile a survey of technology and manufactures. But he was outstripped by the work of Diderot and the Abbé d'Alembert, whose original invitation to edit a collaborative alphabetical dictionary of man's achievements gave them the opportunity to transform it into a work of intellectual genius. The *Encyclopédie* has been described with some exaggeration as the 'Trojan horse' of the *ancien régime*. Still Diderot himself did write that its character was 'to change the common manner of thinking'. It was launched under reputable auspices. It was given a royal licence and printed by the King's printer. By the time it was finished it contained twenty million words and many thousands of illustrations. In the end it had attracted four thousand subscribers and, as R. J. White has noted, 'the demand extended to the western world in general, the book-sellers of France coming to an arrangement with the English when the pirates announced a half-price edition after the first volume'. Later it was to inspire the publication of the *Encyclopaedia Britannica* in England. In 1801 it was to be explained in that *Encyclopaedia* that 'the French *Encyclopédie* has been accused of having disseminated far and wide, the seed of Anarchy and Atheism', which the British volumes now sought to counteract. In fact, like Bayle's dictionary, the *Encyclopédie* was carefully edited. Articles that were written, say, about Noah's ark (whose authenticity had been suspected by Samuel Pepys), were contributed by authors with their tongues well in their cheeks. An attempt by Jesuits to sabotage the work as irreligious was with some difficulty overcome. Diderot, who completed the editing alone, had a flexible and adaptable mind and was intellectually adventurous. Like all good editors, he impressed his own ideas on the volumes. Thus the *Encyclopédie* had a distinctive character. Lord Morley, the English statesman and author, was to write that its moral was that 'human nature is good, that the world is capable of being a desirable abiding-place, and that the evil of the world is the fruit of bad education and bad institutions'.

Modern thought would not accept as readily as did the Victorians that men can be transformed by education and institutions and may believe, what was never believed during the French 'Enlightenment', that heredity plays a major part in individual development. But the utilitarianism which was then very generally accepted in the Western world was salutary enough. Alexander Pope had written in his *Essay on Man* how

God and Nature fixed the general frame
And bade self-love and social be the same

and earlier the Dutchman, Bernard de Mandeville, had argued
in *The Fable of the Bees* (1705) that even passions such as ambition
and greed really served mankind, for they induced people to work
in order to buy wealth and thus to produce general happiness.
Fifty years later Cesare Beccaria, the Milanese author and law
reformer, asserted in *Dei Delitti e delle Pene* (1764) that legislation
should aim at 'the greatest happiness of the greatest number'. By
such laws, he claimed, crimes might be averted; proof of guilt,
he maintained, should not be sought by torture nor could anti-
social activities be prevented by severe punishments. The gravity
of the offence, he thought, should be determined solely by the
harm it did to the state. Undoubtedly his teachings, which were to
be followed by the utilitarian philosopher, Jeremy Bentham, were
ultimately to have a formidable influence on the Western world.

'The eighteenth century', it has been said, 'was the age of
science and history, the age of the triumph of the empirical fact.'
One should perhaps qualify this generalization first by observing
that the *philosophes* (as distinct from Bayle) were not much concerned over traditional history and secondly, by noting that, as has
been the case throughout modern times, a considerable gap
existed between popular historians, often with axes to grind, and
meticulous researchers. One can, for example, contrast the deep
researches of the Abbé Mabillon, who died in 1707, and the work
of other Benedictine monks at the library of St Germain-des-Près
with the history books by Hume and Smollett, which they threw
off at the rate of a chapter a week to earn money. Voltaire, though
a busy and prolific author, took some trouble over collecting the
facts for his *Histoire de Charles XII* (1731) and his *Siècle de Louis
XIV* (1752) and he had the advantage of acquiring information
from his subjects' contemporaries; nevertheless he wrote from a
preconceived point of view: in the case of Charles he criticized
the behaviour of all kings, in the case of Louis XIV he gave praise
not to his victories and conquests but to his patronage of scientists
and artists. That Voltaire's history was regarded as tendentious
was shown by the fact that both books had to be published
surreptitiously, the first in Rouen, the second in Prussia. Another
notable historian was the Neapolitan lawyer, Pietro Giannone,
whose *Storia civile del regno di Napoli* was translated into English
in 1731 as the *History of the Kingdom of Naples* and was regarded

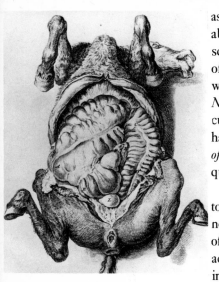

The viscera of a donkey, from Buffon's *Histoire Naturelle*, published in 1749.

as an effective attack on the secular claims of the Papacy. Another able Neapolitan writer was Giambattista Vico, a philosopher and a scientist, who was one of the earliest exponents of a cyclical theory of history. David Hume's *History of Great Britain* (1754), which was not based on serious research, has been overpraised, but his *Natural History of Religion* (1757) may be considered as a precursor of Johann Herder and James Frazer's *Golden Bough*. One has to await the appearance of Edward Gibbon's *Decline and Fall of the Roman Empire* (1776–88) before finding a writer of literary quality and philosophical outlook who was also a great historian.

Science made progress not only because of the impulse given to it by discoveries of the seventeenth century but because it was now recognized as a subject in its own right rather than a branch of philosophy. Scientific academies existed in Paris (where the academy received a new constitution in 1700), in Berlin and later in Moscow. The universities in Italy and Germany taught science. Chairs of various scientific subjects were established at the University of Cambridge. J.M.Hoffman, the first Professor of Chemistry at the University of Altdorf in Switzerland, built a laboratory there for experiments; at Göttingen Albrecht von Haller, an outstandingly versatile scientist, had access to a magnificent library and theatre for study. Haller founded a royal scientific society, while in America two societies concerned with astronomy and other scientific subjects were merged at Philadelphia in 1771; one of these societies – the American Philosophical Society – had been founded by Benjamin Franklin to study the sciences and technology and to undertake research. A group of doctors who graduated at the University of Leyden, one of the oldest European scientific universities, persuaded the University of Edinburgh to set up a faculty of medicine.

Thus science was no longer the hobby of small coteries. It became a subject of conversation in coffee shops and aristocratic salons. Unlike science in the seventeenth century, it was put to a practical use. Physicians and surgeons became more knowledgeable. The value of dieting and even vaccination was recognized and patients were clinically treated and encouraged to describe their symptoms, although modern diagnosis was not developed until the Napoleonic era when the hospitals of Paris revolutionized medicine. In Great Britain William Hunter was a pioneer of modern anatomy, though it had been practised earlier. In chemistry progress was obstructed through the would-be discovery by a German professor of a non-existent substance called phlogiston;

An experiment with electricity in the mid-eighteenth century from a French engraving.

it was not until late in the eighteenth century that the nature of chemical elements and gases was finally resolved in the age of Antoine Laurent Lavoisier.

The scientists of the Western world were firm believers in the value of systematization, particularly in botany. Georges Buffon's *Histoire Naturelle*, published in 1749 before the initiation of the *Encyclopédie*, made its author famous; he presided over the *Jardin des Plantes*, a haven for classifiers. An even more comprehensive classifier than Buffon was the Swede, Carl Linnaeus, in whose *Systema Naturae*, completed in 1758, were to be found vast lists of plants, animals and minerals collected from all over the world. In North America John Bartram was a pioneer of hybridization, while an amateur naturalist, Sir Joseph Banks, who accompanied the expedition of Captain James Cook on its voyage round the world (1768–71), brought back valuable new specimens. Botanical gardens, which began in the seventeenth century, became very popular: the physic garden at Chelsea and the medical garden at Altdorf were counterparts of the *Jardin des Plantes* in France. Engineering also made great strides. Roads, bridges and canals were being built throughout the Western world. In 1750 a Swiss engineer was employed to construct the second bridge across the Thames at Westminster. Finally, tentative experiments were made with oil lamps, gas and electricity. Pieter van Musschenbroek of Leyden produced the jar, named after his university, which condensed electricity and gave out long sparks when a conductor was applied to both sides of it. It became fashionable in society to buy an electric shock and in Italy an attempt was made to cure paralytics with shock treatment. Moved by the new craze, Benjamin Franklin sought to prove that lightning consisted of electricity and he invented a lightning conductor. But it was not until later in the century that Henry Cavendish and Joseph Priestley in England and Luigi Galvani and Alessandro Volta in Italy made really valuable discoveries in electricity, while gas was not used for street lighting in London and Paris before the first decade of the nineteenth century.

Did the *philosophes* of the eighteenth century, who believed optimistically that mankind could be uplifted by knowledge of the useful arts and sciences, share a political philosophy? They held some views in common. They all advocated intellectual liberty and religious toleration. But in other respects Voltaire and Rousseau, the two best-known names in the France of this era, had differing political opinions.

Jean Jacques Rousseau, a self-made genius, was unique; although he contributed articles to the *Encyclopédie* he was a lone wolf. His best known book, *Du Contrat Social* (1762), had an immense influence on later thinkers and was capable of being used to justify both democracy and authoritarianism. He was a poet rather than a profound philosopher; it is doubtful if his teaching had any direct influence whatever on the French Revolution; and his conviction that political equality could be attained only in a small city state had little application to existing conditions in the world. Voltaire, on the other hand, though he was no lover of kings or courts, saw some virtues in absolute monarchy at least for France. He drew a distinction, however, between absolute and arbitrary power; he thought in terms of a philosopher-prince or a benevo-

Opposite: Old Custom House Quay on the Thames: painting by Samuel Scott.

252

lent monarch who submitted to the law. Having himself been ill-treated by the nobility when he was young, he approved of the attempt made during the reign of Louis XV to get rid of the French *parlements* which obstructed reforms. Once he quoted with approval a statement attributed to the Roman Sully: 'If wisdom descended on earth, it would prefer to lodge in one head rather than a body of men.'

Most of the *philosophes* derived their political ideas from Locke or Montesquieu rather than Rousseau or Voltaire. The Swiss popularizer, Jean-Jacques Burlamaqui, who published a book entitled *Principes du droit politique* in 1751, for example, praised the balance of powers and the value of 'mixed government' or limited monarchy, such as he imagined prevailed in Great Britain, and he believed that there were fundamental laws which checked despotic authority. The articles in the *Encyclopédie* on politics favoured a contractual theory of government and a utilitarian standpoint. Thus, in general, approval was given to Locke's view that governments should promote the well-being of their subjects and that if they failed to do so, they could be overthrown. Yet in reality the contractual theory, which defined rights, and utilitarianism were intellectually incompatible and it would be difficult to name any early eighteenth-century figure who had a consistent political point of view, as Hobbes had earlier or Burke later.

Some of the *philosophes* would have liked to trust in the virtues of enlightened despotism, as Voltaire did. The relations between Frederick the Great of Prussia, who was once considered by historians to have been a benevolent autocrat, and Voltaire were mildly comic. Frederick did everything he could to persuade this celebrated author to come to Potsdam, but when at last he succeeded in doing so, they did not get along very well together. Frederick employed Voltaire in correcting his own indifferent poetry and, after an initial honeymoon, the Prussian King said: 'I need him for another year at the most. One squeezes the orange and then throws away the peel.' In the end, Voltaire himself recognized what was up. He wrote in December 1752: 'I see very clearly that the orange has been pressed; I must now think of saving the rind.' At a distance Voltaire had idolized the King; at close quarters he recognized the defects of the Prussian monarchy.

Voltaire was also to admire the Tsarina Catherine II of Russia. Helvétius praised both Frederick and Catherine for their services to humanity. Diderot offered Catherine unwelcome advice on how to run her empire. She was indeed a champion at boasting of

Opposite: 'Morning' from William Hogarth's series of paintings, *The Four Times of the Day*.

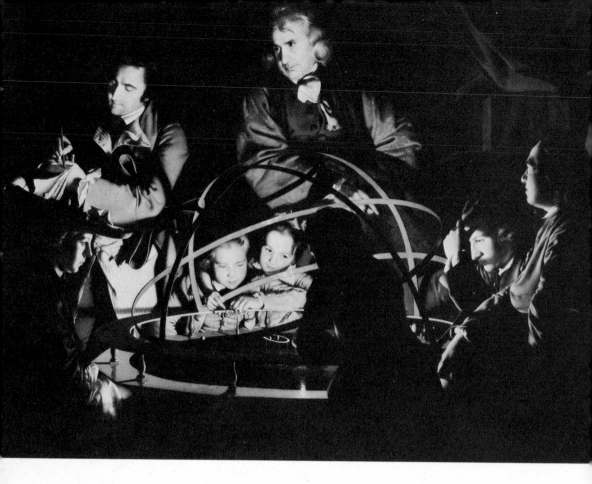

The Orrery, painted by Joseph Wright of Derby in 1766. This depicts a philosopher giving a lecture upon the orrery (a clockwork model of the planetary system), in which the lamp is put in place of the sun. Joseph Wright has portrayed himself on the far left, P. P. Burdett taking notes, and the philosophers Denby and Lawrence Shirley.

her own enlightenment and once assured Voltaire how happy the Russian peasants were. Later Alexander Pushkin was to write of 'the repulsive buffoonery in her relations with the philosophers of her century'. Much of Frederick's and Catherine's liberalism was a façade. If any enlightened despots existed in the eighteenth century they were the Habsburgs, not the Hohenzollerns or the Romanovs. The Emperor Leopold II allowed himself to be painted with a copy of *L'Esprit des Lois* in his hands.

Possibly the reaction among some modern historians against the existence of genuine enlightened despots in the eighteenth century has gone too far. It is certain that Beccaria's views about the reform of the criminal law made a considerable impression upon monarchical governments; religious toleration prevailed in Prussia where the King himself was a sceptic, while Catherine II may, at the outset of her reign, genuinely have intended to pursue reformist principles. But, as Dr Shackleton has written, 'the most important geographical extension of the Enlightenment ... was across the Atlantic'. Locke's teaching, with its stress on inalienable natural (or human) rights, influenced Thomas Jefferson, while the separation of powers, embodied in the American constitution, owes a good deal both to Locke and to Montesquieu.

To sum up, although Voltaire, Rousseau and Diderot differed over constitutional forms, one can detect a broad agreement in French intellectual circles about many important ideas. Rousseau may have believed originally that the progress of the arts and sciences was inimical to human happiness and he may have romanticized the life of the noble savage, but in the *Nouvelle Heloise* and *Emile* he urged the value of moral principles and of educating men for moral ends. All the *philosophes* – Helvétius, for example, though he was no angel – stressed the need for good laws and advocated education and a sound environment as the best way to fashion good citizens. Equally, agreement was reached about the iniquity of religious persecution, the necessity for toleration, and the case for divorcing ethics from revelation. Even if some of the *philosophes* toyed with the advantages of absolutism, they praised the rule of law and thought that laws should be determined by utilitarian considerations. Apart from Rousseau all of them imagined that the greatest happiness could be achieved through technological progress.

One must not, however, overemphasize the importance or the immediate effects of the various ideas put forward in what has been called the Age of Reason or the Age of Enlightenment. Indeed it is doubtful if this age was either the one or the other. The seventeenth century had a better claim to be called the Age of Reason, for it was then that medieval notions about the nature of the universe and scholastic metaphysics were being sloughed off by men of genius like Galileo, Descartes and Newton. Even religious toleration had its beginnings in the earlier century with the growth of nonconformity in England and the welcoming of persecuted minorities in the United Netherlands and Prussia. But philosophical beliefs penetrated society slowly. One may however suggest four developments which were to help shape the immediate future of the Western world. The first was an economic recession which began after the comparative prosperity of agriculture in the first half of the century. The second was the spread of Freemasonry, a charitable and sociable organization with its own secret rites, which swept over much of the Western world during the second quarter of the century. (The first Grand Lodge, that of England, was founded in 1717.) It attracted members of the aristocracy and of the middle classes and although it was not anti-Christian (even if condemned by the Roman Catholic Church), it facilitated the interchange of philanthropic, liberal and, to some extent, deistic thinking. Benjamin Franklin was a typical Mason, who believed that Masonry promoted good fellowship and mutual assistance; undoubtedly it militated against despotism and intolerance. Thirdly, the destruction of the Society of Jesus, initiated by its expulsion from Portugal by the Marquis of Pombal, largely because he considered that the Jesuits were opposed to his colonial policy, was a blow against the Catholic Church. For whatever faults the Jesuits may have had, they were capable evangelists and promoted the unity of the Catholic Church throughout the western hemisphere by combating subversive movements such as Jansenism. The Popes knew all that well enough, yet Clement XIV allowed himself to be bullied into the complete dissolution of the Society in 1773. Fourthly, by contrast, Protestant evangelism made headway through the emergence of the Wesleyans in England and the 'Great Awakening' in America. Religion was brought to the people, with vast meetings held in the open air. George Whitefield warned the unconverted in his congregations that he would not be surprised to see them 'drop down now, this minute into Hell!' It is said that in America Whitefield and his disciples did more 'to divide and diminish the power of the churches than all the discussions and books of the Masons and Deists combined'. Economic factors, the weakening of the Roman Catholic Church by the suppression of the Jesuits, the drawing together of middle class leaders in the Masonic lodges, and the knowledge that emotional oratory could arouse the masses all contributed significantly to the coming revolutions in the Western world.

16 Western Civilization and Culture in the Eighteenth Century

The high baroque style, which is associated with the names of Francesco Borromini and Giovanni Bernini, came late to the Iberian peninsula and later still to Germany. It has been suggested that the aftermath of the Thirty Years' War and the battle on two fronts against the French and the Turks, delayed the German-speaking peoples from playing a leading part in the history of modern culture until the eighteenth century. But, after that, not only Vienna and Berlin but many German princes with their own palaces and petty courts became notable patrons of the arts. They were receptive to the adaptable high baroque style and to the music that came from Italy. It was not until the end of the seventeenth century that the Germans themselves began to produce fine original symphonies and operas.

Among the most creative German architects were the Asam brothers (Cosmas Damian and Egid Quirin) and the Zimmer-manns (Domenikus and Johann Baptist), who began life as village craftsmen, and Johann Balthazar Neumann, whose career started as an artillery officer in the army of the Bishop of Würzburg. Their achievements were mostly in churches and abbeys rather than in palaces, for the German princes usually hankered after miniature Versailles. The Asams' churches (such as the monastery church at Rohr in Bavaria), Sir Nikolaus Pevsner tells us, were naïve, sticking 'to the more ostentatious devices of optical illusion, out-doing Bernini with their melodramatic effects'. Egid Quirin Asam, who was a sculptor, decided to leave a monument to posterity by building a small church, dedicated to St John of Nepomuk, beside his house in Munich. It has been described by Sir John Summerson as 'a sculptor's fantasia' with a concave-convex-concave rhythm and statues of the Holy Trinity floating above the altar, lit from the top east window. The masterpiece of the Zimmermanns was a pilgrimage church at Wies in Upper Bavaria decorated in white and gold except for an elaborate

259

multi-coloured altar with sculptured figures and a ceiling partly picked out in blue and red.

Neumann was sent to learn architecture, to which he graduated from military engineering, in Paris and Vienna. Though he was only partly responsible for the bishop's new palace at Würzburg, Neumann's most highly praised work, lighter, gayer, more mature and less florid than the art of the Asams and Zimmermanns, was the Cistercian pilgrimage church of the Fourteen Saints in Bavaria with an altar in the middle of the nave and an oval choir. In Sir Nicholas Pevsner's view, it is an architect's architecture, just as the fugue is musicians' music.

Neumann's artistry may be described as rococo (the Fourteen Saints was completed as late as 1772); in fact his employment of spaces and manipulation of light were owed to the baroque tradition, while the light colouring and altar style belong to rococo. There is no precise agreement among art historians over the relationship between baroque and rococo. Some say that

Opposite above: The choir of the pilgrim church at Wies in Upper Bavaria, the work of Domenikus and Johann Baptist Zimmermann.

Above: The chapel of the Residenz, the bishop's palace in Würzburg, the architectural masterpiece of Johann Balthazar Neumann.

rococo was purely a style of interior decoration, some that it was indeed a distinct successor to baroque, and others that rococo is to baroque what the decorated style is to Gothic. Whereas baroque stemmed from Italy, rococo originated in regency France, though it actually received a welcome from Louis xiv before he died. The word rococo derives from the French *rocailles* meaning rockwork. One of its chief characteristics was asymmetry or zigzag work, using such motifs as arabesques, loops, ribbons, arrows, leaves and shell-like formations. On the whole, the use of colour was less brilliant and more delicate than in the baroque style. Its emphasis on conscious artistry in decoration has been said to make it heartless at times.

Though rococo came from Paris and was to some extent a reaction against the Louis xiv classical style, its practitioners in the West were international. Among the artists whose work was essentially rococo Gilles Marie Oppenord was the son of a Dutchman and was trained in Italy, Juste Aurèle Meissonier was born in Turin, and Antoine Watteau, the supreme rococo painter, was by birth a Fleming. In Germany, the three-dimensional curve was the *leit-motif* of rococo and was exemplified particularly by the Zwinger palace built in Dresden for the Elector Augustus (who was also King of Poland). Experts on rococo draw attention especially to the magnificent staircases of the period, such as that in the Bishop of Speir's palace at Bruchsal. Neumann had been instructed to redesign the staircase, which was surmounted by a vast vault lit from many windows, painted with gay frescoes and decorated in stucco. The paintings were by Giambattista Tiepolo, while the stucco work was carried out by Johann Michael Feictmayr, who learned his art in a Bavarian village. Another example of the cosmopolitan character of European art is to be found in Spain. When Carlos ii decided to decorate the Escorial with frescoes he sent for the Italian Luca Giordano, an energetic and showy painter, much to the annoyance of the Spanish practitioners of late baroque. Philip v, being French, naturally sent to Paris for artists, but only one of them, Michel-Ange Houasse, captured the Spanish spirit. Philip's successor, Carlos iii, employed another Italian, Raphael Mengs, who worked in the classical style. Indeed the main factor in the development of Spanish art until the time of Goya was the founding of an academy in the middle of the century to promote culture and train native artists. But broadly it was foreigners, particularly French and Italians, who were the aesthetic leaders in Spain in the eighteenth century.

Thus rococo, like the high baroque, combined many artistic elements, architecture, sculpture, painting, stucco work. Antoine Watteau and Giambattista Tiepolo were its finest painters. Watteau, who was born at Valenciennes in 1684, was tubercular and, like Mozart, died young. He represented a reaction in favour of nature and most of his paintings are set in gardens or parks. His colour was influenced by Rubens and Van Dyck (he paid a short visit to England) and he is most famous for his *fêtes galantes*, though he also painted religious pictures and represented himself as the pale, tragic clown, Gilles. His painting inspired a number of less talented artists, including Jean Baptiste Simeon Chardin, who was considered a realist by Diderot, the voluptuous François Boucher, favourite of Madame de Pompadour, and Jean Honoré Fragonard, the last an able exponent of rococo painting. Tiepolo's decorative style was a fusion of Italian baroque and French rococo: above all, he was a supreme religious artist. Other examples of rococo in Italy were the coloured sculptures of the Sicilian Giacomo Serpotta and the famous Spanish Steps in Rome.

The O'Murphy, Louis xv's girl mistress, as portrayed by François Boucher.

263

Rococo was a style of the salon and of sophisticated living, reflecting the tastes of the petty princes and aristocrats who ruled Europe in the eighteenth century. But it was not the only aristocratic style. Great Britain, for example, never took to either baroque or rococo as enthusiastically as did the Roman Catholic countries. It had its own architectural traditions deriving in particular from Inigo Jones. Sir Christopher Wren, who dominated English architecture until his death in 1723, offered a mild form of baroque, as did his successor, James Gibbs. Possibly Sir John Vanbrugh, who was both a dramatist and architect in the English semi-amateur fashion, with his grandiose style and expansive temperament, came nearest to embracing Italian baroque. Blenheim palace, which the widowed Duchess of Marlborough did not allow him to complete, has towers reminiscent of Borromini. Vanbrugh was no believer in functionalism or even comfort. Pope said of Blenheim: ''tis very fine. But where d'ye sleep, or where d'ye dine?' The kitchen was far from the dining room and, as Pevsner has observed, 'servants may have had to walk a long way, and hot dishes may have got cold before they reached their destination'. However, no shortage of servants prevailed in the eighteenth century.

As early as the reign of George I a reaction set in against baroque in Great Britain. The Scotsman, Colin Campbell, published an illustrated book entitled *Vitruvius Britannicus* expounding classical thought on the subject of architecture, while the third Earl of Burlington collected drawings by Andrea Palladio, the Italian Renaissance architect, and financed a book of drawings by Inigo Jones, edited by Burlington's own protégé, William Kent. Under their influence Palladianism became the rage in aristocratic England. Burlington designed his own house at Chiswick as a free copy of one of Palladio's villas, while Campbell's Wanstead house in Essex belongs to the same genre. One of the main features of the façade of these houses was the classical triangular pediment above the lintel which was supported by Doric or Corinthian columns. It is remarkable, however, that the patrons of architects wanted both a formal Palladian house and an informal English garden of the kind that is associated with the names of William Kent and 'Capability' Brown. According to Horace Walpole, Kent, who helped to plan the magnificent park surrounding Blenheim palace, was the first 'to leap the fence and show the whole of Nature is a garden'. No doubt the combination of formal house and informal garden exemplified English eclecticism or

Monticello, Thomas Jefferson's Virginia home, which he designed on the basis of Palladio's drawings.

even empiricism. The Palladian style in Great Britain reached its apogee with the Georgian squares designed by John Wood and his son. They still survive for the delectation of posterity in Bath and Edinburgh, but Robert Adam's neo-classicism at the Adelphi in London was uprooted for the benefit of twentieth-century commercial profit. The Palladian style crossed the Atlantic, where it was adapted to meet the needs of Virginia by the future President, Thomas Jefferson, who is said to have owned the only copy of Palladio's book in America. From what Jefferson learned of Palladio he designed his own house, Monticello, and the original buildings of the University of Virginia. On the other hand, Mexico and South America preferred baroque where it was the characteristic style of eighteenth-century city churches, monasteries and convents. Four of the finest baroque buildings in the Western world are in Mexico.

In painting as in architecture the British followed a path largely of their own. Although foreign artists were made welcome, such as the two Germans, Godfrey Kneller and Johann Zoffany, one can speak of 'the sudden birth of a genuine English school of painting' in the first half of the eighteenth century. The victories of the first Duke of Marlborough, leading to the satisfactory peace treaties of 1713, the prosperity which grew during the pacific Prime Ministership of Robert Walpole, the ability of the landed

aristocracy to invest their profits from rents and investments in self-glorification, all contributed to the amassing of cultural treasures as well as to the enlightened patronage of painters and sculptors. Walpole himself was a lavish collector. He employed the income he gained from offices and the agents that he had at his disposal in the diplomatic representatives abroad to stock his house of Houghton Hall in Norfolk with many masterpieces. He could write, for example, to the British ambassador in Paris offering £400 for a painting of the Holy Family by Poussin, which Walpole believed to be the highest price ever paid for a picture by that artist. James Brydges, who amassed a fortune out of the office of Paymaster of the Forces in the reign of Queen Anne, possessed four large houses in or near London which he could fill with pictures. Paintings by Rubens, Paolo Veronese and Van Dyck could still be picked up cheaply – in fact Brydges could afford to give away Van Dycks as presents – but he hankered after Michael-angelos and Raphaels as well. One has the impression that some of these patrons of the arts were fairly eclectic in their tastes and since they were often ready to buy speculatively, without even seeing the pictures for which they negotiated, they were sometimes fobbed off with fakes. About native artists, however, they could obtain reliable information. Brydges had his wife's painting done by Kneller for fifty guineas and employed William Kent to decorate his palatial house, Canons.

Portrait painting was naturally the most profitable line for professional artists. A fashionable portrait painter such as Kneller or Joshua Reynolds (as Lely before them) could do extremely well. But other painters were more ambitious. Thomas Gainsborough was possibly influenced by the work of Watteau to undertake open-air painting, while Richard Wilson was persuaded, while on a visit to Venice, to give up portraits in favour of landscape. George Stubbs was extremely skilful in the painting of horses, while William Hogarth, disgusted by what he considered to be the favouritism shown to Italians, turned to his unique commentaries on the social life of his time in paintings which comprised moral lessons elegantly presented, as in *Gin Lane* or *The Rake's Progress*. A market existed for anecdotal or historical paintings. Benjamin West, who was American by birth, made his name with his imaginative painting of *The Death of Wolfe* (1770). Another American history painter, John Singleton Copley, sent over his work for sale in England.

Sir Kenneth Clark has made some fascinating comparisons

Opposite: Portrait of Handel by Thornhill. Born in Germany, he spent most of his adult life working in England, under the patronage of the Hanoverian Court.

between the rococo style and music. He says that some of the qualities of eighteenth-century music – its melodious flow, its complex symmetry, its decorative invention – are reflected in contemporary architecture, but not its deeper appeal to the emotions. He links the music of Johann Sebastian Bach with the baroque interiors of Dutch painters and the music of Handel with the architecture of Neumann. Bach of course was a universal genius, though he was better known in his lifetime not as a composer, but as a virtuoso of the organ, and he was also overshadowed at the time by Georg Philipp Telemann. Much of his finest music in chorales, cantatas and oratorios is religious. We now see him as the greatest artist ever produced by the Lutheran Church and his achievement was in the Lutheran tradition, for Luther himself composed and sang. George Frederick Handel was not a universal genius like Bach, but was a brilliant child of his age and probably had a happier and more profitable career than Bach. He did not lack astuteness. Like Bach, he began as an organist. When he visited Dietrich Buxtehude, another considerable musician, at Lübeck, it has been related that he was offered the succession to the post if he undertook to marry the organist's twelve-year-old daughter. But 'thinking this too great an honour', he quickly returned to Hamburg where Telemann was to make a name for himself. Later Handel left Hamburg to seek his fortune in England under Hanoverian patronage.

Handel wrote many operas of which his first, *Rinaldo*, was written in Hanover and was thought to be his best. The numerous operas that he wrote after he became a naturalized British subject in 1726 never really caught on at the time in London. More interest attached in London society to the rivalry of two Italian singers, Cuzzoni and Faustina, whom Handel pitted against one another. The Royal Academy of Music, which was created to encourage the opera, quickly went into a decline. It has been suggested that operas, whose libretto was in a foreign language, were seldom successful in the eighteenth century. That was why Handel failed, while Gay's light entertainment, *The Beggar's Opera*, with music selected from old English melodies, was a striking success. Handel then turned to the oratorios which earned him an enduring reputation.

In the mid-eighteenth century Handel dominated English music and it was a long time indeed before there was another great native English composer to follow in the footsteps of Henry Purcell and gain an international reputation. The English were

more famous as patrons than as composers. Johann Mattheson, who was himself a composer, then wrote: 'The Italians exalt music; the French enliven it; the Germans strive after it; and the English pay for it well.' The patterns of German music were set by the Italians, notably by Alessandro Scarlatti. Dresden, Berlin and Vienna were the leading musical centres in eighteenth-century Germany. Bach used to take his favourite son to Dresden to hear Italian opera; Frederick the Great revived the opera in Berlin and was said by a contemporary to perform 'the part of director-general as much as of generalissimo in the field'. In Vienna the Emperor Charles VI and his daughter, Queen Maria Theresa, were keen patrons of music. The father conducted and the daughter sang. Christoph Gluck's dramatic *Orfeo*, performed in Vienna in 1762, changed the direction of opera and had a deep historical importance. Dr Charles Burney, a prolific writer on music, thought that of all the German towns Vienna was 'most

William Hogarth's painting of a scene from John Gay's *Beggar's Opera*, first performed in 1728.

269

remarkable for its fire and invention'. By the end of the century Vienna was unquestionably the greatest musical centre in the Western world. When the infant prodigy, Wolfgang Amadeus Mozart, played the piano at the Court of Vienna in his seventh year, it was a presage of glories to come.

Eighteenth-century French music, like English painting, had a character of its own. French musicians who visited Italy were surprised that concertos had no solo violin parts, that ballets were not included in operas, that dancing consisted mostly of high jumps and that the Italians maintained the voice of boy sopranos by a barbarous operation. French operas eschewed long dry recitatives; Dr Burney, who was pro-Italian, wrote that 'the French voice never comes further than from the throat'. French music was clear, neat and precise. Rousseau (by birth a Genevan) thought that it lacked strict time and melody. Indeed he asserted that the French had no music and never could have it. Jean Philippe Rameau, perhaps the greatest French composer of the century, paid only a brief visit to Italy and in his operas, the first of which was *Hippolyte et Aricie* (1733), he deliberately departed from conventional Italian forms by strengthening harmony. His operas met adverse criticism from the followers of Jean Baptiste Lully (Louis XIV's favourite musician, who was an Italian by birth) and from Rousseau. Rameau, for his part, thought poorly of the articles on music which Rousseau contributed to the *Encyclopédie*. But perhaps Rousseau may be said to have had the last word, since the Parisians found Rameau rather heavy going, while Rousseau's own opera *Le Devin de Village* (1752) was welcomed as melodious and charming. Spectacular opera remained in vogue in Italy: Venice had four opera houses and Naples three. On the other hand, in England the great Dr Johnson pronounced that opera was 'an extravagant and irrational entertainment'. So opera varied in character from country to country, but it appears that after the middle of the eighteenth century a general reaction took place in favour of lighter or comic operas. In 1770 Dr Burney watched the *Comédiens ordinaires du roi* performing comic opera in Paris where the audience hissed 'as much mixed with horse laughs', he wrote, 'as ever I heard at Drury Lane or Covent Garden'. In Milan he saw 'the opera buffo or dramma giocoso' since serious opera was put on there only at carnival time. In fact on this tour of Europe most of the best music he heard was performed in churches. Light opera had become the fashion in the theatre. Even Mozart's operas were later to be regarded as heavy.

Opposite: French rococo painting: Antoine Watteau's *Harlequin and Columbine*.

On the whole, eighteenth-century art was aristocratic. Except in England, where concerts in Vauxhall Gardens, for example, were open to all who could afford to pay the price for admission, the public concert scarcely existed. Music was performed in large churches, in small theatres and, above all, in the private houses of the nobility or at Courts. In Hamburg, which has been called the cradle of German opera, the ordinary public were allowed into the theatre, but by contrast Lady Mary Wortley Montagu, the widely travelled daughter of an eccentric millionaire, described how early in the century in Vienna the operas were performed in the open air with the stage built over a canal; the royal family alone was provided with a canopy and the opera had to stop when it rained. Opera, then as now, was extremely expensive and had to be subsidised by kings and princes. Only in Leipzig was music easily accessible to the ordinary citizen. The performances at the opera house there took place at the time of the annual fair, but in 1743 a regular 'Grand Concert' was established by public-spirited nobles and merchants, which had considerable success. But, broadly, as Dr Lindsay has written, 'one characteristic common to the musical life of all princely capitals was that the concerts and operatic performances were private entertainments given by a prince for his guests'. At the other end of the scale European peasants had their own folk songs and dances, performed in village greens or taverns, though church music was available to them in Roman Catholic, Greek Orthodox and Lutheran countries.

One may reflect that in spite of the growth of scepticism about orthodox religion which was prevalent, say, at the Courts of Peter the Great and Frederick the Great, and despite the deism which was becoming common, at any rate in intellectual circles in France and England, the Christian religion remained the most important direct influence on music in the first half of the eighteenth century. Organ music, it has been said, was one of the means by which ordinary men and women 'could enter the world of spiritualized emotion' and organs themselves were 'expressions of municipal pride and independence' and were often built by local craftsmen. Big organs, such as that at the Groote Kerke in Haarlem, decorated with cupids and other symbolic statues, were a physical link between music and architecture. Baroque and rococo church architecture was intended to arouse the religious emotions of the faithful in the days of heretics and sceptics. As Pevsner has written, 'To restore the first to the fold, to convince the others, religious architecture had both to inflame and to mesmerize.' Just as the first half

Opposite: Italian rococo painting: *The Banquet of Anthony and Cleopatra* by Giambattista Tiepolo.

of the eighteenth century saw the building of vast monasteries and towering churches throughout southern Germany and Austria, so too two outstanding composers, Bach and Handel, began their careers as organists and were responsible for a tremendous output of religious music of all kinds. Not only these two men of genius but lesser lights, such as Telemann and George Gebel the elder, poured out cantatas, settings of the Passion and oratorios. In England the Reverend Arthur Bedford in a tract called *The Great Abuse of Music* (1711) complained of the loss of ancient church music since the deaths of Purcell and Dr John Blow; Handel may be said to have redressed the balance, for he learned from Purcell how to use simple means to achieve massive effects. His stream of oratorios, culminating in his famous *Messiah* of 1743, was well calculated to stir religious emotions, as much as Wesley and Whitefield did by their oratory.

If music, especially organ music, appealed to the masses, domestic architecture reflected the changing tastes of the ruling classes. French classical architecture of the reign of Louis XIV, as exemplified in the rebuilt Louvre of Perrault and, to a lesser extent, in the palace of Versailles, represented the grandeur of the authoritarian state. Rococo was warmer, lighter and less redolent of responsibility and certainly constituted a reaction against Colbert's and Le Brun's methods of pleasing their master. It could, no doubt, be claimed that rococo was too playful and too irrespons- ible, that it reflected the light-mindedness of the privileged French nobility who were to perish on the guillotine. One may perhaps even compare the palace of Versailles, built for Louis XIV, with the Petit Trianon, so much prettier and more charming, which was built for Louis XV. By contrast the British aristocracy with their love for Palladianism created an air of social permanence and political security; they built their palaces and country houses, confident that their descendants would dwell in them proudly, undisturbed by revolutionaries.

However, all such speculations about the relations between art and society are dangerous and can no doubt be disproved by specific instances. But what is fairly certain is that by the middle of the eighteenth century rococo vanished, quite suddenly, after the death of Neumann in 1753. 'Between Neumann's world and that of Goethe', writes Pevsner, 'there is no link.' Classicism or neo-classicism, whose triumph culminated in Napoleonic France, took the place of baroque. In 1756 the Italian Giovanni Battista Piranesi published his book *Le Antichità Romane* and urged that

Roman architecture was the best. In Germany, on the other hand, the influential art historian Johann Winckelmann advocated a return to Greek ideals. He wrote his books in Dresden and later in Rome and never went to Greece at all. In fact no one knew very much about either classical Greek architecture or sculpture, although two British architects produced weighty volumes on the *Antiquities of Greece* in 1762 which were preceded in France by Le Roi's shorter *Ruines de Grèce* of 1758. In England it was ingeniously suggested that Greek and Roman architecture stemmed from the Etruscan, which antedated both. When Josiah Wedgwood established his potteries in Staffordshire in the 1770s he was inspired to manufacture Etruscan vases and to name his own works Etruria. The controversies between Romanists, Grecophiles and the Etruscan party waxed furious in the 1760s and 1770s and paved the way for romanticism. The ancient Greeks and Romans were republicans; Brutus assassinated the authoritarian Caesar. If one wishes to draw parallels between artistic trends and political history, one can argue that the wave of republicanism that swept over the Western world during the last quarter of the eighteenth century was symbolized in revolutionary neo-classical art which reached its peak in the French painter Jacques Louis David's dramatic pictures that proved equally pleasing to the triumphant republicans and to Napoleon Bonaparte.

17 Two Young Giants: Russia and North America 1763-75

Though Great Britain and France remained the two richest and most influential kingdoms in the Western world, by the third quarter of the eighteenth century can be discerned, at any rate by hindsight, the rise of two young giants who were to become dominant two hundred years later – the Russian empire and the United States of America. Under Peter the Great Russia had begun to expand both to the west and to the south and the Tsar had first become fully conscious of the possibility of his empire emerging stronger and more important through the study of Western technology and the adoption of the latest military techniques. His daughter Elizabeth (who reigned from 1741 to 1762) has perhaps been underestimated as a monarch, for she honestly attempted to fulfil the programme drawn up by her father. Not only did she secure the western frontier of her empire by defeating the Swedes, vainly seeking revenge, but she promoted education and literature at home; the first Russian university, at Moscow, was founded during her reign. The error that she committed, however, was to allow her country to become involved in a long and pointless war against Prussia, which was of no future advantage whatsoever and from which the Russians eventually withdrew. But the glory of the Romanovs – and Elizabeth was in fact the last of them but one – was symbolized by the magnificent palaces built for her by her favourite architect, the Italian Bartholomeo Francesco Rastrelli, who designed or redesigned a Summer Palace and a Winter Palace (the latter completed in 1762) as well as the Tsarkoe Selo Palace just outside the city of St Petersburg, all of vast length – the palace of Tsarkoe Selo being notable for its Corinthian pillars picked out in gold and decorated in the rococo style.

Elizabeth was the beautiful though poorly educated daughter of Catherine I, the peasant girl from Livonia, who for two years had carried on her husband's rule. Not being unduly impressed

by blue blood, Elizabeth chose as a wife for her son, the future Peter III, the lively daughter of an obscure German prince, who was to become Catherine II. Catherine arrived in Russia during 1744 when she was only fourteen and was married in August 1745. She was a girl devoured by ambition and had benefited from a useful practical education. She had travelled widely in Germany and met Frederick the Great before she settled down in St Petersburg. Her tutors had been mainly French Huguenots. She quickly taught herself Russian and entered the Orthodox Church. Her favourite amusements were riding horses and making love. The Tsarina Elizabeth came to suspect that Catherine and her mother were Prussian spies, and the statesman Alexis Bestuzhev-Ryumin, a secretive and ruthless character, was instructed to keep a close watch on Catherine. What Elizabeth wanted above all was a grandson, but after ten years of marriage Catherine was still childless; it was not her fault, for her husband was impotent. However, she met the need by giving birth to the future Tsar Paul, whose father was a handsome Russian courtier (though which one is not entirely clear) belonging to the earliest but not the first of Catherine's string of lovers. She afterwards declared that if her husband had only loved her, she would have remained faithful to him. But she was unable to live without love.

Tsarkoe Selo Palace, built outside St Petersburg for the Tsarina Elizabeth by her favourite Italian architect, Bartholomeo Francesco Rastrelli. From a contemporary engraving.

277

When as a result of a palace revolution in 1763 Catherine was recognized as empress and her husband was assassinated a week later she soon proved herself at the age of thirty-three to be a superb administrator and diplomatist. During the forty-four years that had elapsed since the death of Peter the Great his projected domestic reforms had been largely abandoned, the nobility relieved of their obligations to serve the state, and an economic decline had set in; for example, the output of iron, which had been one of Russia's principal exports, had fallen off. At first Catherine was obliged to feel her way cautiously, but she resisted the claim of the leading Russian nobles, headed by Nikolas Panin, that she should govern as the figurehead of an oligarchy. She was compelled to cope with a number of plots against her by groups of conspirators, who backed other claimants to the throne or pretended to be claimants themselves. She also had to overcome the opposition of the Archbishop of Rostov, whom she nicknamed Andrew the Babbler, and who abused and excommunicated her when she stood by her murdered husband's decision to sequester ecclesiastical lands and to reaffirm that the Church was a department of state.

It is clear that at the beginning of her reign Catherine seriously considered introducing new liberalizing reforms such as universal education and municipal self-government. She was a voracious reader and a voluminous writer – indeed she not only wrote thousands of letters but composed plays and satires and produced articles for magazines as well as dabbling in history. Her reading included Sir William Blackstone, the English lawyer, and Georges-Louis Buffon, the French naturalist, and Voltaire as well as Montesquieu and Beccaria, whose theories about constitutional and legal changes she absorbed. In December 1766 she summoned a big elected commission to meet in St Petersburg with a view to drawing up a new Russian code of laws; and she wrote instructions for it principally embodying the ideas of Montesquieu and Beccaria. But though there was a lot of talk, nothing was done; after a year and a half the commission was suspended indefinitely. The only positive achievements during the first years of Catherine's reign were the setting up of one or two model schools and a behest to the women of upper-class Russia to improve their manners. Although Russian historians are not agreed about this, the impression one receives is that Catherine learned from painful experience that it was difficult to westernize her Russian subjects quickly: she therefore came to prefer a more practical approach.

Opposite: The Tsar Peter III with his wife, who was to rule Russia as Catherine the Great, and her son, the future Tsar Paul. Portrait painted in 1756 by Rosine Mathieu.

278

The state of Poland in 1773. This allegorical print shows Catherine the Great of Russia, Joseph II of Austria and Frederick II of Prussia, each indicating the portion of Poland they propose to take.

She acquiesced in most of the nobility being relieved of their obligations to the state; she allowed the serfs, who constituted half the population of Russia, to be further degraded: their masters were permitted not merely to flog them but to punish them for offences in other ways – from 1765 they could send them to do forced labour in Siberia; and she gave up efforts at internal reforms in order to pursue an aggressive foreign policy.

The Russian government's main expansionist aims were

twofold: first, to extend the boundaries of the empire westward beyond the rivers Dvina, Sozh and Dnieper, which would provide it with frontiers protected by broad rivers against an enemy advance eastwards; secondly, to gain access to the Black Sea, which would be not only a military but also a commercial advantage. To fulfil the first purpose required the seizure of part of the eastern territories of Poland-Lithuania. Ever since the time of Peter the Great Poland had been, if not a Russian protectorate, strongly under the influence of its increasingly powerful neighbour. The Russians possessed a perpetual pretext for intervening in Poland because of their anxiety to support members of the Greek Orthodox Church, some of whom were Russians, against the Roman Catholic majority despite the Polish-Lithuanian agreement between the Orthodox and Roman Catholics embodied in the native Uniate church. Russia's policy was to obtain toleration for all 'dissenters' in Poland. Moreover, it was to the Russian interest to keep Poland weak. In fact the Saxon kings of Poland – Augustus II and Augustus III – were unable, much as they might have wished to do so, to win centralized autocratic control over the so-called Commonwealth. Thus it was accepted that Poland must remain an 'oligarchic anarchy' rather than an autocratic or even constitutional monarchy. Catherine II reckoned that the Polish constitution, which sanctioned the anarchy, must be maintained. An army of thirty thousand Russian soldiers was kept on the Polish borders to impress the Tsarina's strength on her neighbour; the Russian ambassador at Warsaw was able to exert enormous influence; and from 1717 no attempts had been made by the Polish Seym (or Parliament) to reform the constitution or to contravene Russian demands for limiting the size of the royal Polish army.

If in order to expand westwards the Russians were obliged to terrify, fight or subdue the Poles, to reach the Black Sea they had to confront the Turks. Although neither the Janissaries nor the Spahis were what they had once been, the Turks could still command formidable armies. Their supremacy stretched from Bosnia in the western Balkans to the frontiers of Persia. Although defeated by the Austrians at the end of the seventeenth century, they in turn had defeated the Russians under Peter the Great, the Venetians, and the Austrians during the reign of the Emperor Charles VI. They had regained Azov from Russia and much of Serbia and Hungary from Austria. They resented the Russian domination of Poland, which threatened their position in the

Balkans and they were most reluctant to relax their grip on the Black Sea.

Catherine II's foreign policy, like her domestic policy, vacillated. At first she contemplated withdrawing into glorious isolation, which she thought would enable Russia to exert its influence without prior commitments. Her adviser Panin, on the other hand, adumbrated a scheme for a northern alliance consisting of a number of relatively small powers which Russia could lead and which would act as a balancing force against the Roman Catholic countries of France and Austria. The only result of this scheme was that in April 1764 a defensive treaty was signed between Russia and Prussia by which it was agreed that they should support one another in the event of an attack by a third party. More important from the Russian point of view was that Catherine was committed to consulting Frederick the Great over her policy in relation to Sweden and Poland. Thus Russia ceased to have a free hand in Poland because of the treaty and Frederick was able ultimately to link western Pomerania with east Prussia by way of Polish Prussia.

Before that treaty was signed Catherine succeeded in removing the son of Augustus III of Poland from the duchy of Courland and replacing him by a Russian nominee, thus reinforcing the Russian frontier to the north-west. Secondly, after the treaty was signed, she persuaded Frederick to let her nominate one of her numerous lovers, Stanislas Poniatowski, to succeed Augustus III (who died in October 1763) to the Polish throne. Stanislas was a native Polish nobleman (or *piast*) and though he conducted himself cautiously he did not in fact prove to be a mere Russian puppet. To secure the 'free election' of Stanislas Russian troops were moved into Poland, while the Russians did what they could to extend their influence there by demanding concessions for their fellow-religionists and for other dissenters and by ensuring that no attempt was made to overhaul the anarchic Polish constitution. Finally, it proved necessary in order to secure liberties for non-Catholics, to station more troops on the Polish frontier and to send a force to the Polish capital. After that, the Polish Seym was obliged to agree to a treaty with Russia whereby Catherine was recognized as the protector of the Polish constitution and political rights were conferred on religious dissenters. This treaty, signed in February 1768, did not please Frederick the Great at all. It was obviously a breach of the spirit of the earlier Russo-Prussian treaty of alliance.

In her Polish policy Catherine had in fact to choose between two alternatives: either she could try to make Poland into a Russian protectorate or she could come to an agreement with her neighbours, Prussia and Austria, to partition Poland between them. The idea of partition was a commonplace of eighteenth-century diplomacy. The Spanish empire had been partitioned in 1713, while part of the Persian empire had been partitioned between the Russians and the Turks in 1724. The partition of the weak and ill-governed Polish Commonwealth had long been foreseen. It was, in fact, Austria which made the first intervention when in 1769 Austrian troops seized the territory of Zips, which was an enclave into Hungary. It is not absolutely certain who was responsible for setting the negotiations on foot; apparently a light-hearted suggestion by the Russian Tsarina was taken up with enthusiasm by Frederick the Great's brother, Prince Henry, when on a visit to St Petersburg. A pretext for intervention was presented soon after the signature of the Russo-Polish treaty when a group of anti-Russian nationalists had been constituted into what was known as the confederacy of Bar (in Podolia in southern Poland) which determined upon a nationalist resistance movement by means of guerrilla warfare and also sought constitutional reforms. Similar confederacies sprang up elsewhere and by the end of 1769 a General Confederacy was formed. But it failed to win foreign support (though incited by the French, who sent a military mission to give it advice) and the Russians were able to intervene on behalf of the Polish King to defend the 'evil old constitution', and to restore order. Nevertheless the Russian troops did not find the going smooth; though they were able to capture towns, they were harassed in the countryside. Moreover the Turks, who had earlier promised to aid the Poles, were provoked by frontier incidents into declaring war on the Russians.

Although the Russians won victories over the Turks both in the Balkans and in the Crimea, the war lasted for nearly five years. The Russians possessed capable generals and trained soldiers, but they had to cope with the continuing Polish rebellion, with the Turks and Turkish allies in the Crimea, and with an internal rising, headed by the Don Cossack, Emelyan Pugachev, who in 1773 captured many towns on the Volga and in the Urals. Pugachev first allied himself with the Tartars and other non-Russian subjects in the south, but in 1774 the revolt of the Cossacks and nomads was transformed into a peasant war. Catherine was obliged to divert soldiers from other fronts to put down the rising.

It was not until the beginning of 1775 that Pugachev was captured and executed in Moscow. Catherine was never to forget the fright that Pugachev gave her.

The rebellion, together with the war against the Turks which brought a terrible plague across the frontiers into Russia in 1771 and spread from the south-west as far as Moscow, killing a hundred thousand people, combined to persuade the Tsarina that she could not act on her own; she therefore agreed to divide up a large part of Poland with the Prussians and Austrians. The Poles were unable to resist the threats from three great military powers. The Polish Seym was compelled to surrender about two-sevenths of the Commonwealth's territory and five-twelfths of its population. Russia occupied White Russia, to which some ethnic claims could be made; Prussia took the area lying between eastern Pomerania and East Prussia and, further to the east, Ermeland, and the Austrians received a large part of Galicia. Frederick the Great observed of Queen Maria Theresa 'the more she wept for Poland, the more she took of it'.

Two years after the treaty of partition was signed the Russo-Turkish war came to an end. By the treaty of Kutchuk-Kainardji (July 1774) the Crimea, hitherto under Turkish suzerainty, was declared independent, Kerch and Yenikale, to the east of the Crimea, were surrendered to the Russians, who also obtained Azov, Kunam and Terek to the north of the Caucasus. Furthermore the Tsarina was given the right to protect the Christians in Moldavia (part of modern Romania), while the Sultan promised in general terms not to persecute his Christian subjects. Thus Catherine not only attained her immediate ends, but the disruption of Poland and the treaty with the Turks afforded her the opportunity for further territorial gains after her empire recovered from eight years of armed exertions.

One may notice how these events in eastern Europe had comparatively little effect upon the west. It is true that the French had long thought of themselves as the allies of the Poles. For a time Louis xv's father-in-law, Stanislas Leszczynski, had been King of Poland until he was compensated for the loss of his throne by being made Duke of Lorraine in 1736. But the French rulers came to realize, after the abortive war of the Polish succession in 1733, that the country was too far distant for them to do more than exert intellectual, cultural and diplomatic influence in eastern Europe. In fact their efforts to stir up trouble for Russia in Poland and Turkey met with comparatively little success. In 1766 after the death of Stanislas Lorraine became part of France; in 1769 the French bought the island of Corsica from the Genoese Republic; and from 1763 onwards under the influence of the Duke of Choiseul and Charles Gravier, Count of Vergennes the French were preparing for a war of revenge against Great Britain because of their humiliating defeat in the Seven Years' War. The British, especially during the short ministry of William Pitt, Earl of Chatham, in 1766, tried to find allies in case of a possible new war with France in Russia and Prussia, but they were rebuffed. For the overriding concern of these governments was Poland. There seemed to be no common interests between Eastern and Western great powers at the time.

As for Catherine II, who was henceforward to be known as the Great, she had through her brilliant diplomacy and her ability to find good ministers and generals, as well as to sustain large armies and fleets, successfully carried on the foreign policy of her predecessor, Peter the Great. Russia now ruled the eastern Baltic, could dominate Finland, withstand the Swedes and the Turks, and extend the frontiers of its empire westward and southward. Catherine II, however, had been obliged to abandon the policy of seeking to make Poland into a protectorate (a policy which was later to be resumed by both Tsar Alexander and the Soviet Union) and she had been driven to neglect internal reforms. Henceforward her attitude was essentially autocratic. That is why she was to sympathize with the British during the war of American independence and to dislike the French revolutionaries who reminded her forcibly of the peasant followers of Pugachev and of the Polish rebels.

With Catherine [wrote Sir Bernard Pares], we go a great step further in the glaring contrast between Russia at home and Russia abroad, a contrast which led and was meant to lead to a complete mystification of Europe as to the realities in Russia. It is the monstrously unequal march of a great giant, whose one leg is sinking further and further into the morass created by serfdom, while the other stretches further and further afield to cover new territory and to meet new problems with which the Russian government is increasingly incompetent to deal.

Besides Russia the other young giant that could be discerned in the 1760s was British North America. 'It had become a young giant', observes Professor Lawrence Gipson, 'as a result of the extraordinarily favourable conditions under which it had been permitted to flourish.' But it had not yet emerged as a nation. At the end of the Seven Years' War the thirteen disparate colonies formed a part of the British empire. Though the population of Great Britain was only eight million, its government ruled over a bigger empire than that of the Russians, the French, the Spaniards, the Portuguese or the Dutch. Because of recent victories over the French the way was cleared for the subjection of the whole of India to the British Raj; the British also controlled valuable parts of the west coast of Africa; and, above all, their sway covered North America from Hudson Bay to east Florida. They possessed the largest fleets in the world and owned many essential naval bases from Minorca in the Mediterranean to Port Royal in Jamaica. Great Britain at that time has been compared with ancient Athens both in its naval strength and in its wide-flung colonies, built upon commerce and protected from the sea. Yet this empire had been acquired, at any rate until the days of William Pitt, more or less in a fit of absence of mind. British Governments possessed no clearly formulated ideas about the future of imperial government nor did they think merely in terms of economic exploitation. Any difficulties with which they were faced perplexed rather than angered them.

The thirteen North American colonies that existed in 1763 formed a unique part of this growing empire. They contained over two million inhabitants of which the bulk were white Europeans (perhaps there were some 350,000 black slaves). Most of the colonists were pioneers whose aim was to get rich quickly. Thus in so far as class distinctions were to be found at all in North America they were based on wealth rather than lineage. In effect all men – except for the slaves – were equal before the law; Jack was as good as his master and was anxious to make himself better. On the western frontier only ability and enterprise counted. American women, who performed invaluable services for the economy, were freer and more independent than those in the Old World.

In 1763 this community was already becoming rich. In New England industry as well as agriculture was flourishing. For example, a shipbuilding industry was successfully established. American sailing ships were constructed from native oak and white pine. Naval stores, such as pitch, tar and cordage, which Great Britain had previously imported from the Baltic countries, were in abundant supply and constant demand. It cost half as much to build a ship in New England as it did in Old England. Americans also employed the ships which they built to develop a fishing industry that comprised the catching not merely of cod and mackerel but also of whales. An iron industry had also grown up, centred in Pennsylvania, which benefited from unlimited supplies of iron ore and of hardwood from which charcoal was made. Rum manufacture was also an expanding trade, the potent alcohol being distilled from molasses imported cheaply from the West Indies; Boston was the chief producer of American rum. The southern colonies still relied on the sale of tobacco, rice and indigo, while the middle colonies did a huge trade in provisions, exporting biscuits, flour and barrels of beef and pork as well as wheat and timber. The high standard of living enjoyed by southern planters was mainly financed from Great Britain which handled their products for resale. Thomas Jefferson estimated that Virginia, which was twice the size of England, owed two to three million pounds of private debt to Great Britain at the time when the war of independence began.

The growing wealth, the rising population, which doubled every twenty-five years, the cheapness of land, and the sense of golden opportunities to be grasped combined to make the American colonists reasonably satisfied with their lot so long as they were left to look after their own business. But many of the colonists were not English; some, like the Irish, hated the English, yet the prevalence of the English language and the English common law gave a feeling of belonging to a distinctive Western community. Between 1763 and 1775 over forty newspapers were published, ranging from the *Boston News-Letter* to the *Virginia Gazette* and these helped to create an American public opinion. John Adams may have exaggerated when he claimed that 'the revolution was in the minds of the people' before it actually began, but certainly the concept of American independence and to a lesser extent the idea of Union were in the minds of many people during the decade after the end of the Seven Years' War.

This growing sense of Americanism was one of the long-term causes of the war for independence. So was a consciousness of economic and fiscal grievances. The northern colonies were annoyed by the restrictions imposed upon their commerce and industry. Americans were, for instance, forbidden to manufacture hats and they were not supposed to buy sugar directly from the French, Dutch or Spanish West Indies: the Molasses Act of 1733 introduced prohibitive duties on the import of their sugar. Duties were also levied on imports from Great Britain, though these were not onerous and did not even cover the salaries of customs officers. The southern colonies disliked the 'enumeration' clauses of the British navigation acts which meant that nearly all the principal exports might be sent to Europe only by way of England, thus giving the British importers a monopoly; furthermore European and East Indian goods had to be imported into North America via Great Britain or in British ships. Most of these restrictions were in fact evaded in one way or another. When in 1761 an attempt was made to put an end to smuggling by the use of writs of assistance, which were in effect general warrants allowing customs officers to search suspected premises, James Otis of Massachusetts claimed that 'the navigation acts' were 'a taxation law made by a foreign legislature without our consent', that they could not be reconciled with the colonial charters, and that they violated the laws of nature. Though the court allowed the writs to be issued, they proved ineffective. Smugglers were heroes, not villains.

Finally too sharp a contrast should not be drawn between the situation before and after the accession of George III in 1760. The 'salutary neglect' of the American colonies, which was practised by the Whig governments of Walpole and the Pelhams during the first half of the eighteenth century, was not without its limitations and irritations. The Privy Council could and did veto colonial legislation; the British Parliament could and did try to tighten the laws dealing with commercial relations; the King nominated the governors and councils of eight out of thirteen colonies (Pennsylvania, Delaware and Maryland were still proprietory colonies, while Connecticut and Rhode Island as corporate colonies appointed their own governors). But as James Henretta has shown in a recent book, British politicians and society ladies jockeyed for the right to nominate office-holders in America from governors to naval officers stationed there. Giving sinecures in the colonies was one means of solving delicate political problems at home. It was Robert Walpole who started the rot; the Pelhams, writes Henretta, 'inherited an inefficient and corrupt system when they came to office in 1742; they did not create it'. The conferring of patronage in colonial offices was thus one of the principal factors in Anglo-American relations, and in the eighteenth century patronage was power.

Such was the background. What happened after the signature of the treaty of Paris in 1763, which enabled Great Britain to acquire the whole of Canada, to extend the settlements in North America, from the Atlantic to the left bank of the Mississippi (except for New Orleans) and to transform Florida, formerly Spanish, into a part of the British empire? In the first place, direct threats to the security of the North American settlers had been removed. It has been said that until then the armed holdings of the French had half-encircled the British colonies 'as with a jagged scythe'. The military history of North America during the first half of the eighteenth century was mainly one of contests with the French and pro-French Indians immediately south of Canada and along the Ohio. American historians have questioned whether in fact the removal of pressures from the French in the north or the Spaniards in the south materially influenced Anglo-American relations. It has been suggested that although one or two foreign observers, such as the Swede Peter Kalm, predicted that once the French menace was removed from the frontiers the colonists would no longer need to rely on British military or naval power but would quarrel with the British as soon as they felt inclined to do so, American public opinion was not much moved by that consideration. But even if it cannot be conclusively proved, one can hardly doubt that the American sense of mission or of manifest destiny was enhanced, that with the removal at any rate of the French threat Americans began to feel that nothing could now impede their western expansion. The great British historian, Sir Lewis Namier, has quoted a letter written from New York in December 1759 by the brother of a member of the British Parliament in which he said:

If at the peace we can retain Cape Breton, Crown Point, Oswego, Niagara and Pittsburg we shall secure the frontiers and engross the fur and fish trade. Many are of the opinion that occupying this barrier would be of more advantage than actually possessing all Canada, as the colonies would then be under no restraint, more difficult to be managed, and might push trades detrimental to Great Britain, while the poorer sort of inhabitants, having nothing to fear, would retire far into the woods, free from the Government, rent or taxes, where they could raise and manufacture everything for their own use, without consuming anything from Britain, or being of the least benefit to that country.

Sir Lewis commented that it was to the honour of British statesmen that they took no notice of warnings that the removal of the presence of the French, which acted as a check on the colonies, would pave the way to independence.

Secondly, public-spirited Americans began to realize during the French and Indian war that a case could be made out for colonial union. In 1754, on the eve of the war, Benjamin Franklin, who had been appointed American Postmaster-General, advocated uniting the colonies in a federation and urged through the newspapers: 'join or die'. He believed that this would not only be a means of resisting the attacks of the French and Indians in war, but could also be a guarantee of prosperity in peace. The idea was that the King should appoint a governor-general to take care of immediate matters of defence, while a council of representatives from each colony should deal with questions of general defence, relations with the Indians, and taxation, thus anticipating confederation. A conference actually met at Albany in 1754 to draw up proposals and received the approval of the Governor of Massachusetts. But as a whole the scheme was welcomed neither in America nor in Great Britain. In America the existing assemblies did not wish to sacrifice their independence, while in Great Britain it was feared that such a colonial union, however valuable in time of war, might be damaging to British interests during peace. Yet in spite of the failure of the Albany Congress, a sense of inter-colonial solidarity began to develop.

Another thought in American minds was the recognition that the colonists no longer needed to depend for their security on British professional soldiers. The humiliating defeat of General Edward Braddock in 1755 made a deep impression in Virginia. Was not young George Washington quite as good an officer? During the war amateur soldiers from more than one colony – such as the Virginians and North Carolinans – had fought victoriously side by side. So Americans came to believe in voluntary rather than aristocratic or conscripted armies. The Americans, it has often been said, are a military but not a militaristic people. After the war was over North America possessed many battle-hardened veterans who would be found capable of fighting for their own rights.

A question that was cognate to this was the cost of defence. The British had undertaken to reimburse the American colonies for their expenditure upon the war. This they did and consequently the North American colonies got rid of public debts which had mounted during the hostilities. On the other hand, the British public debt increased to nearly a hundred and fifty million pounds. George Grenville, who became Prime Minister in April 1763, determined that it was his duty to limit future government expenditure. Of Grenville it has been said that 'his mind had no great depth, his speeeches no eloquence, his methods no finesse'.

He was, nevertheless, stubborn. The contemporary Spanish ambassador in London observed he 'would lose all he has in the world rather than suffer diminution of the honour of the King his master or of the commerce of the kingdom'. Members of the British Parliament were by now deeply concerned over finance and trade so that when Grenville proposed that in order to maintain a standing army of ten thousand men to police North America the colonists should be asked to contribute a third of its cost, about £360,000 a year, no opposition was aroused. An act which took effect from 1765 introducing a stamp duty upon American newspapers and official documents, however, met with the disapproval of the Earl of Chatham and of other British statesmen, while in America, although it was admitted that the financial burden was small and even John Adams agreed that the British Parliament had taxed the colonists for a hundred years, an uproar arose over questions of principle. 'No taxation without representation' was the battle-cry, first to be heard in Virginia. Was not such internal taxation the thin edge of the wedge? Patrick Henry, a Virginian lawyer, tabled four resolutions in the Virginian assembly. In the course of his supporting speech he declared: 'Tarquin and Julius had their Brutus, Charles had his Cromwell', and he did not doubt that some good American would stand up in favour of his country.

George Grenville was popular neither with the King, whose influence on politics he tried to restrict, nor with his ministerial colleagues. He attempted to offset his own unpopularity by putting public finances in order and by reducing the land tax. He therefore carried through wholesale economies on the army and navy and a scheme for cutting down the floating debt. His treatment of the American colonies was a byproduct of his general policy. Besides the Stamp Act, he introduced a Sugar Act, increased the number of 'enumerated articles' which the colonies had to export via Great Britain, and published a proclamation on the western frontier. The Molasses Act of 1733 had been so widely evaded in America that it was virtually a dead letter. Grenville lowered the tax on foreign sugar imported into America from six pence to three pence a gallon and instructed the navy to help to enforce it. The articles added to the enumeration included lumber, logwood, raw silk, potashes and whalefins. Finally, by a proclamation issued in 1763 the British government laid down that, for the time being, all colonial settlement must stop at the crest of the Appalachian mountains. The main object was to pacify the native Indians who

In 1764, Grenville introduced a Stamp Act to pay part of the cost of the British garrison in North America. This proved to be an unpopular act on both sides of the Atlantic. In America there was rioting in several cities and customs houses were burned. A boycott on English goods was organized and American debtors repudiated loans due to British merchants, causing bankruptcies in Bristol and Liverpool. Thus this cartoon celebrating the repeal of the Stamp Act by the Rockingham ministry in 1766 not only expressed the American view but also that of the Whigs in England.

feared that they were to be deprived of their lands. Grenville did not want to have to pay for and employ more troops to cope with fresh Indian wars. He hoped that once the Indians quietened down, these lands could be reopened to settlement. Though it was only a temporary measure, it was not rescinded and caused offence to all sorts of white Americans.

But the principal resistance of the colonists was concentrated against the stamp duties. Six months after the act had been passed, the Massachusetts assembly summoned a congress to meet in New York City in October 1765. Although the addresses drawn up for presentation to George III and Parliament were moderate in tone, this congress, which did not include representatives from all the colonies, passed some pretty sharp resolutions and inaugurated a resistance movement which effectively sabotaged the act. Before this the King, who for various reasons was irritated with Grenville's behaviour, dismissed him. The new ministry, headed by Charles Watson Wentworth, Marquess of Rockingham, was compelled to repeal the Stamp Act, though it did not admit that this was done under American pressure, but because of opposition to it from both William Pitt and London merchants who traded with North America.

Before the Rockingham administration repealed the Stamp

Act it sponsored a declaratory act which 'asserted the authority of the legislature of this kingdom, supreme and unlimited over all members of the British Empire', while condemning its 'unwarrantable use'. Only Pitt, who was now ill, lonely and cantankerous, opposed the Bill. Though the new government tried to follow a conciliatory policy, it was divided against itself and was perplexed by the movements of resistance in America. For example, New York had proved uncooperative over the quartering of British soldiers there. In August 1766 George III again sent for Pitt to form a Cabinet. To the consternation of his friends he chose the honorific office of Lord Privy Seal and took the title of the Earl of Chatham. Though in March 1767 he managed to struggle up to London, as Edmund Burke unkindly put it, he lay on his back and 'talked fustian'.

Chatham was determined to pacify the Americans and thought that if money must be obtained from them as a contribution to the cost of the British garrison it should be sought from voluntary subscriptions – an optimistic view. Chatham, who regarded himself as 'above party', had difficulty in forming a government by selecting individuals out of the heterogeneous groups of politicians. Burke, the able Irish orator and pamphleteer, later wrote in his *Thoughts on the Present Discontents* that to try to govern without party support was a mistake. At any rate Chatham soon retired to Bath to nurse his gout, leaving the government in the hands of younger men, one of whom was Charles Townshend, the brilliant Chancellor of the Exchequer.

In Chatham's absence Townshend produced a plan for levying taxes on a number of imports into America including tea. It was not a very wise scheme because while the cost of the upkeep of the American colonies was estimated at over £400,000 a year, the duties were likely to yield only a fraction of this amount. Townshend had imagined that the colonists would pay these duties since they were 'external' taxes. He was mistaken. The colonists had tasted blood. Non-importation agreements were framed, while Americans started drinking coffee instead of tea, which they have done with curious consequences for their meals ever since. Moreover, it was known that if smugglers were caught, they were certain to be acquitted in the colonial law courts.

Though the resistance movement in North America was not entirely effective, public opinion there was aroused against the imposition of the new import duties and the conduct of British soldiers. In 1767 Frederick, Lord North, a typical sprig of the

English aristocracy, succeeded Charles Townshend on his death as the Chancellor of the Exchequer and in 1770 he became First Lord of the Treasury and effective Prime Minister, for Chatham once more resigned and retreated into opposition. Partly because the merchants who traded with America complained about the alarming state of their business, North repealed all the Townshend duties except that on tea, which was remodelled. The East India Company was given permission to carry tea directly to North America where it was to pay a duty of three pence a pound. But even before the repeal of the other Townshend duties an incident took place in Boston which revealed the temper of the Americans. Angered at Customs House informers and at the behaviour of the British garrison the men of Massachusetts began rioting, the soldiers fired on them, and a few citizens were killed or wounded. Though the offending soldiers were brought to trial and acquitted of premeditated murder, the affair became known as 'the Boston massacre' and was used for anti-British propaganda.

In the following year the Bostonians became involved in another incident. A band of men disguised as Mohawk Indians boarded ships bringing in tea, and the contents of 342 chests of tea were thrown into the sea. In London Lord North's government was determined to enforce law and order: the Massachusetts charter was abrogated; General Gage, the British commander-in-chief in North America, was authorized to quarter troops in Boston and to close the port until the tea had been paid for. The news of these measures spread throughout North America; the leaders in other colonies promised their help. At the same time the British Parliament passed an act, known as the Quebec Act, for the reorganization of Canada. Among its provisions was that Illinois and Detroit were included within the Canadian frontier. This exasperated the Americans on the north-west seaboard who considered that they had been cut off from the fur trade. General Gage warned the British government that the temper of the Americans was now so fierce and unruly that only a big army could restore order.

The warning came too late. On 5 September 1774 the first continental congress met in Philadelphia; all the colonies except Georgia were represented. The delegates included such men as Franklin, Washington and John Adams. The Congress addressed a mild resolution to George III asking for peace, liberty and safety. The Americans did not even protest against commercial regulations, but insisted that they must have the exclusive right to

The Boston Tea Party, a famous incident before the war of American Independence. In December 1773, a tea-ship belonging to the East India Company was attacked in Boston harbour by a large number of citizens disguised as Mohawk Indians. The cargo, worth £18,000, was thrown into the sea and destroyed.

legislate upon their own affairs. Furthermore it was agreed that a ban should be imposed on the importation of British goods until their grievances were met. Massachusetts was promised the support of the whole of North America in their resistance to Gage's soldiers.

When George III heard of what was going on he wrote: 'the die is now cast, the colonies must either submit or triumph ...'. It now needed only a spark to light the flame of war. Both sides started making military preparations. In the spring of 1775 General Gage sent a contingent to Concord near Boston to seize the stores that were held there. On their way to Concord the British force ran into a body of militiamen, farmers armed with shotguns. In a skirmish men were killed on both sides. The incident took place on 19 April. The war of independence had begun.

How might a historian of Europe, writing in 1775, have speculated about the future? He is likely to have believed then that France would long remain the outstanding power in the Western world. For its population was growing, it had fertile lands to cultivate, expanding industries and a navy which had been built up by Choiseul to assert its imperial authority. The French peasants were relatively prosperous. France was the intellectual centre of Europe with the handsome buildings of the Louvre and the palace of Versailles symbolizing the glories of the Bourbon monarchy. One cannot say that such a historian would have been wrong since under Napoleon I France was in fact to rule much of the Western world. On the other hand, a perceptive historian might have pointed to Russia as a future mighty empire. After the first partition of Poland its population reached over twenty million. It was known to have resources to tap; iron and timber, vast wheatfields, the furs of Siberia. It was ruled by an able and resourceful Tsarina who by 1775 had made herself secure on the throne of the Romanovs and commanded a large army and a useful navy which in 1770 sailed round Europe and defeated the Turks at the battle of Chesmé.

What of North America? It then had a population of only about two and a half million; was it really likely that the flow of immigrants would suffice to develop an enterprising and wealthy community which could spread westwards to the Pacific and populate almost the whole of the continent? True, like France, it had become a prospering community, though cut off from the fur trade of Canada and forbidden by the British government to pioneer beyond the Appalachian mountains. But could it remain secure from European invaders? Up till 1775 the American people had depended upon the protection of the British navy. Supposing that they became sufficiently strong to establish unity and independence, they would still require to be shielded from assaults across the Atlantic. No other colony had yet thrown off the yoke of the mother country, though precedents were to be found in the Athenian empire. No other country had yet been changed into a great power by a vast flow of immigrants. So the idea of a United States of America dominating the Western world can hardly then have been contemplated.

18 Summary and Conclusions

Historical generalizations are always dangerous. In the first place, historians, unlike statesmen, can forecast the run of events. Secondly, the historian looks at the happenings of the past through spectacles manufactured in the present. Nowadays French historians are obsessed with sociological problems because they live in a sociological world; many British historians seek to measure social and economic facts about the seventeenth and eighteenth centuries by means of quantitative analysis, for they are accustomed to a Parliament in which politicians brandish statistics against one another. Finally, American historians today write what they call 'modern' histories of Europe, by which presumably they mean that they re-examine the Old World, from which their ancestors came, in terms of democracy and egalitarianism.

Thirdly, it is virtually impossible for one historian to master all the known facts about the Western world or any other world; consequently those historians who have ventured to make a bold sweep, as H. A. L. Fisher did in his *History of Europe* or Lord Acton did in his *Lectures on Modern History* and, above all, as Dr Toynbee has done in his stimulating *Study of History*, are liable to face criticism from specialists on the ground that the authors have failed to understand the *minutiae* of some particular subject or period. Nevertheless unless one eschews broad generalizations altogether, history is liable to degenerate into mere chronicle. So one has to attempt to evaluate the past. It can scarcely be wrong to try to point a moral or to adorn a tale.

The first thing that may be said about the years 1648–1775 is that they witnessed the rise or decline of various states. By the last quarter of the seventeenth century France appeared to be ascendant in the Western world, while Spain had lapsed into a stately old age. Spain experienced some moments of revival, as when the Bourbon King was firmly established at Madrid in 1713, but in spite of its considerable possessions, the years of greatness had gone. Whether the decline of Spain was caused by over-exertion during the reigns of Carlos I and Philip II or by the drying up of the flow of silver across the Atlantic or by the demoralization of the mercantile and landed classes outside Catalonia is disputable, but a decline undoubtedly took place in wealth as well as political influence. The French, who had previously lived in dread of the Spanish *tercios* and had adopted Spanish customs and fashions at the Court of Paris, themselves became the cynosure of every eye. Louis XIV was admired and feared throughout the Western world. And though the French conquests did not stretch beyond Germany, the rulers of eastern Europe were all affected by French culture and French literature.

Just as the Spaniards were exhausted by their efforts to hold what they had in the Netherlands, in Portugal, in Italy and in Central and South America, so the French suffered from forty years of war. Of course it can be argued – and here is a difficulty typical of generalizations – that war can be of advantage to a country (whether victorious or not) first because it stimulates industry and invention, secondly because it syphons off surplus population and creates full employment, lastly because it can buy security for the future. That is why French historians pride themselves on the achievements of Richelieu, Mazarin and Louis XIV, even though it is hard to prove that any one of them had a consistent foreign policy other than that of traditional enmity to the Habsburgs. Even then, in the long run, the attempts by the French to hem in the Austrian Habsburgs by alliances in parts of Germany, Poland and Turkey were a failure, though that policy was to be revived in a somewhat different guise in the twentieth century.

The Dutch Republic flourished at the same time as France; indeed French statesmen like Colbert were frankly jealous of the affluence of the 'cheese merchants'. The Dutch, however, did not believe that war was good for business, at least their own wars, not other people's. But because their frontiers were vulnerable they had to go on fighting even after they had finally wrenched their independence from the Spanish monarchy in 1648. The wars of 1672–8, 1688–97 and 1702–13 put a strain on their resources. While it is a fact that their supremacy as merchants trading abroad and as shippers who served other nations was maintained until beyond 1775 – a Dutch historian has claimed that the East Indian trade nearly doubled during this period – their maritime strength and financial power declined, while the barrier of fortresses, for which they had fought so long and so courageously, was to prove of little use in the future when the Netherlands were invaded by a Napoleon or a Hitler. On balance, the 'periwig period' of Dutch history in the eighteenth century was one of comparative stagnation.

Great Britain, having experienced twenty years of revolution took advantage of the period of peace under Charles II and James II. It is true that two wars were fought against the Dutch, but they were largely naval wars and did not interfere with either agriculture or industry while commerce began to boom. Charles II, who was a shrewd if lazy monarch, was anxious to see the Dutch, the chief trading rivals of the British, have their economy disrupted; he also aimed to keep in trim a navy at least as big as that built up in the time of Oliver Cromwell. He just about managed to do so, though Parliament was reluctant to vote money for the purpose except during the first Dutch war. When, after King James II lost his throne in the revolution of 1688, Dutch William won the succession, it did not prove to be a Dutch conquest of Great Britain. For William had become king of a more populous country and had to spend much time in London to make sure that the British held firm to his foreign policy. After his death British fleets and armies, sustained by public finance, grew even more formidable. The treaty of Utrecht laid the foundation upon which Pitt the Elder was to fashion an empire. This empire was built on trade. British exports doubled between 1660 and 1700 and again between 1714 and 1750. After the middle of the eighteenth century the navy was expanded. It was the British navy which for a long time was to protect the growth of the United States of America and was to contribute to the downfall of the French empire established by Napoleon. Finally, these years, as was pointed out in the previous chapter, saw the emergence of two very young giants who now dominate the Western world.

Yet much as one might like to forget the fact, these years were filled with wars, great and small. They were not yet organized upon a national scale nor were they fought so intensely as in later times. Armies were growing in size, but it was not until the American and French Revolutions that large volunteer armies went into the field. Moreover, as has been noticed, most of these wars were not particularly damaging to the national economy (at least in modern terms) and, in the long run, stimulated trade and industry. But the character of war was gradually changing. Soldiers wore uniforms and underwent drill. Armies consisted for the most part of the dregs of the population, including criminals who cost the governments less if they were forced to serve than if they were kept in prisons. Again, mercenaries were widely employed, particularly in western Europe. The French, the British and the Dutch all hired professional soldiers from Switzerland, Sweden, Italy and a variety of German principalities. Because the criminals deserted whenever they could and the professionals were liable to change sides if they thought it was profitable enough, a strict watch had to be kept by officers upon them if armies were to be prevented from melting away. Frederick the Great instructed non-commissioned officers to kill men who tried to run away.

Strict drill was needed to control the movement of the armies thus composed. Uniforms were also an aid to discipline. A French officer named Martinet became a byword for strictness in both the French and British armies. But training was needed for another reason. The increasing employment of missile weapons, it has been said, dehumanized warfare. The invention of the flintlock musket and the socket bayonet meant that the infantry was coming to take a larger part in battles. Infantry as well as engineers had always been required for siege warfare, but now they were more important in the open field. What has been called a military revolution began with the methods used by Gustavus Adolphus in the Thirty Years' War to enhance his striking power. In the middle of the seventeenth century infantry consisted of pikemen and slow-firing musketeers. Artillery fired even more slowly and it created more noise than damage. Battles were won by fast trotting cavalrymen, stationed on the wings of an army, who acted as a shock force that won battles. But during the eighteenth century with the improved muskets available a higher rate of fire could be maintained. Though the infantry were still lined in three rows, one firing, one loading, and one unloading, Marlborough and other generals organized firing by platoons instead of by rows. The cavalry was often kept in reserve to be thrown into the battle at a critical time. It was characteristic of this change of tactics that at the battle of Mollwitz Frederick II of Prussia, who was still an inexperienced officer, thought that after his cavalry had been beaten all was lost. But in fact his infantry won the battle – a decisive battle in the history of the Western world.

Thus an extraordinary contrast can be drawn between the armies that fought under Cromwell and Prince Rupert in the English civil wars, with their cumbrous armoured cavalry and relatively untrained infantry, and the professional soldiers of the late seventeenth and eighteenth centuries. Because armies needed to be highly trained, mercenaries had to be well paid, and it proved impossible for soldiers to live off the country, thus requiring food to be purchased or carried with them in wagons, generals were obliged to take care that they did not fritter away their soldiers or allow these armies to suffer heavy casualties. The preference that was shown on the whole for siege warfare was largely because it was less costly to both sides. In battles the casualty rate was kept as low as possible – much lower than it was to be in later centuries – and battles such as Malplaquet were exceptional. Indeed after his heavy losses at Malplaquet Marlborough refused to fight another battle during the next two years while he remained in command. Nor was it at all easy for generals to outmanoeuvre each other. An army had to halt every three or four days to bake bread. Artillery drawn by horses over bad roads and cumbrous supply trains handicapped swift and surprising movements. That was why Frederick the Great was satisfied with what he called small advantages.

Two other consequences arose from the military revolution. The first was that though war became comparatively cheap in terms of casualty rates, its dehumanization through the intensification of firepower meant that the civil populations in the countries over which wars were fought came to suffer increased cruelty. It was difficult to check the behaviour of troops after a hard-fought battle or long-contested siege. Devastation was used to bring an enemy to heel. Previously – or at least so it has been argued – religious and moral restraints imposed themselves on the behaviour of soldiers. Indeed up to the time of Malplaquet a good deal of bowing and scraping took place between rival generals. Presents of food and wine were dispatched across the lines along with polite messages, while if a garrison surrendered at the appropriate time the defenders would be allowed to march away carrying their side-arms instead of being taken prisoners. The Swiss international lawyer, Emeric Vattel, who was also a practising diplomatist, argued that the restraints imposed by 'natural law' had become insufficient and that what was needed was an agreed code limiting the ferocity of warfare, especially as it affected civil populations. In the first half of the seventeenth century, the Dutchman Hugo Grotius and his successors had already been anxious to establish agreed limits to the interference of navies with the mercantile marine and to define the laws of war and peace generally. The British, who aimed to win wars by blockade and the rigorous search of neutral ships carrying enemy goods, resisted such attempts by men like Grotius to protect the freedom of neutral shipping. British methods provoked the Dutch and were to lead both to the fourth Anglo–Dutch war and to the formation of an armed neutrality during the war of American independence.

One last consequence of the military revolution or at any rate of the increased professionalisation of warfare was that standing armies became characteristic of many countries in the Western world in the eighteenth century. Governments were reluctant to disband armies or at any rate to deprive themselves entirely of military forces in times of peace. The successful autocrat needed an army to maintain his own position. Though standing armies were unpopular in Great Britain, particularly after the reign of James II, in fact a small army was necessary for policing purposes at home and a garrison had to be kept in North America: the cost of this garrison – or how it was to be met – was one of the immediate causes of the war of independence. The modern idea of a civil police force was held hardly anywhere in the West; in the last resort an army was needed to keep internal order. Peter the Great of Russia used his army to free himself from the power of the Streltsi in Moscow and many years later a Turkish Sultan employed his army to repress the influence of the Janissaries. Finally, the existence of a standing army was helpful to Machiavellian diplomacy. Louis XIV kept a substantial standing army after the ending of the war of 1672–8 and thus for a time was able to fasten his aggressive policy on Germany and elsewhere. Nearly a hundred years later the Tsarina Catherine II required a standing army not only to suppress revolutionaries but also to frighten the Polish Seym into acquiescing in the first partition of their Commonwealth, and lastly to continue expansion against the Turkish empire.

Principles of Christian morality therefore scarcely entered into dealings between States. The attitude adopted – notably in the case of Poland – was

> The good old rule, the simple plan
> That they should take, who have the power,
> And they shall keep who can ...

Although undoubtedly many believers in Christianity still existed throughout the Western world right up to the time of the French Revolution, it is clear that the influence of Christianity on politics was steadily being eroded. Naturally one must not exaggerate this theme. It has sometimes been said that the Thirty Years' War was the last war in the West to be fought over religion, but that generalization can be refuted. The Thirty Years' War combined a German civil war with the continuation of the long-drawn-out struggle between the Bourbons and the Habsburgs. Though religious considerations played a part, if not a major part, in the intervention of Gustavus Adolphus in the affairs of Germany, Cardinal Richelieu in effect rejected the concept of a united Catholic Europe when he declared war on the Holy Roman Emperor. On the other side, it may be contended that the expulsion of the Muslim Turks from Austria and Hungary forty years later was the last Christian crusade, backed by the Pope. Nevertheless the authority of the Papacy was declining. Louis XIV was one of the last European monarchs to claim to rule by divine right. Yet his relations with the Papacy were equivocal. When Pope Clement XIV was persuaded to dissolve the Society of Jesus in 1773 he abandoned one of the most potent instruments of the Counter-Reformation. At the same time the influence of the Roman Catholic Church among educated men was being undermined by the secularization of thought. It is doubtful if any of the 'enlightened despots', apart from Queen Maria Theresa, was a sincere Christian.

The Christian religion, which, as was argued in the first chapter of this book, had been a unifying factor in the Western world, was attacked from various angles. First, political philosophers from Machiavelli to Thomas Hobbes – and to some extent the Jewish Spinoza – had argued that for a state to flourish it needed to possess a unified and all-powerful government which had to be ruthless in its methods if it were to stand a chance of survival. It could not afford to tolerate a state within a state. Therefore the secular government must be supreme over the Church. And so it was, for the most part, from London to St Petersburg. The only theocracy, curiously enough, was to be found for a time in the Land of the Free in Massachusetts. The medieval notion that the Pope was the sun and the Emperor the moon went by the board. Yet it is fair to remember that the Pope and the Patriarch of the Greek Church still commanded large followings. It may be hazarded that apart from Spain, where superficially at any rate Catholicism was still devoutly practised, orthodox religion was stronger in eastern than in western Europe. Although Gotthold Ephraim Lessing, the German philosopher, declared in a book written in 1750 that 'a true Christian has become rarer than in the dark ages', Friedrich Heer has argued that in Germany the Enlightenment was confined to 'small élites' while a huge wave of pietism, aimed at purifying the Lutheran Church, swept over the north and the east, paralleling the Wesleyan movement in Great Britain and North America.

These appeals were essentially emotional. But intellectually the philosophers, except for Bishop Berkeley, were undermining Christianity. Though Descartes had claimed to have proved the existence of God – and his proof was accepted by his followers, while later John Locke argued in favour of the reasonableness of Christianity – philosophers as a whole rejected the traditional teaching of the Christian Churches. Locke, for example, did not believe in the doctrine of the Holy Trinity. Generally, philosophers were either deists or sceptics. The truth of the Old Testament and, above all, the reality of miracles was questioned by all the *philosophes,* that is to say the popularizers of the sciences and mechanical arts, though only a few of them were atheists. The famous dictionary of Bayle and the encyclopedia of Diderot chipped away at the accuracy of biblical stories. Although the view that the writings of the *philosophes* and of Voltaire and Rousseau were a major influence on bringing about the French Revolution is no longer generally accepted by historians, they all contributed to the growth of the spirit of scepticism at any rate among the rising professional classes, who were to take a leading part in the Revolution. It is hardly an exaggeration to say that the whole intellectual atmosphere of the West was changing. A mechanical universe left little room for divine intervention in human affairs.

But it would be wrong to speak of a revolution in thought even on a practical level. It needed the best part of two centuries for the discoveries of pure science to be translated into technological terms. Medieval misconceptions lingered a long time, the bulk of mankind was conservative in its habits, and inertia was not easily overcome. To take one example, chemistry. Though the medieval notion of four elements was abandoned by Robert Boyle, it was not until nearly a century later that Lavoisier and other scientists established the constituents of elements and of gases. The methods of agriculture also changed slowly: to talk about an agricultural revolution is misleading until quite modern times. Equally the popular phrase 'the Industrial Revolution' merely reflects an acceleration in the discovery of relatively elementary inventions such as the spinning jenny. Even the idea of a commercial revolution having taken place during this period is questionable. Certainly international trade was expanding, but it must have been checked by the attempts of European governments, notably the British, Spanish and Portuguese governments, to maintain their

305

trading monopolies. For their colonies were thought of simply as communities from whom raw materials could be cheaply purchased and to whom manufactured goods could be profitably sold. The triangular trade, whereby Negro slaves were carried from West Africa to the West Indies and the Americas, and their products – particularly sugar and tobacco – were then carried to Europe, was perhaps the most typical example of commercial expansion during the eighteenth century.

But man does not live by bread alone. To those people (no doubt one is likely to be reminded that they usually belong to the affluent or leisured classes) for whom the gross national product is not the most important end in life, the chief values are likely to be found in the arts. Although the period from 1648 to 1775 was not as outstanding as the Renaissance or the first half of the seventeenth century the fact is that baroque and rococo have left the Western world some wonderful buildings, paintings, sculptures and music. We do not need to think immediately of Versailles: indeed Versailles was not of the first importance. And although it may readily be admitted that Rubens and Borromini at their best were artists beyond compare, this is even more true of Raphael, Michelangelo and Leonardo da Vinci. But Westerners can also pride themselves for example on the later Rembrandt and Bernini, Vermeer and Watteau, Fischer von Erlach and Wren. The rococo palaces of Russia or the monastic buildings in Germany are splendid achievements of a magnificent artistic age. Many lovers of classical music consider that Johann Sebastian Bach was the finest composer who ever lived. Purcell, Monteverdi and Handel also belong to the pantheon of musicians. It is true that Haydn, Mozart and Beethoven were still to come, but they were in fact products of the aristocratic eighteenth century not – Heaven forfend – of the so-called Industrial Revolution. Newcomen and Kay are mere names at the best. But no cultured Westerner can fail to have heard of Rembrandt or Bach.

To return finally to economic history. Because of growing wealth the standard of living was rising. But it was only slowly that medical treatment improved and agriculture, through the use of new fertilizers and the adoption of sensible rotations, stimulated the output of food and offered a better diet for people at large. In general, population went up and life expectation rose above the thirty years which was still accepted as normal at the beginning of the eighteenth century. Yet enlightened thinkers honestly believed in the possibilities of progress in every sphere of life. It would be wrong to deny that material or intellectual progress was taking place or to assert that the eighteenth century before the two great political revolutions was stagnant and uninspired. It was in fact because throughout the Western world mankind was conscious of economic growth that the inequalities of the existing political and social system were being more insistently realized. Political reforms were being advocated in England, agricultural reforms were being attempted in France, and enlightenment was genuine in Vienna. Finally, the prospering American colonists were unwilling to accept selfish economic policies or to obey the orders of a government three thousand miles away. The French peasants, who had enjoyed a considerable improvement in their standard of living during the first three-quarters of the eighteenth century, became more and more restive about the privileges of the aristocracy and of the Church. Men saw that revolutions were coming, though few guessed their extent.

Bibliography

There are no histories of the Western world as such covering this period. A sound new book on European history comprising both politics and culture is Eugen Weber, *A Modern History of Europe: Men, Cultures and Societies from the Renaissance to the Present* (1973) chapters 6–10. An earlier book, also by an American historian, is E. J. Knapton, *Europe 1450–1815* (1958), reliable but mainly political. A third American historian who has written about Europe and is an expert on the eighteenth century is R. R. Palmer, *A History of the Modern World* (1958). Three highly suggestive books are Denys Hay, *Europe: the Emergence of an Idea* (1957); Fernand Braudel, *Civilisation materielle et capitalisme XVe – XVIIIe siècles*, vol. 1 (1967), which has recently been translated into English; and P. Chaunu, *La civilisation de l'Europe classique* (1966) covering the years from 1620 to 1760. There are various series of books on European history published in the United States, Great Britain, France and Germany: one of the latest and best is the Fontana paperback series (Collins) which includes John Stoye, *Europe Unfolding 1648–1688* (1969), Stephen Baxter, *Europe 1689–1715* and David Ogg, *Europe of the Ancien Regime 1715–1789* (1965). E. N. Williams, *The Ancien Regime in Europe 1648–1789* (1970) is excellent, particularly on political and constitutional history. Maurice Ashley, *The Golden Century 1598–1715* (1969) and George Rudé, *Europe in the Eighteenth Century* (1972) are two recent contributions to the Weidenfeld History of Civilization series.

For economic history there is the *Cambridge Economic History of Europe* and the Fontana *Economic History of Europe* (edited by Carlo M. Cipolla): neither of these series is yet complete and the contributions vary in quality. For agriculture B. H. Slicher van Bath, *The Agrarian History of Europe* (English trans. 1963) is a good introduction. The relevant volumes of the *New Cambridge Modern History* are concerned with economic, social, cultural and demographical history as well as political and constitutional history: these are *The Ascendancy of France 1648–1688* (ed. F. L. Carsten 1961), *The Rise of Great Britain and Russia 1688–1725* (ed. J. S. Bromley 1970) and *The Old Regime 1713–1763* (ed. J. O. Lindsay 1966).

For the history of the North American colonies up to the war of independence L. H. Gipson, *The British Empire before the American Revolution* (1955–67) in thirteen volumes is comprehensive and up-to-date. A shorter book, the first volume of the Cambridge history of the British Empire by C. M. Andrews (1929), is an excellent introduction. C. P. Nettels, *The Roots of American Civilization: history of*

American cultural life (2nd ed. 1963) may be recommended. Louis B. Wright, *The Cultural Life of the American Colonies 1607–1763* (1957) is also concerned with this subject.

For European cultural history there is V. L. Tapié, *The Age of Grandeur: Baroque and Classicism in Europe* (1960) and *La Baroque* (1961), but perhaps Michael Kitson, *The Age of Baroque* (1966) is a better general introduction to painting and sculpture. The volumes so far published in the Pelican arts series may be consulted; the two volumes on France are particularly good. For music see Manfred F. Bukofser, *Music in the Baroque Era* (1947) and (more general) Paul S. Lang, *Music in Western Civilization* (1942). Nikolaus Pevsner, *An Outline of European Architecture* (1951) is a fine introduction to the subject.

For science A. R. Hall, *The Scientific Revolution, 1500–1800* is a valuable discussion; David Landes, *The Unbound Prometheus* (1969) is stimulating. For philosophy Bertrand Russell, *A History of Western Philosophy* (1946) though provocative is a clear and entertaining introduction to the subject; another book giving the general background is Jacob Bronowski and Bruce Mazlish, *The Western Intellectual Tradition: From Leonardo to Hegel* (1960). Ernst Cassirer, *The Philosophy of the Enlightenment* (English trans. 1960) and R. J. White, *The Anti-Philosophers* (1970) deal with the encyclopedists and *philosophes*. There is no satisfactory book on political science; the most up-to-date interpretations will be found in the Pelican monographs on Spinoza, Hobbes, Locke etc. For the seventeenth century Stuart Hampshire, *The Age of Reason* (1956) may be recommended. Paul Hazard, *The European Mind: the Critical Years 1680–1715* (1953) links the seventeenth and eighteenth centuries. For the development of political thought in the eighteenth century Alfred Cobban, *In Search of Humanity* (1960) is stimulating and valuable.

For the Balkans see I. S. Stavrianos, *The Balkans since 1453* (1958). For France Ernest Lavisse (ed.) *Histoire de France depuis les origines jusqu'à la Révolution* is still as good an introduction as any. For Louis XIV see the biography by J. B. Wolf (1968) and for Louis XV's reign Henri Carré, *La France sous Louis XV* (1891). Ragnhild Hatton, *Louis XIV and his world* (1972) is stimulating and provocative. For Germany and Austria H. Holborne, *A History of Modern Germany* vol. II 1648–1840 (1964), Adam Wandruszka, *The House of Habsburg* (1964) and F. L. Carsten, *Princes and parliaments in Germany from the fifteenth to the eighteenth century* (1959) and other books by Professor Carsten are sound introductions. For Great Britain the best guide is the Oxford series which includes G. N. Clark, *The Later Stuarts 1660–1714* (1956), Basil Williams, *The Whig Supremacy 1714–1760* (2nd edition revised by C. H. Stuart, 1962) and Steven Watson, *The Reign of George III 1760–1815* (1960). For Sir Robert Walpole see the uncompleted biography by J.H.Plumb, and for William Pitt the Elder the biography by Brian Tunstall (1938) is a good introduction. Sir Lewis Namier's masterpiece, *England in the Age of the American Revolution* (1930) is indispensable. For Poland see O.Halecki, *History of Poland* (1955). For Portugal H.V.Livermore, *A History of Portugal* (1947) is a sound introduction. For Russia V.O.Klyuchevsky, *A History of Russia*, vol. III and Bernard Pares, *A History of Russia* (revised 1965) are unprejudiced. For Scandinavia R.Bain, *Scandinavia* (1900), Ingvaar Anderson, *A History of Sweden* (1956) and Paul Lauring *A History of the Kingdom of Denmark* (1960) cover the subject adequately. For Spain see J.H.Elliott, *Imperial Spain 1469–1716* (1963) and J.H.Parry, *The Spanish Seaborne Empire* (1966). For the United Netherlands B.H.M. Vlekke, *The Evolution of the Dutch Nation* (1945) is a good introduction, but the standard works (mainly political) are by a great historian, Pieter Geyl, which have been translated into English. C.R.Boxer, *The Dutch Seaborne Empire 1600–1800* (1965) is illuminating on this period.

Chronological Tables

1648	*Jan*	Peace of Münster between Spain and Netherlands
	April	Outbreak of Second Civil War in England
	July	Swedes capture Prague
	Aug	Cromwell defeats Scots at Preston
		Outbreak of the First Fronde in France
	Oct	Peace of Westphalia ends Thirty Years' War
1649	*Jan*	Charles I of England beheaded
	Mar	Treaty of Rueil between French government and Frondeurs
	May	England declared a Commonwealth
	Dec	Outbreak of Second Fronde
1650	*June*	Charles II lands in Scotland
	Sept	Cromwell defeats Scots at Dunbar
1651	*Jan*	Charles II crowned at Scone
	Sept	Cromwell defeats Charles II at Worcester
	Oct	English Parliament passes First Navigation Act
1652	*June*	First Anglo-Dutch War breaks out
	Oct	Louis XIV returns to Paris
1653		John de Witt becomes Grand Pensionary of Holland
	April	Cromwell expels Parliamentary Rump
	July	End of Second Fronde in France
	Dec	End of Barebones Parliament
		Cromwell establishes the Protectorate under the 'Instrument of Government'
1654		Dutch finally replaced by Portuguese in Brazil
	April	Peace of Westminster ends war between Dutch and English
	June	Christina of Sweden abdicates; throne passes to Charles X
		Coronation of Louis XIV of France
	July	Treaty between England and Portugal
	Sept	Tsar Alexis takes Smolensk
1655	*May*	English expeditionary force captures Jamaica from Spaniards
	July	Charles X of Sweden invades Poland and captures Warsaw
1656	*Feb*	Spain declares war on England
	July	Charles X defeats Poles at Warsaw
	Sept	Alliance between England and France against Spain
	Nov	Treaty of Vilna between Poland and Russia against Sweden
1657	*Mar*	Treaty of Paris between England and France against Spain
	April	British Admiral Blake defeats Spanish fleet off Cadiz
	July	Swedes invade Denmark
1658	*June*	Spanish defeated by French and English at battle of Dunes
		Capture of Dunkirk

		Aug–Nov Charles x besieges Copenhagen
	Sept	Cromwell dies; succeeded as Lord Protector by his son Richard
1659	*May*	Richard Cromwell resigns as Lord Protector
	Nov	Peace of the Pyrenees between France and Spain
1660	*Feb*	Charles x of Sweden dies; succeeded by Charles XI
	May	Charles II proclaimed king by Parliament and returns to England
		Peace of Oliva ends First Northern War between Poland, Brandenburg and Sweden
	June	Peace of Copenhagen between Sweden and Denmark
	Dec	Royal Africa Company founded
1661	*Mar*	Death of Mazarin; personal rule of Louis XIV begins
	April	Charles II crowned in London
	June	Treaty of Kardis between Sweden and Russia
1662	*Aug*	Act of Uniformity passed in England
	Oct	Charles II sells Dunkirk to France
1663	*April*	Turkey declares war on Austria
	June	Portugal and England defeat Spain at Ameixal
1664	*May*	Conventicle Act passed
	Aug	English seize New Amsterdam (New York) from the Dutch
		Turks defeated at battle of St Gotthard by Austrians and Poles
1665	*Feb*	Second Anglo–Dutch war breaks out
	April	Outbreak of great plague in London
	June	English fleet defeats Dutch off Lowestoft
	Sept	Death of Philip IV of Spain; succeeded by Carlos II
1666	*Jan*	France declares war on England in support of Holland
	Dec	Cleves acquired by Brandenburg
1667	*May*	French attack Spanish Netherlands
	June	Dutch fleet enters River Medway
	July	Peace of Breda ends war between England and Holland
	Aug	Treaty of Andrussovo between Poland and Russia
1668		Fort William founded near Calcutta
	Jan	Alliance between England and Holland against France
	Feb	French occupy Franche-Comté
	May	Treaty of Aix-la-Chapelle ends war between France and Spain
	Sept	John Casimir of Poland abdicates
1669		Foundation of Carolina
1670	*June*	Secret treaty of Dover between Charles II and Louis XIV
1672	*Mar*	Outbreak of war between England and Dutch Republic
	May	English fleet defeats Dutch at Southwold Bay
	July	William of Orange becomes Stadholder of Holland
	Aug	De Witt brothers assassinated in The Hague

1673	Aug	Alliance of Habsburgs with Holland and Lorraine against France
	Nov	John Sobieski of Poland defeats Turks at Chotim
1674	Feb	Treaty of Westminster; England withdraws from war against Dutch
	May	John Sobieski elected King of Poland
1675		King Philip's war between Indians and colonists in New England
	June	Alliance between France and Poland
		Great Elector defeats Swedes at Fehrbellin
	July	French general Turenne killed at Sassbach
	Dec	Colonists attack Indian stronghold in Rhode Island
1676		Bacon's Rebellion in Virginia
	Feb	Secret agreement between Charles II and Louis XIV
	Aug	End of King Philip's war
1677	Nov	William of Orange marries Mary, daughter of James, Duke of York
1678	Aug	Peace of Nymegen between France and Holland
	Sept	The Popish Plot anti-Catholic scare begun in London by Titus Oates
1679	Jan	Dissolution of Cavalier Parliament
	Feb	Catholic Duke of York banished to Brussels
		Peace of Nymegen between France and the Empire
	June	Monmouth defeats Scottish Covenanters at Bothwell Bridge
		Peace of Brandenburg between Brandenburg and Sweden
	Sept	New Hampshire created a separate province from Massachusetts
		Peace of Fontainebleau between Denmark and Sweden
1680	May	House of Commons passes Exclusion Bill against the Duke of York; rejected by Lords
1681	Mar	Charter of Pennsylvania granted
	Sept	French seize Strasbourg and occupy Casale
1682	July	Philadelphia laid out under direction of William Penn
1683	June	Rye House Plot against Charles II discovered; Monmouth exiled
	July–Sept	Turks besiege Vienna
	Sept	Colbert dies in France
	Dec	War between France and Spain
1684		Annulment of Massachusetts charter
		French Mississippi Company formed
	June	French take Treves and Luxembourg
	Aug	Truce of Ratisbon between France and Empire
1685	Feb	Death of Charles II of England; succeeded by James II
	May	Elector Palatine dies; Louis XIV claims Palatinate for his sister-in-law

	Oct	Louis XIV revokes Edict of Nantes; many Protestants flee from France
1686	*July*	League of Augsburg formed in Germany to maintain treaties of Münster and Nymegen
1686	*April*	James II issues Declaration of Indulgence
1687	*Aug*	Turks defeated at Mohacs and evacuate Hungary
1688	*May*	Death of the Great Elector of Brandenburg
	Sept	French attack the Emperor; Nine Years' War begins
	Nov	William III of Orange invades England
		Louis XIV declares war on Dutch
	Dec	James II flees to France
		William enters London
1689	*Feb*	English crown accepted by William and Mary
	May	England and United Netherlands join the Grand Alliance against France
	Oct	Bill of Rights passed in England
1690	*June*	Spain joins Grand Alliance
	July	William III defeats James II in Ireland
		Allies defeated at Fleurus
	Aug	Piedmontese defeated at Staffarda
	Oct	Savoy joins Grand Alliance
1691	*April*	French capture Mons
1692	*May*	English defeat French fleet off Cape La Hogue
	Aug	French defeat William III at Steenkerke
1693		Carolina divided into North and South
	July	William III defeated at Neerwinden
1694	*Jan*	Peter I becomes sole Tsar of Russia
1695	*Sept*	William II takes Namur
1696	*July*	Peter the Great takes Azov from the Turks
	Oct	Savoy withdraws from the Grand Alliance
1697	*April*	Death of Charles XI of Sweden; succeeded by Charles XII
	Sept	Prince Eugene defeats Turks at Zenta
		Treaty of Ryswick ends Nine Years' War
	Sept–March 1698	Peter the Great tours western Europe
1698		Scots establish Darien colony
	Oct	First Partition Treaty concerning Spanish succession
1699		Failure of the Darien colony in central America
	Jan	Peace of Carlowitz between the Empire, Poland, Turkey and Venice
	Feb	Electoral Prince of Bavaria dies
1700	*Mar*	Second Partition Treaty
	May	Outbreak of the Great Northern War
	Nov	Charles XII of Sweden defeats Peter the Great at Narva
		Carlos II of Spain dies

	Nov	Treaty between Empire and Brandenburg
1701	*Jan*	Frederick of Brandenburg crowned Frederick I, king in Prussia
	April	Outbreak of war of the Spanish succession
	June	Act of Settlement settles future of English throne on the Protestant House of Hanover
	June–July	Charles XII occupies Livonia and Courland and invades Poland
	Sept	James II dies; his son, James Edward (the Old Pretender) acknowledged as King of Great Britain and Ireland by Louis XIV
1702	*Mar*	William III dies; succeeded by Anne
	May	England declares war on France in alliance with the Dutch and the Emperor
		Charles XII takes Warsaw
	July	Charles XII defeats Poles at Klissow
1703		Delaware becomes a separate colony
	May	Charles XII defeats Peter the Great at Pultusk
		St Petersburg founded
		Portugal joins Great Alliance
		Marlborough occupies Cologne
1704	*July*	Stanislas Leszczynski elected King of Poland
	Aug	English capture Gibraltar
		Marlborough and Prince Eugene of Savoy defeat French at Blenheim
1705	*May*	Emperor Leopold dies; succeeded by Joseph I
	Oct	English navy takes Barcelona
1706	*May*	Marlborough defeats French at Ramillies
	June	English and Portuguese capture Madrid
	Sept	Eugene defeats French at Turin
		Peace of Altranstadt between Sweden and Saxony
1707	*April*	French win battle of Almanza in Spain
	May	Union of England and Scotland
	Aug	Imperial troops take Naples
1708	*Mar*	The Old Pretender lands in Scotland; soon returns to France
	July	Marlborough and Eugene defeat French at Oudenarde
	Sept	English take Minorca
		Russians defeat Swedes at battle of Lesnaja
	Oct	Allies take Lille
1709		First mass emigration of Palatinate Germans to Pennsylvania
	July	Peter the Great defeats Charles XII at Poltava
		Marlborough and Eugene capture Tournai
	Sept	Marlborough and Eugene defeat French at Malplaquet
	Oct	Allies take Mons
1710	*Feb*	Dutch 'barrier' discussed at Gertruydenberg

1711		English South Sea Company formed
	April	Emperor Joseph I dies; succeeded by Charles VI
	May–Oct	Unsuccessful English expedition against Canada
	July	Peter the Great forced to conclude treaty of Pruth by Turks
1712	*Jan*	Peace Congress opens at Utrecht
	Feb	Duke of Burgundy, heir-apparent to Louis XIV, dies
	July	Austrians defeated at Denain
1713	*Mar*	By Asiento Treaty Spain grants England right to supply slaves to Spanish America
	April	Peace of Utrecht ends war of the Spanish succession
		Emperor Charles VI issues Pragmatic Sanction giving right of succession to Habsburg possessions to his daughter Maria Theresa
	July	Peace of Adrianople between Russia and Turkey
1714	*Mar*	Peace of Rastatt between France and Empire
	Aug	Queen Anne of England dies; succeeded by Elector of Hanover as George I
1715	*Feb*	Peace of Madrid between Spain and Portugal
	Sept	Louis XIV dies; succeeded by Louis XV
		Jacobite rising in Scotland
	Nov	Jacobites defeated at Preston and Sheriffmuir
		Barrier Treaty between Austria and Dutch Republic
1716	*May*	Treaty of Westminster between England and Austria
	Aug	Prince Eugene defeats Turks at Peterwardein
	Nov	Defensive alliance between England and France
1717	*Jan*	Triple Alliance between England, France, and Dutch Republic to uphold peace treaty
	Aug	Prince Eugene captures Belgrade
1718		New Orleans founded
	July	Spanish capture Sicily
		Peace of Passorowitz between the Empire and the Turks
	Aug	Quadruple Alliance between Emperor, French, English and Dutch
		British Admiral Byng defeats Spanish at Cape Passaro
	Dec	England declares war on Spain
		Charles XII of Sweden killed in Norway; succeeded by Ulrica Eleanora
1719	*Jan*	France declares war on Spain
1720	*Feb*	Peace between Quadruple Alliance and Spain
		Treaty of Stockholm between Sweden and Prussia
	May	John Law's Mississippi Scheme collapses in Paris
	Sept	South Sea Bubble burst in London
1721	*April*	Robert Walpole becomes Prime Minister of Great Britain
	June	Defensive alliance between England, France and Spain
	Sept	Treaty of Nystad between Sweden and Russia

1723	Dec	Death of French Regent
1724	June	Treaty of Constantinople between Russia and Turkey
1725	Feb	Peter the Great dies; succeeded by Catherine I
	May	First treaty of Vienna between Austria and Spain
	Sept	Alliance signed between Great Britain and France to counterbalance alliance of Spain and the Empire
1726	June	Cardinal Fleury becomes first Minister in France
	Aug	Russia and Austria ally against Turkey
1727	Feb	War between England and Spain
	May	Tsarina Catherine I dies
	June	George I of England dies; succeeded by George II
1728	Mar	Convention of Pardo ends Anglo-Spanish war
	Dec	Treaty of Berlin between Empire and Prussia
1729	Nov	Treaty of Seville between England, Spain, France, and Dutch Republic
1730	Feb	Peter II of Russia dies; succeeded by Anna
	Sept	Victor Amadeus of Savoy abdicates; succeeded by Charles Emmanuel I
1731	Jan	English and Dutch guarantee Pragmatic Sanction
	July	Second treaty of Vienna between England, United Netherlands, Austria, and Spain
1732	Jan	Empire guarantees Pragmatic Sanction (excluding Saxony, Bavaria, Palatinate)
1732–3		Foundation of Georgia
1733		Outbreak of war of the Polish succession
	Nov	Treaty of Escorial between France, Spain, and England
1734		8000 Protestants emigrate from Salzburg to Georgia
	Jan	Emperor declares war on France
	June	Russians capture Danzig
1735	Oct	Third treaty of Vienna ends war of the Polish succession Augustus III recognized as King of Poland
1736	Feb	Maria Theresa, daughter of Emperor Charles VI, marries Francis Stephen of Lorraine
	May	Spain accedes to the treaty of Vienna Outbreak of Russo-Turkish war
1738	Oct	Alliance between France and Sweden
	Nov	France guarantees Pragmatic Sanction
1739	Jan	Secret treaty between Austria and France
	April	Secret treaty between Prussia and France
	Sept	Treaty of Belgrade between Russia and Turkey
	Oct	Outbreak of war of Jenkins's Ear between England and Spain
	Nov	British capture Portobello
1740	May	Frederick William I of Prussia dies; succeeded by Frederick II (the Great)

	Oct	Emperor Charles VI dies; succeeded by Maria Theresa as ruler of Habsburg dominions
	Dec	Frederick the Great occupies Silesia starting war of the Austrian succession
1741	*April*	Frederick the Great defeats Austrians at Mollwitz
	May	Secret alliance of Nymphenburg between France, Bavaria, Spain, and Austria
	Aug	French invade southern Germany
	Nov	France, Bavaria, and Saxony capture Prague
1742	*Jan*	Charles Albert, Elector of Bavaria, elected Emperor Charles VII at Frankfurt
	May	Frederick the Great victorious over Austrians at Chotusitz
	July	Peace of Berlin between Austria and Prussia
	Nov	Alliance between England and Prussia
1743	*June*	George II, commanding the Pragmatic Army, defeats French at Dettingen
	Aug	Peace of Abo between Russia and Sweden
	Sept	Treaty of Worms between England, Austria and Sardinia
	Oct	Alliance of Fontainebleau between France and Spain
1744		Clive arrives at Madras
	Mar	France declares war on England
	June	Alliance between France and Prussia
	Aug	Frederick the Great invades Saxony
1745	*Jan*	Emperor Charles VII dies
	April	Peace of Füssen between Austria and Bavaria
	May	French defeat Pragmatic Army under the Duke of Cumberland at Fontenoy
	June	Americans capture Louisbourg
		Frederick the Great defeats Austrians at Hohenfriedberg
	July	Charles Edward (the Young Pretender) lands in Scotland
	Sept	Francis Stephen, husband of Maria Theresa, elected Emperor
	Nov	Young Pretender wins battle of Prestonpans
	Dec	Young Pretender reaches Derby
		Prussians defeat Saxons at Kesselsdorf
		Treaty of Dresden between Prussians and Austrians
1746	*April*	Young Pretender decisively defeated at Culloden
	June	Alliance between Austria and Russia against Prussia
	Sept	French take Madras
		Young Pretender flees to France
	Oct	French defeat Austrians and their Dutch and British allies at Roucoux
1747	*May*	Alliance between Prussia and Sweden
	July	French defeat Duke of Cumberland at Lauffeldt
1748	*April*	Preliminary peace of Aix-la-Chapelle between France, Great Britain and Dutch Republic

	Oct	Peace of Aix-la-Chapelle ends war of the Austrian succession
1749	Mar	Ohio Company obtains Royal Charter
	June	Georgia becomes a Crown Colony
1750	Oct	Britain renounces Asiento Treaty
1751	Mar	Frederick, Prince of Wales, dies
	Sept	Clive captures Arcot
		Great Britain joins Austro-Russian alliance of 1746
1752	June	Clive takes Trichinopoly
		Treaty of Aranjuez between Spain and Austria
1753		Duquesne, Governor of Canada, establishes French forts in Ohio valley
1754	June	Albany Convention held to form common defence for British North America against the French
	Dec	French abandon conquests in India
1755	June	Anglo-Russian convention signed at St Petersburg
	July	French defeat British at Fort Duquesne
	Aug	Alliance between Britain and Austria ends
	Sept	British defeat French at Lake George
	Nov	Lisbon earthquake
1756	Jan	Treaty of Westminster between Britain and Prussia
	May	Alliance of Versailles between France and Austria
		England declares war on France
	June	Siraj-ud-Daula siezes Calcutta
		French take Minorca
	Aug	Outbreak of Seven Years' War
		French general Montcalm takes Oswego
		Frederick the Great invades Saxony
	Oct	Frederick the Great defeats Austrians at Lobositz
		Saxon army surrenders to the Prussians at Pirna
1757	Jan	Empire, Russia, Poland, and Sweden join in war against Prussia
		Clive takes Calcutta
	Mar	British Admiral Byng executed
	May	Second Treaty of Versailles between France and Austria
		Frederick the Great defeats Austrians at Prague
	June	Austrians defeat Frederick the Great at Kolin
		Clive wins battle of Plassey
	July	French defeat British at Hastenbeck
	Aug	Russians defeat Prussians at Gross Jägersdorf
		Montcalm captures Fort William Henry
	Sept	British surrender at Klosterzeven
		Swedes invade Pomerania
	Nov	Frederick the Great defeats French and Austrians at Rossbach
		Austrians defeat Duke of Brunswick-Bevern at Breslau
	Dec	Frederick the Great defeats Austrians at Leuthen

1758	April	Great Britain agrees to subsidize Frederick the Great
	July	French defeat British under Abercromby at Ticonderoga
		British take Louisbourg
	Aug	Frederick the Great defeats Russians at Zorndorf
		British general Bradstreet takes Fort Frontenac
	Oct	Austrians defeat Prussians at Hochkirch
	Nov	British capture Fort Duquesne
		Choiseul becomes French Foreign Minister
1759	April	French defeat Prussians at Bergen
	Aug	Russians defeat Prussians at Minden
		Russians and Austrians defeat Prussians at Kunersdorf
		Ferdinand VI of Spain dies; succeeded by Carlos III
	Sept	Wolfe defeats Montcalm outside Quebec; both generals killed
	Oct	George II dies; succeeded by grandson George III
		Russians burn Berlin
	Nov	Frederick the Great defeats Austrians at Torgau
		British navy defeats French at Quiberon Bay
1761	Jan	Coote takes Pondicherry
	Aug	Alliance between France and Spain
	Oct	Resignation of William Pitt as Secretary of State
	Dec	Russians capture Kolberg in East Pomerania
1762	Jan	Elizabeth of Russia dies; succeeded by Peter III
		Britain declares war on Spain
	April	British cease subsidizing Frederick the Great
	May	Peace between Russia and Prussia
		Treaty of Hamburg between Sweden and Prussia
	July	Peter III of Russia assassinated; succeeded by Catherine II
	Oct	Prussians defeat Austrians at Freiburg
	Nov	Truce between Prussia, Austria and Saxony
1763	Feb	Peace of Paris between Britain, France, Spain, and Portugal
		Peace of Hubertusburg between Prussia and Austria; Seven Years' War ends
	April	No. 45 of John Wilkes' *North Briton* published in London
	Oct	George III issues a proclamation temporarily closing America west of the Allegheny mountains to white settlement
		Augustus III of Saxony dies
1764	April	Treaty between Russia and Prussia to control Poland
1765	Mar	Stamp Act passed by British Parliament
	Aug	Emperor Francis I dies; succeeded by Joseph II
	Oct	Stamp Act Congress meets in New York; adopts Declaration of Rights and Liberties
1766	Feb	Lorraine incorporated into France
	Mar	Stamp Act repealed; Declaratory Act asserts right of British Parliament to make laws for British colonists

1768–71		Captain James Cook explores east coast of Australia; names it New South Wales
1769	Feb	John Wilkes expelled from House of Commons
	Aug	Napoleon Bonaparte born
1770	Mar	Boston 'massacre' occurs
	May	French Dauphin marries Marie Antoinette
	July	Russians defeat Turks at sea off Chesmé
1771	Jan	Spain cedes Falkland Islands to Britain
1772	Feb	Boston Assembly threatens secession from British Empire unless rights of colonies are observed
	Aug	First Partition of Poland
		Coup d'état by Gustavus III in Sweden
1773	Feb	Alliance between France and Sweden renewed
	Dec	Boston 'Tea Party'
1773–75		Pugachev's rebellion in south-eastern Russia
1774	Mar	Coercive Acts against Massachusetts passed
	May	Louis XV dies; succeeded by Louis XVI
	June	Quebec Act closes Ohio country to seaboard settlers
	July	Peace of Kutchuk-Kainardji between Russia and Turkey
	Sept	First Continental Congress meets in Philadelphia; Declaration of Rights and Grievances drawn up
	Oct	Delegates to Congress adopt non-importation of British goods programme
	Nov	Robert Clive dies
1775	Feb	Lord Chatham (William Pitt the Elder) presents plan to Parliament for reconciliation with British North American colonists; rejected
	April	Skirmishes of Lexington and Concord; war of American Independence begins

List of Illustrations

The author and publishers would like to thank the museum, agencies and photographers listed below for their help in supplying the illustrations and for permission to reproduce them.

326

Picture research by Philippa Lewis

Index

334